The Permanent Tax Revolt

The Permanent Tax Revolt

**HOW THE PROPERTY TAX TRANSFORMED
AMERICAN POLITICS**

Isaac William Martin

Stanford University Press
Stanford, California

Stanford University Press
Stanford, California
©2008 by the Board of Trustees of the Leland Stanford Junior University. All rights reserved.

Printed in the United States of America on acid-free, archival-quality paper

Library of Congress Cataloging-in-Publication Data

Martin, Isaac William.
   The permanent tax revolt : how the property tax transformed American politics / Isaac William Martin.
     p. cm.
  Includes bibliographical references and index.
  ISBN 978-0-8047-5870-3 (cloth : alk. paper)—ISBN 978-0-8047-5871-0 (pbk. : alk. paper)
  1. Property tax—United States.   2. Taxation—United States.   3. United States—Politics and government.   I. Title.

HJ4120.M37   2008
320.973—dc22   2007044494

Typeset by Westchester Book Group in 10/14 Minion

Part of Chapter 4 first appeared in Isaac Martin, "Does School Finance Litigation Cause Taxpayer Revolt? Serrano and Proposition 13," *Law and Society Review* 40 (3): 525–557, © 2006 Law and Society Association, published by Blackwell Publishing.

To Amaha

CONTENTS

ACKNOWLEDGMENTS

"THE PUBLIC FINANCES are one of the best starting points for an investigation of society," Joseph Schumpeter wrote in 1918, "especially though not exclusively of its political life."[1] They are also one of the best starting points for the acknowledgment of my many debts. The research for this book was supported financially by many public institutions. Foremost among them was the University of California, including the Institute for Labor and Employment (now the Labor and Employment Research Fund); various branches of the University of California at Berkeley, including the Graduate Division, the Townsend Center for the Humanities, and the Department of Sociology; and the University of California at San Diego, including the Division of Social Sciences and the Department of Sociology. The National Science Foundation supported the early data collection for the statistical analysis of tax limitation. So did the Lincoln Institute for Land Policy—a private institution, but, like every not-for-profit organization, one that is subsidized by a federal tax exemption. So my first and greatest debt of thanks is to the taxpayers who made this possible.

The book owes a tremendous intellectual debt to people who did pioneering research on the American property tax revolt. David Sears and Jack Citrin wrote the book on who voted for Proposition 13 and why. Clarence Lo's research demonstrated that Proposition 13 was the endpoint of a long evolution and taught me to pay attention to how the movement's social base changed over time. Robert Kuttner's research first drew my attention to the importance of assessment reform. And Harold Wilensky's comparative research on "tax-welfare backlash" inspired my own, comparative approach to understanding the property tax revolt. Careful readers will notice places where my judgments differ from some of the judgments of these scholars, but anyone who knows their work will also recognize my debts.

I am indebted to several people for conversations about my research design in the early stages: Tony Chen, Robin Einhorn, Jerry Karabel, Clarence Lo, Cathie Jo Martin, Jeffrey Stonecash, Kim Voss, and Margaret Weir.

The people who helped in various ways with the research process include Peter Brownell, who bought me an autographed copy of Howard Jarvis's autobiography; Tony Chen, who put me up during a research trip to Ann Arbor; Peter and Judi Kleinman, who also put me up on that trip; Rebecca Hyde, who discovered the eerie parallels between Dixwell Pierce and Malcolm Davisson; Ji Sung-Jin, who collected and hand-entered much of the data for the quantitative analysis reported in Chapter 5; Paul Garcia-Reynaga, Eric Van Rite, and Nadav Gabay, who helped to collect some of the data on tax revolts around the world that informs the comparative discussion in Chapter 7; and Elisabeth Oxfeldt, who taught me Danish. I also depended on the labor and kindness of many librarians and archivists whose names I do not know. The Massachusetts tax rebels Barbara Anderson, Charles Faulkner, Don Feder, and Edward F. King graciously agreed to be interviewed early in my research, and I am deeply grateful for the time and kindness of these passionate activists.

Several people read the whole manuscript, sometimes more than once, and deserve special thanks. Margaret Weir read and commented on more early drafts of this project than anyone else and offered expert guidance at every stage. Robin Einhorn, Jerry Karabel, and Kim Voss also offered superb advice and generous encouragement. So did Tony Chen, Amy Hanser, Roger Haydon, Peter Katzenstein, Anna Korteweg, Ben Moody, Kimberly Morgan, Chris Rhomberg, Lynn Rivas, Teresa Sharpe, Jonathan Vanantwerpen, and Melissa Wilde, along with my mother, Ann Martin, and several anonymous reviewers. All of these people read most or all of the manuscript at least once and gave me kind and useful suggestions. People who read and offered helpful comments on shorter sections include Jørgen Goul Andersen, Balder Asmussen, Richard Bensel, Paul Burstein, Andrea Campbell, Nitsan Chorev, Bernhard Ebbinghaus, Davita Glasberg, Bill Hurst, Jan Bendix Jensen, Michael Baggesen Klitgaard, Martha Lampland, Asbjørn Sonne Nørgaard, Thomas Pallesen, Steve Pfaff, Kent Redding, Barbara Wejnert, and John Witte. Some of these people will be relieved that I am done sending them drafts. Others will be surprised to see their names here, because the chapters or conference papers they read many years ago are transformed beyond recognition.

I received excellent comments on parts of this project from audiences at the American Sociological Association, the Social Science History Association, the Policy History conference, the Center for Comparative Welfare Studies at the University of Aalborg, and the sociology departments at Indiana University, the University of California at San Diego, Harvard University, the University of California at Berkeley, and Columbia University.

I am grateful to everyone who helped me navigate the world of academic publishing, including Margaret Weir, Tony Chen, Melissa Wilde, John H. Evans, John Skrentny, Steve Erie, Jerry Karabel, Peter Katzenstein, Roger Haydon, and Kate Wahl.

The title is due to the fertile imagination of Amaha Kassa. He suggested some others, too, that are probably best not repeated here. He also told me it was a good idea to study the tax revolt and kept me focused on what was at stake. The book is dedicated to him.

The Permanent Tax Revolt

1 INTRODUCING THE TAX REVOLT

TAXATION IS one of the most basic political issues. Taxes help to determine who gets what, when, and how. Tax policy also defines what government can do about every other issue, from health care to the environment to national defense—because doing things takes money, and money means taxation.

For Americans in the twenty-first century, however, taxation is not just an important issue. Taxes, and tax *cuts* in particular, are the central domestic issue of our time. Candidates for Congress and the Presidency regularly campaign on the promise of tax cuts. Big, high-profile tax cuts appear like clockwork at the top of the domestic policy agenda. Since 2001, Congress has voted to abolish the tax on inherited wealth and has passed a major income tax cut almost every year, including two of the three largest income tax cuts in American history. Congress wrote sunset provisions into these laws that will keep tax cuts at the top of the political agenda for the foreseeable future. Influential politicians are openly pushing for even more tax cuts as a way to shrink the government by starving it of resources. Some politicians, including President George W. Bush and several Republican presidential candidates, have floated the idea of repealing the income tax altogether.[1]

It was not always this way. Americans have a tradition of tax protest—every schoolchild has heard of the Boston Tea Party—but our politicians' current obsession with tax cuts is something new. For three decades after World War II, tax revenues rose to levels that were historically unprecedented. Elected officials from both major parties were happy to let taxes rise. They rarely fought over taxes. They rarely even mentioned the word at election time. American voters, for their part, rarely considered tax policy when they were deciding whom to vote for.[2] They mostly paid their taxes without protest. Our national obsession with tax cuts is not a timeless cultural trait. It is a new political development.

How did taxes—and tax cuts in particular—come to be such a central issue in American political life? The answer lies in a short-lived but intense wave of anti-tax fervor that swept over American politics in the 1970s. After decades of supporting the growth of government with their votes and their taxes, Americans rebelled against the local property tax. Hundreds of thousands of homeowners across the United States picketed, petitioned, and even withheld payment. The movement caught politicians by surprise. Officials scrambled to position themselves as champions of the taxpayer. They voted to cut taxes. They voted to limit the future growth of taxes. And they ushered in a new era in American politics.

This wave of tax protest was a defining moment for many politicians who lived through it. Political entrepreneurs—mostly in the Republican Party—seized on tax cuts as a populist issue that they could use to define themselves and their party in the political marketplace. They led the charge for what would become the largest income tax cut in American history, the Economic Recovery Tax Act of 1981 (ERTA). The political scientists Jacob Hacker and Paul Pierson recently described the memory of this campaign and that tax cut as "the guiding light" of President George W. Bush's domestic agenda. And that tax cut was only possible, they wrote, because President Ronald Reagan had "the popular anti-tax tide of the late 1970s at his back."[3]

This is a book about that anti-tax tide: what it was, where it came from, and what it did to our politics.

WHAT THE TAX REVOLT WAS

The anti-tax tide of the 1970s was a tax revolt. The phrase may conjure images of backwoods revolutionaries priming their muskets or peasants parading around with the tax collector's head on a pike. These images are only partly misleading. To be sure, the tax revolt of the 1970s was something less than an armed rebellion. But it was much more than a trend in public opinion. It was what sociologists call a social movement: a sustained, collective, and unconventional challenge to authority.[4]

Social movements are politics by other means. They are unconventional in the sense that they take place outside official channels and depart from the usual norms of political participation.[5] To grasp what makes a social movement different from the political process you learned about in high school civics, picture some scenes from the tax revolt: a dozen senior citizens assemble to burn their assessment notices on the steps of the county courthouse; thousands of people pack into an auditorium and pledge not to pay their property taxes; a mob of homeowners take to the streets and smash the mayor's car; a crowd of protesters interrupt a county board meeting to seize microphones and shout down their elected tax assessor. The tax rebels did all this and more. They also did the ordinary stuff of politics—they wrote letters, signed petitions, and voted—but they did even these familiar actions in ways that broke with business as usual. The letters flowed in a deluge. The petitions expressed radical new demands to abolish old taxes. And the voters rejected establishment politicians in favor of grassroots ballot measures. One of the rebels' most characteristic demands was to take property taxes out of the ordinary political process altogether—to bind the hands of elected officials by establishing a constitutional limit on how much they could tax. Many of the protesters may have secretly wished for muskets and pikes, but they challenged the old order effectively enough without them.

Tax policy is usually made by elites, but the tax rebels came from all walks of life. A composite portrait would show a homeowner who was typically—but by no means always—a middle-aged white man, married, with an income slightly above the median. His occupation might be almost anything. Mike Rubino, one of the movement's first leaders in California and in the country, drove a beer delivery truck. Robert Tisch, one of the movement's most influential leaders in Michigan, was a former tax assessor and a drain commissioner on the Shiawasee County payroll. George Wiley, one of the movement's earliest spokespeople in the national media, was a former professor of chemistry who is best remembered for his welfare rights activism. Public employees and college professors were underrepresented, but, as these examples suggest, even they were present and participating. Real estate professionals were overrepresented, but they were a small minority in a big and diverse movement. Anyone might be a tax rebel. The tax protesters saw themselves as average people, and surveys from that era suggest that they were basically right.[6]

Like any other movement, the tax revolt had a hard core of leaders and organizers who were especially committed to the cause. These organizers had more political experience than the average person, but they came from all walks of life, too, and from all parts of the political spectrum. Some, like the Massachusetts homemaker Barbara Anderson, had cut their teeth campaigning for conservative causes at a time when this was seen as a fringe activity even in the Republican Party. Others, like George Wiley and the California social work professor Timothy Sampson, were leftists who had learned their politics in the movement for welfare rights. Even the most committed tax rebels shared little beyond a conviction that property taxes were intolerable.[7]

Their protest made headlines all around the world. The fact that voters dislike taxes is not in itself newsworthy, and incumbent politicians everywhere expect voters to turn against them when they raise taxes. But the American tax revolt was unusually ferocious, and it looked like an unprovoked assault. Policy makers had not raised taxes. They had not passed new taxes. The tax that aroused the rebels' anger—the local property tax—was the oldest tax levied in the United States. Its legal basis was enshrined in nineteenth-century state constitutions, but in fact and in administrative practice it was older still.[8] It may even have the distinction of being the only colonial-era tax that survived into the 1970s. Americans had put up with this tax for hundreds of years. Why on earth were they suddenly demanding its abolition? Where, in short, did the tax revolt come from?

At the time, political commentators on the right had a favorite answer: taxpayers rebelled because taxes were just too high.[9] The trouble with this explanation is that it does not fit the facts. American taxes were not very high compared to taxes in other countries that did not have tax revolts. The local property tax was not very burdensome compared to the income taxes that Americans paid without protest. And the people who protested the property tax were not taxed very heavily compared to the people who did nothing.[10] It is true that the tax rebels wanted lower property taxes, but high taxes are not the explanation for why they rebelled.

Some observers on the left argued that taxpayers rebelled because the tax system was riddled with loopholes that unjustly favored the rich and powerful.[11] The trouble with this explanation is that people rose up in protest against the property tax after reformers tried to fix the worst injustices. In state after state, the tax revolt followed closely on the heels of reforms that made the property tax less arbitrary and more progressive than ever before. The movement was not a protest against distributive injustice.

This book shows that taxpayers rebelled because the very same reforms that increased the fairness of the property tax also exposed taxpayers to new income shocks. By modernizing and standardizing tax assessment, the reformers did away with traditional and informal tax breaks that dated from the late nineteenth century. Local tax assessors had dispensed these informal tax privileges unevenly and often arbitrarily. But most homeowners received substantial benefit from them. When they were swept away, homeowners fought to restore them in a new and permanent form.

WHERE THE TAX REVOLT CAME FROM:
INFORMAL TAX PRIVILEGES AS SOCIAL PROTECTION

The central argument of this book is that state officials caused the tax revolt by doing away with informal tax privileges, and people fought to restore those privileges because they had provided a kind of social protection from the market.

A tax privilege is a specific exception to the normal rules of taxation that is designed to benefit a particular person or group of people.[12] For some readers, the term may call to mind prerevolutionary France, where the king routinely granted special tax exemptions to "clergymen, courtiers, nobles, military officers, magistrates and lesser officers" and many other groups called *privilegiés*. (On the eve of the French Revolution, one sure way to insult a nobleman was to call him a "*taillable*," or taxpayer, because only common people paid the tax called the *taille*.)[13] But tax privileges are common in the modern world as well. A well-known example from the contemporary United States is the income tax deduction for mortgage interest on owner-occupied dwellings—the so-called home mortgage interest deduction. This deduction is a special rule that applies to homeowners: before you calculate the tax you owe on your annual income, you may first reduce your taxable income by the amount of interest that you paid on your mortgage. This deduction is different from the tax privileges of prerevolutionary France in many ways, most importantly in that it favors a middle class instead of a hereditary aristocracy. It is nonetheless a tax privilege. It specifically exempts some people (namely, homeowners) from the normal taxes that they would otherwise owe.

These examples are *formal* tax privileges. A formal tax privilege is codified in law—whether in a written constitution, in a statute, or in the procedural regulations that define how a statute is implemented. For example, the federal income tax code today enumerates some 160 specific privileges, called "tax expenditures" or "tax preferences," that provide hundreds of billions of dollars in benefits to defined constituencies that range from low-income college students to wealthy oil companies.[14]

An *informal* tax privilege, by contrast, is one that is not codified in law but that is nevertheless part of the tax system in practice. Many tax systems incorporate informal privileges. Informal tax privileges exist because most countries permit tax officials the leeway to adjust how much they collect from particular taxpayers, and in practice, these officials often go especially easy on certain categories of people. There is anecdotal evidence, for example, that tax collectors in the Internal Revenue Service routinely go soft on delinquent taxpayers who have the right political connections. You will not find this tax break written anywhere in the tax code—but, if the stories are true, it is a real tax privilege with real benefits for the politically well-connected.[15] Even though informal tax privileges like this are not codified, they tend to become institutionalized in custom. The taxpayers who benefit from informal tax privileges come to expect that special rules apply to them. They also tend to react strongly if their special treatment is threatened.

The property tax rebels rebelled because a series of state tax reforms threatened to take away an informal tax privilege called *fractional assessment*. This tax privilege refers to the custom of taxing people on a fraction of the value of their taxable property. Most local governments in the United States levied property taxes in the twentieth century, and most state constitutions had "uniformity clauses" dictating that all owners of real estate should pay taxes on the full market value of their property. In practice, however, homeowners received special treatment. They were typically taxed on a small fraction of the true value of their homes. When the federal government first began collecting information about the quality of local tax administration, in the late 1950s, it found that fractional assessment was legal in only twenty-two states but nearly universal in practice. Even in states where the constitution permitted taxing homeowners on less than the full value of their homes, the true fraction they were taxed on was almost always less than the law dictated and less than the fraction applied to other property owners.[16]

Officials could dispense this privilege because the American property tax was, and is, levied on something invisible. The property tax is a tax *ad valorem*, meaning a tax on value, rather than on some other characteristic of real estate, such as its land area, or the number of windows it has, or the number of bushels of grain it yields at harvest time. A tax *ad valorem* has advantages for the government, one of which is that it is elastic: the tax base grows automatically as the economy grows. But it also has one key disadvantage. Unlike acres of land, windows, or bushels, value is not something you can observe directly, except during the rare and fleeting instant when a property is actually being sold. At all other times— that is, almost always—the value of a property refers to the purely hypothetical price that it *would* sell for if it were sold. Tax officials have to use various techniques to estimate that value indirectly, for example by calculating what it would cost to replace a structure at current construction prices or by observing the price of comparable land parcels that sold in the recent past. Any such technique of estimation opens room for error and disagreement—or for deliberate manipulation and favoritism. That is one reason why political thinkers as astute as James Madison and Alexander Hamilton thought that real estate values were a "chimerical" basis for taxation.[17]

Since the nineteenth century, the officials in charge of estimating property values had dispensed informal tax privileges because it was in their interest to do so. Assessors were generally local elected officials or political appointees. They typically used their discretion politically, rewarding favored constituencies by assessing their property at a fraction of its true value. In exchange, they received votes, campaign contributions, and sometimes even bribes. Although some big commercial property owners benefited from fractional assessments, the most favored constituency was actually homeowners, who were a big, stable, and potentially loyal voting bloc. Of course, not all homeowners benefited equally. There were gross inconsistencies among communities because local assessors in different places were subject to little standardization or state supervision. There were also inconsistencies within communities because assessors often traded particularly favorable assessments directly for political contributions or bribes. Most assessors also had the habit of copying the assessment rolls from year to year and ignoring changes in the market value of homes—a practice that was good for most homeowners when the market was strong and homes were appreciating in value, but bad for those homeowners, often poor or black, who lived in areas of declining property values. Still, despite all these inequities, most homeowners paid tax on a small fraction of the true market value of their homes.[18]

Fractional assessment was more than just a tax break: it was a kind of hidden social policy. By subsidizing homeownership, fractional assessment provided a valuable form of protection against the risk of income shocks, whether those shocks were due to unemployment, sickness, or retirement. As the sociologists Dalton Conley and Brian Gifford note, we may think of homeownership as a kind of safety net: "When unemployment or other financial crises strike," they write, "family net worth—primarily housing equity—may assist in riding out the tough times." Perhaps most important, homeownership can provide a kind of insurance against poverty in old age. Most homeowners in the postwar United States, for example, had fixed-rate mortgages and therefore faced declining payments for housing over the term of the loan. This meant that homeownership promised substantial income security in retirement. Comparative studies suggest that voters and politicians treat tax subsidies for homeowners as a substitute for direct social insurance programs like Social Security: the more that a government spends on one, the less it spends on the other.[19]

Although homeownership appears to be a private alternative to public social provision, the widespread private ownership of homes in the postwar United States actually depended on a variety of public subsidies. The best known of these policies were federal mortgage loan guarantees and the home mortgage interest deduction.[20] A lesser-known policy, but one that was just as important, was the local assessor's unofficial policy of fractional assessment. Homeowners could count on inexpensive housing in retirement because they could count on the assessor to keep their property tax bills low and stable.

By describing tax privileges as a kind of social policy, I am building on recent scholarship that describes formal tax expenditures as a core element of the American social policy regime. Tax expenditures and direct expenditures are alternative ways to achieve similar social purposes. From the point of view of the budget, they are perfectly equivalent—as the political scientist Christopher Howard points out, a tax privilege affects the budget just as if "taxpayers write a check to the government for their full tax liability, and the government issues them a check to cover those activities exempted from taxation." American politicians have taken advantage of this equivalence to build a "hidden welfare state" of tax expenditures that is almost half as large as the federal budget for direct spending on social welfare.[21] Some of these tax expenditures, like the earned income tax credit, supplement direct spending for social welfare by transferring cash to beneficiaries. Others, like the tax exemption for employer-provided health insurance, accomplish social purposes indirectly by subsidizing private organizations that provide either services or income support to individuals in need. Recent scholarship by Christopher Howard and by Jacob Hacker has shown that these tax expenditures for housing, health, and income security are great enough to change our traditional picture of the American welfare state. Scholars once thought of the American welfare state as small and stingy compared to the developed welfare states of Europe; we now see it as middling in size and generosity—but as unusually reliant on tax expenditures that favor middle- and upper-income groups.[22]

To understand the origins of the tax revolt, however, we need to expand our conception of the American social policy regime even further to include the informal tax privileges dispensed by local government. For most of the twentieth century, these informal tax privileges were even more important than formal tax privileges as a source of social protection for most Americans. Because informal tax privileges are not written down, no one keeps statistics on how much they are worth, but even a rough estimate is instructive. I estimated the value of fractional assessment for three points in time—1940, 1956, and 1971— by comparing the property values recorded on local assessment rolls to estimates of the total residential wealth in the United States and calculating how much tax would have been owed on the unassessed wealth if it had been assessed at its true value.[23] The results of the calculation, illustrated in Figure 1.1, show the total property tax revenues lost to fractional assessment of residential property other than farms, in comparison to the budget of selected other social programs. Figure 1.1 shows that the informal tax privilege of fractional assessment saved residential property owners more than \$39 billion in taxes in 1971. The calculation suggests that the fractional assessment of homes was easily the largest single government housing subsidy in the postwar era, and it was among the largest categories of social expenditure of any kind, direct or indirect. Fractional assessment of residential property provided a subsidy that was forty times greater than federal spending for public housing. It was ten times greater than the home mortgage interest deduction. It was five times as costly as more

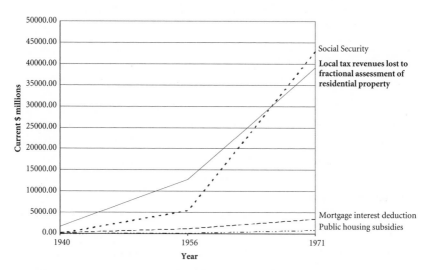

Figure 1.1. Local assessors provided a greater subsidy than most federal social programs, 1940–1971

Sources: *Historical Statistics of the U.S.* and author's calculations (see Appendix 1).

controversial "welfare" programs like Aid to Families with Dependent Children. Although fractional assessment did not show up on official government budgets, on the eve of the tax revolt it was providing more benefits than any other social policy in America except for the twin blockbusters of the federal budget, Social Security and Medicare.

The idea that fractional assessment was a kind of social provision still might seem surprising. Is a corrupt or lackadaisical tax assessor really the same thing as a social security program? Not exactly. Social Security is what I will call *formal social insurance*: a government program that provides people in an explicitly defined risk category (in this case, the elderly) with a legally enforceable entitlement to government income support. Fractional assessment does not meet this definition because (in most states, for most of the twentieth century) it was *informal*: that is, it was not codified in law, so it did not explicitly define risk categories, and—even more important—it did not create an entitlement that the courts would enforce. The latter difference between fractional assessment and formal social insurance was crucially important, as we will see below.

Nevertheless, I will emphasize the similarities between fractional assessment and Social Security by referring to fractional assessment as an example of *informal* social provision. I define *social provision* in very general terms as any customary subsidy provided by government that redistributes resources "to protect against widely distributed risks to income and well-being."[24] The fractional assessment of homes fits this definition because it was a customary subsidy; because it was dispensed by government officials; because it redistributed resources, taking from some taxpayers to subsidize others; and because it did so in order to provide homeowners with income security (in implicit exchange for votes). Although fractional assessment did not provide a legal entitlement, it did have the stability of a deeply entrenched custom. Homeowners expected that the assessor would continue to subsidize their housing by billing them for a small fraction of the taxes that the law prescribed.

The Politics of Fractional Assessment

Thinking of fractional assessment as a kind of social policy helps us to understand how this informal tax privilege survived so long and why taxpayers rebelled when it was threatened. Social policies tend to generate constituents who fight to preserve them and who rally to their defense when they are threatened. There are at least two mechanisms by which social policies create this kind of lock-in effect.[25]

The first mechanism is information asymmetry. Social policies tend to con-centrate benefits on a defined constituency while spreading costs thinly over a broad and less clearly defined population. This combination creates a powerful informational bias in favor of maintaining the policy. Beneficiaries acquire a strong motive to pay attention to the policy and to advocate on behalf of main-taining it: each person who benefits from the policy benefits a great deal and therefore notices, and cares, a great deal about what happens to it. By contrast, each person who pays for the policy pays only a small amount and is therefore likely to be inattentive or indifferent to the question of whether the policy is maintained.[26] This asymmetry creates a logic of blame avoidance. Savvy politi-cians learn that they can dispense benefits in exchange for political support, be-cause the people who benefit will notice and be grateful, and the people who pay will not be especially put out. By the same logic, politicians will try to avoid blame for cutbacks. Cuts to a social policy predictably provoke a noisy outcry from the beneficiaries of that policy without generating much notice or enthu-siasm among other voters who pay for it.[27]

This informational asymmetry and the political logic of blame avoidance that follows from it help to explain why fractional assessment persisted so late into the twentieth century. The benefits of this informal tax privilege were con-centrated among electorally influential groups. The greatest benefits went to affluent homeowners—that is, frequent voters who were concentrated in partic-ular neighborhoods and electoral districts. By contrast, the costs of this tax priv-ilege were more widely distributed and difficult to trace. Who exactly paid more taxes so that homeowners could pay less? Many business owners probably recog-nized that they did not get the same tax break on their business property that they did on their homes, but they may not have recognized that their business taxes were high *because* their home taxes were low. Few tenants presumably paused to think through the long causal chain that ran from homeowners' tax privileges through the landlord's property tax bill to their rent payments. Many consumers of public services might have preferred that property taxes were col-lected and spent on something other than tax privileges for homeowners, but fractional assessment was not listed as an expenditure in local government bud-gets, so it is understandable that few people perceived the budget trade-offs clearly. Fractional assessment provided a tangible benefit at little political cost.

The second mechanism that locks in social policy is material interest. Social policies are often designed in ways that ensure expanding coverage and increas-ing benefits over time. The longer such a policy is entrenched—the more people who come to benefit, and the more valuable the benefit comes to be to them—the stronger the incentive to maintain the policy.[28] Fractional assessment illustrates this process. This tax privilege grew in importance over the twentieth century until it was impossible to dislodge without provoking an outcry. In the early decades of the century, homeowners were a minority of American households, and fractional assessment provided comparatively little benefit to those homeowners. Because property values were low by today's standards, an exemption from property taxes was not especially valuable. By 1970, however—partly as a consequence of this informal subsidy—a majority of American householders had become homeowners, and property values had increased many times over. Fractional assessment was worth more to more people than ever before.

These similarities between informal tax privileges and formal social insurance help us understand how fractional assessment lasted until the late twentieth century. It is the differences, however, that help us understand why fractional assessment did not last forever. Because fractional assessment was informal, it did not create a legal entitlement. The benefits depended on the whim of the assessor, and in most states a homeowner's claim to the benefits of fractional assessment was not enforceable in the courts. This absence of entitlement is important because the growing demand for local spending in the postwar era—particularly on schools—increased conflicts over the distribution of the property tax burden, and these conflicts eventually wound up in court. When the growing demand for local spending came into conflict with the growing tax privilege for homeowners, it created a serious legal problem for state officials. The informal tax privilege gave way.

The states ultimately did away with informal tax privileges by modernizing the property tax. Modernization meant increasing *centralization, professionalization*, and *standardization* of property assessment. State officials centralized authority for assessment, for example by instituting new lines of supervision and by consolidating small jurisdictions. They standardized assessment, by enforcing new procedures—for example, by requiring all assessors to use the same forms to collect information and using new computer-assisted techniques to evaluate all homes according to the same mathematical function. And they professionalized property assessment, for example by replacing elected with appointed officials and by requiring assessors to undergo training and certification.[29]

The reforms deprived local assessors of the discretion that they had used to grant informal tax privileges. They thereby ensured that the tax bill reflected the market value of a property rather than the social status or political party of the taxpayer. The reforms made the tax fairer. But they also took away the informal social policy that had protected homeowners. For the first time, homeowners were effectively taxed on the market value of their property. People whose taxes had been stable for years found that their tax bills—and their welfare—suddenly depended on the whims of the housing market.

Consider what this meant from the perspective of an ordinary homeowner. If you were someone like Mike Rubino, your home was your biggest investment. It was your hedge against uncertainty, your main retirement fund, and one of your main forms of security against a sudden loss of income. And all of this was possible because of fractional assessment. You bought your home secure in the expectation of a low tax bill. Even when the market drove your home's value up, the assessor promised to hold your tax bill down. That was the deal—until the tax reforms of the 1960s took matters out of the assessor's hands.

If you were someone like Mike Rubino, you did not just sit there and watch while your tax privileges disappeared. You got together with your neighbors, who saw their own tax privileges disappearing too. And then you rebelled.

WHAT THE TAX REVOLT DID TO AMERICAN POLITICS

The tax revolt transformed American politics by popularizing a new public policy—tax limitation—that helped to place tax cuts permanently on the policy agenda.

Voters and politicians at first embraced property tax limitation as a way to restore tax privileges for homeowners. A property tax limitation was a law that established a fixed limit on the annual percentage increase in the property tax levy—often by combining a legal limit on the property tax rate and a legal limit on the annual increase of assessed valuation. Tax limits effectively forbade local governments from increasing property taxes rapidly, even if the market value of taxable property increased rapidly. If you were a property owner, this meant that the longer you held your property, the more of a tax privilege you enjoyed. Property tax limitations created a tax privilege much like the old, informal tax privilege provided by local assessors, who had simply copied the tax rolls from year to year without reappraising property. The difference was that now the tax privilege was formal: it was codified in statute and sometimes in state constitutions.

Property tax limitation laws did more than just restore a tax privilege for homeowners. They locked in a new and growing tax privilege for *anyone* who held onto real estate for a long time. Property tax limits thus created especially big tax breaks for business owners and the affluent. The more valuable that a property was, the more that the tax break would be worth in the long run. Property tax limits also limited the revenues available for public social spending—most particularly, spending on public schools.

These laws were not the only possible response to the movement. The property tax protesters demanded the restoration of their traditional tax privileges, but there were many possible ways to meet their demands. The federal structure of American government allowed policy makers at the state level to experiment with every alternative that showed any promise of quieting the protests. Some legislators amended state constitutions to authorize fractional assessment for homeowners. Others targeted tax privileges to elderly and low-income people. Still others passed tax limitation laws that limited the annual growth of property tax bills. Each of these alternatives had its proponents among the protesters. For a time, they competed on equal footing.

Once tax limitation won a popular referendum, however, it became the tax rebels' favorite strategy. The turning point was the California primary election of June 6, 1978. The property tax rebellion had made property taxation into the central issue on the state's policy agenda, and the major question in that election was which alternative property tax relief policy the voters would approve. California voters approved the most conservative alternative, a ballot initiative called Proposition 13. This initiative amended the state constitution to limit the growth of the property tax. Before Proposition 13, liberal and conservative policy solutions to the property tax crisis competed on equal footing. "After Proposition 13," the columnist Russell Baker wrote, "there were only about four liberals left in the country."[30]

The policy changed what activists and legislators thought was possible—and therefore which policies they thought it worthwhile to pursue. Those conservatives who preferred other ways of limiting government decided to pursue Proposition 13–style limits on the property tax because they were winnable. Even liberals who preferred other ways of reforming the property tax began to rethink their opposition to tax limitation when they saw how well it did at the ballot box. Policy makers began to position themselves as allies of Proposition 13. Other remedies fell by the wayside as state after state passed property tax limits like Proposition 13.

The ripple effects spilled over to other tax policies. California's Democratic Governor Jerry Brown, who had opposed Proposition 13, declared himself "born again to the spirit of austerity and tax cut" after it passed.[31] Brown and other officials throughout the country began to entertain proposals to limit other taxes. Tax and expenditure limitations of all kinds spread through the states more rapidly after 1978. Conservative activists began making headway with plans for constitutional limits on federal spending.[32]

In short, officials saw Proposition 13 as a symptom of public hostility to government in general, rather than the property tax in particular, and concluded—wrongly—that more tax cuts were the cure. For decades, policy makers had treated tax cuts like a carefully regulated prescription medication, a tool of Keynesian demand management to be employed with care, under expert guidance, when the economy was ailing. After 1978, some politicians started selling tax cuts over the counter as an all-purpose remedy.

Tax limitation ultimately changed American politics by changing the terms of competition between the parties. The success of property tax limits at the ballot box persuaded many entrepreneurial politicians—including the presidential candidate Ronald Reagan—that big tax cuts were good politics. Reagan ran on a pledge to cut taxes, and his landslide victory persuaded people in both parties that he had a mandate for cuts. The Economic Recovery Tax Act of 1981 embodied his proposal for a deep reduction in tax rates. The existence of state tax limits helped to keep tax cuts in the public eye. Although Reagan later signed legislation to raise income taxes (as did his successor, George H. W. Bush), the historic tax cut of his first term—and the state tax limitations that inspired it—cemented an anti-tax constituency within the Republican Party. The experience convinced many young Republican legislators and lobbyists that tax cuts were good politics. These politicians worked hard to keep taxes in the public eye and fought with moderates in their own party to redefine the G.O.P. as the party of tax cuts. To say that their motives were political is not to impugn their sincerity. Many of today's most influential Republicans are true believers who look back on the tax cuts of Reagan's first term as the symbol of a revolution in government. It was a golden moment that the faithful are still trying to re-create.

THE LESSONS OF THE TAX REVOLT

The tax revolt has important lessons for anyone who wants to understand American politics in the twentieth century. It also has more particular lessons for policy makers and scholars. Three of these lessons are particularly important.

Americans Want Their Government to Protect Them from the Market

One of the most important lessons of this story is that American taxpayers like their invisible welfare state—indeed, that they will fight to defend it. The tax revolt was a rebellion fought to defend a regime of tax privilege that was also a regime of social protection. The policies that tax rebels demanded, including Proposition 13, were not attempts to dismantle the welfare state. They were attempts to restore a customary form of welfare for homeowners.

This lesson is important because it contradicts some other popular stories that are told about the tax revolt and American politics in general. Some commentators on the tax revolt have drawn the conclusion that Americans will not tolerate big government. This story traces the tax revolt to America's long tradition of "anti-statism," or generalized hostility to government.[33] It is a short step from this argument to the conclusion that would-be social policy reformers in America should scale back their ambitions. Reforms that require substantial government intervention in the market are doomed from the start, in this view, because they are ill-suited to our anti-statist traditions.

This book will show to the contrary that the tax revolt was not at first especially anti-statist. The movement included liberals alongside libertarians. Protesters' proposed solutions to the property tax crisis varied, but few were anti-statist in the sense that they would actually constrain the state's ability to tax. Most protesters simply wanted to restore tax privileges. Even those wings of the movement that proposed to abolish property taxation altogether were typically proposing that it be replaced by some other form of taxation they regarded as more just or more sustainable. The fight was not about whether to tax. It was mainly about how to tax, and whom.

Other commentators on the tax revolt have drawn the conclusion that Americans will not tolerate government redistribution of income. The most influential version of this story traces the tax revolt to Americans' hostility to means-tested public assistance (or "welfare"). There was a much-discussed backlash of white working-class voters in the 1970s against what they saw as the excesses of the liberal welfare state in President Lyndon B. Johnson's Great Society programs. But the welfare backlash was not the tax revolt, and it did not cause the tax revolt.[34] The tax revolt was not directed against federal welfare programs. It was directed against the local property tax. And some of the earliest and most stalwart tax rebels—including, for a time, the most successful ones—were actually veterans of the struggle for welfare rights who continued to think that the Great Society had not gone far enough. Welfare rights organizers like George Wiley and Tim Sampson stoked the fires of the property tax revolt because they hoped it would spark a broader movement for income redistribution.

Yet another lesson that some commentators have drawn is that Americans re-belled against the property tax because activist judges were equalizing the fi-nances of rich and poor school districts. The story has it that people in wealthy school districts happily paid property taxes only as long as they could keep those taxes for their own schools. Beginning in the 1970s, several state courts overturned this system of local school finance on the grounds that it violated the constitu-tional rights of children in poor districts. A California legislator described the tax revolt as a backlash against one such court order: "This is the revenge of wealth against the poor. 'If the schools must actually be equal,' they are saying, 'then we'll undercut them all.' "[35] The lesson, if this story is correct, is that we should tolerate the unequal financing of public schools, because that is the only way to keep middle-class taxpayers from rebelling against public education altogether.

This, too, is a plausible story but not a true one. The tax revolt was not lim-ited to states with school finance decisions. In California—the state that had the most famous equalization decision, *Serrano v. Priest*—the tax revolt pre-dated school finance equalization, and surveys show that the tax rebels were neither concentrated in wealthy school districts nor especially hostile to school finance equalization.[36]

The tax rebels were not opposed to government action, even government ac-tion that redistributed income. They *wanted* government to redistribute income in order to protect them from income shocks that resulted from the rising price of housing. The tax revolt, in short, was a social protectionist movement—much like the movements of farmers, workers, and poor people that gave rise to the first welfare states.[37]

Good Government Can Cause Social Protest

The second important lesson of this case is that even good government can pro-voke social protest. By good government, I mean the ideal of modern public ad-ministration: a rational, bureaucratic system, with clear lines of authority, standardized procedures, and professionally qualified administrators, that guar-antees equal treatment for citizens in a democratic state. State officials modern-ized the administration of the property tax in the 1960s and 1970s to bring it closer to this ideal. They improved the state's ability to collect and redistribute re-sources without favoritism. But they also supplanted traditional tax privileges—an earlier, informal mode of redistribution—and thereby triggered the tax revolt.

This conclusion has broader relevance to social movement theory, because it suggests that a common assumption about the relationship between government and protest needs to be revised. Many social movement scholars have assumed that the relationship between public administrators and protesters is cooperative rather than conflictual. Modern public administration increases the state's ability to distribute the collective goods that many protest movements demand, such as civil rights enforcement, welfare benefits, or environmental protection. Bureaucrats may also secretly welcome protesters as allies, because protesters' demands for more benefits can help bureaucrats justify larger budgets. For these reasons, social movement scholars generally treat good government as a dimension of the "political opportunity structure." Good government, according to this view, invites protest by promising that it will be rewarded.[38]

This study shows that good government may also provoke protest by threatening to impose new costs on citizens. This argument builds on a small but growing body of social movement research into the mobilizing power of threats. People may protest if they believe that their protests will be rewarded, but they will weigh the perceived rewards of action against the perceived costs of inaction. A government that increases the costs of doing nothing—or merely threatens to do so—may therefore provoke protest even if protesters think their chances of success are low. Several empirical studies have demonstrated the mobilizing power of threats. Most of these studies, however, focus on the extraordinary threat of repression in undemocratic states—that is, on very bad governments—rather than on the routine costs of government in modern democracies.[39]

The case of the tax revolt reminds us that good governments also impose costs that can cause protest. Even the least repressive states must impose collective burdens as a routine part of what they do. Redistribution creates losers as well as winners; the collective benefits distributed by government are always paid for by someone. In modern, democratic states, the costs of government are widely distributed.[40] The resistance to these costs may therefore inspire broad-based collective action. If we want to understand the spread of social movements in democratic countries, we would do well to attend to the *routine policy threats*, a category that includes not only taxes but all of the costs imposed by the ordinary activities of government—from the siting of hazardous landfills, to the routing of traffic, to the teaching of painful truths in public schools.[41]

The property tax revolt responded to political opportunities, too, as classic social movement theory would predict. The openness of electoral institutions and the availability of elite allies affected the form of the protest and the outcome of the protest, just as scholars have found for a variety of other social movements.[42] But if we ask what gave rise to the movement in the first place, then political opportunities alone cannot answer the question. There were protest mobilizations against local property taxation in the United States, where electoral institutions were decentralized, the political system was presidential, and voters could make use of the ballot initiative; and in Britain, where electoral institutions were centralized, the political system was parliamentary, and voters did not have access to the ballot. In the United States, protest mobilization peaked in California in the late 1970s—where and when government was (and was widely perceived to be) especially *unresponsive* to the needs of property taxpayers.[43] It was the push of a routine policy threat, not the pull of political opportunity, that led to protest.

The Configuration of American Political Institutions Can Help Outsiders Win

Finally, the tax revolt has an important lesson about American political institutions. The American political system—particularly the combination of federalism and direct democracy—gives protesters and other political outsiders many access points to the policy agenda. It may therefore promote dramatic changes in public policy, for good or ill.

This lesson is important because many scholars of social policy and social movements have assumed the contrary. The fragmented American political system is supposed to block policy change by providing many constitutional "veto points," or opportunities to block new policy proposals. The obvious example is the presidential veto, but other American political institutions also create veto points. Bicameralism permits either house of Congress to block legislation. Federalism means that policy proposals of the national government often require the cooperation of the states—so that states have an opportunity to block policies they oppose. At the state level, the institution of direct democracy, or the referendum, may permit voters to block acts of the legislature. The more such veto points there are, the story goes, the harder it is for any proposed bill to clear all the necessary hurdles before it becomes law. The usual outcome, in the words of one social movement scholar, is "policy stalemate."[44]

This "veto points" view of the American polity is a partial truth. The American political system does have many constitutional veto points. This book will show that these veto points did indeed allow state and local officials to block proposed policies that they opposed. It will show that the dispersion of authority in the American polity also contributes to policy stability in another way: by diffusing blame for failed policies. The fragmentation of authority in the American polity creates many opportunities to pass the buck.[45] It thus helps to explain why the modernization of property assessment was delayed so long into the postwar era. It also helps to explain why protesters' demands to abolish the local property tax failed.

But the existence of multiple veto points does not mean that the American political system is doomed to policy stalemate. For in other ways the fragmentation of authority may actually *increase* the rate of policy innovation.[46] Many of the veto points in the American political system are also access points that enable protesters to promote new policies they favor.[47] Federalism, for example, does not just add veto points; it also multiplies opportunities to initiate policy. As the Supreme Court Justice Louis Brandeis famously remarked, "It is one of the happy accidents of the federal system that a single courageous state may, if its citizens choose, serve as a laboratory, and try novel social and economic experiments without risk to the rest of the country."[48] Just so, the political diversity of the states encouraged legislators to experiment with different ways of responding to property tax protests. Direct democracy, too, is more than just a veto point: in many American states, voters may not only veto acts of the legislature, but may also initiate new legislation by petition. Property tax rebels made frequent use of the ballot initiative. They circulated petitions to abolish the property tax, to formalize homeowners' tax privileges, and to limit the tax. Protesters thereby directly influenced the policy agenda and the alternatives in play. They also provided lawmakers with crucial information about which policies were potential vote-getters. Even the presidency is not just a veto point. The president not only vetoes legislation: he or she also sets the policy agenda.

So does institutional fragmentation help or hinder social movements? This book argues for a conditional answer: it depends. One thing that it depends on is the *specific* set of powers that the relevant institutions confer on actors in a particular policy domain. A social scientist cannot predict whether institutions will promote or inhibit new social policy simply by counting up veto points or access points, because similar institutions may have different rules about who is empowered to veto what kinds of legislation under what circumstances. There are different varieties of federalism, for example, that assign decision-making responsibilities differently across policy domains, and it is important to the story of the tax revolt to understand that American federalism (unlike, say, German federalism) reserves property tax legislation to the states.[49] This book might tell a very different story if it were about a German property tax revolt—or if it were about an American protest movement that was concerned with monetary policy, war, or interstate commerce.

The effects of institutions also depend on the strategies that protesters employ to get their way. This argument draws on the recent work of social movement scholars who have shown that protesters have the greatest impact on public policy where they match their behavior to their institutional environment.[50] But the case of the tax revolt illustrates a further point. Finding the right fit between behavior and institutions is not only a matter of tactics, or choosing *how* to engage in conflict—for example, by calibrating the degree to which protests should be disruptive or assertive. It is also a matter of strategy, or choosing *where*, *when*, and *in what sequence* to make demands. The tax rebels discovered that beginning with the president was a recipe for failure: a proposal for property tax relief that started here would have to clear multiple veto points at the state level. Starting with the states was a better recipe for success, because the president could not veto state action. And the pathway through the states would ultimately put the demand for tax relief back on the president's desk—though ultimately in a form that few protesters would have recognized.

Finally, the effects of institutions may depend on their configuration in relation to one another. A particular package of institutions may be greater than the sum of its parts. This does not mean that institutions always fit together into a smoothly functioning system, or that political scientists should abandon their efforts to identify how a particular institution, such as, say, the referendum, shapes political outcomes. But it does mean that our theories should do more than catalog the effects of institutions considered in isolation.[51] We should also consider how institutions work in combination. Configurations matter. For example, a ballot initiative may assume special symbolic importance if it takes place in an important electoral district; its impact may then be magnified by that district's position in a federal system; and it may ultimately reshape presidential politics. That, anyhow, is the story of Proposition 13.

The general lesson of the property tax revolt, then, is that the effects of political institutions on protest movements are domain specific, strategy dependent, and configurational. At least sometimes, the configuration of American political institutions not only allows outsiders access but also helps them to win. This book will focus on two American political institutions in particular: federalism and direct democracy. When challengers make the right policy demands and use the right strategies, the combination of these institutions can facilitate radical changes in policy.

WHAT IS TO COME

Today, most people probably associate anti-tax sentiment with the American right. The politicians who promote tax cuts with the greatest enthusiasm are the politicians who also want to limit government intervention in the market. It may seem surprising, then, to trace the origins of the tax revolt to a progressive movement for social protection from the market, or to describe the tax revolt, as this book does, as a defensive rebellion begun when the state undermined traditions of informal tax relief.

To make the case for this surprising conclusion, the rest of this book presents two kinds of evidence. The first is historical narrative. The book tells the stories of many little-known tax protests. The property tax revolt included working-class homeowners in the inner-city Midwest and poor farmers in the South. It included radicals and liberals alongside moderates and conservatives. One justification for focusing on these untold stories is that they help to fill in our picture of the tax revolt: most published histories of the movement focus narrowly on conservatives in a few California suburbs. But these stories do more than just fill in the details in a picture whose broad outlines are already familiar. This book's focus on the progressive wing of the tax revolt changes the big picture, too. I put progressives front and center in this book's narrative because, at the outset, these groups really were front and center in the property tax revolt.

The second kind of evidence that the book presents is analytic. The book makes use of social-scientific methods. Experiments are impossible in history, but historically oriented social scientists are sometimes able to use comparisons to isolate causes—in something like the way that experimental scientists isolate causes by comparing treatment and control groups.[52] For the purposes of this book, it is a happy accident that the property tax is regulated separately in each state. This fact creates a lot of variation from state to state that we can exploit for the purposes of comparison. We can also use a comparison to Britain, the only other rich democracy to rely as heavily on real property taxes; and one penultimate chapter assesses how exceptional the American tax revolt was by situating this story in an even broader comparative perspective. At a few key points, this book also presents the results of original statistical analyses, although it should be possible for readers to follow and evaluate the main argument without reading the technical appendices.

Because the book covers a lot of ground, a brief outline may help. Chapter 2 sets the stage for the story of the tax revolt by demonstrating how policy lock-in and the logic of blame avoidance preserved fractional assessment late into the twentieth century. Chapter 2 relies heavily on a case study of California, but it also makes selective comparisons to other high-tax states, Massachusetts and New York. These states presented best-case scenarios for the development of modern property tax administration: they were innovative, liberal states that spent heavily on public education, and they were states where pressure to modernize the tax was therefore strongest. But even with all of these advantages, it took intervention by the courts to undermine the custom of fractional assessment. Chapter 3 presents case studies of the property tax revolt—with a special focus on two more typical states, Illinois and Missouri—to show how the modernization of property assessment led to the growth of a social movement.

The next chapters show how American political institutions transformed the movement. By 1972, property tax protesters on the right and the left were united in demanding the abolition of the local property tax. Chapter 4 follows this movement as it splintered on the federal structure of American government. Federalism had two faces. On one hand, federalism blocked policy innovation at the national level. On the other hand, federalism also allowed many different policies to flourish at the state level, thereby revealing the underlying diversity of the movement and promoting policy innovation. The chapter illustrates the process of fragmentation by following the development of three alternative forms of property tax relief—progressive policies that restored property tax privileges for low-income people; centrist policies that restored fractional assessment for homeowners; and conservative policies that created new tax privileges for *all* property owners, but especially the affluent.

Chapter 5 presents evidence that the California ballot initiative called Proposition 13 was a crucial turning point, when the most conservative policy option began to capture the allegiances of protesters and politicians around the country. Chapter 5 also presents evidence that direct democracy was the key to explaining this outcome. Proposition 13 captured the imagination of policy makers and the public because it passed at the ballot box—thereby ratifying property tax limitation as a political winner. Property tax limitation laws, and state and local tax limitations more generally, began to spread rapidly throughout the states.

What consequences did tax limitations have for American politics? Chapter 6 traces the story to the present, by showing how state and local tax limitations transformed politics at the federal level. These policies made possible the largest income tax cut in American history. They also elevated tax cuts to prominence as a partisan issue, by inspiring a group of politicians who thereafter worked hard to redefine the Republican Party as the party of permanent tax rebellion. This chapter, in short, shows that the right turn in the property tax revolt of the 1970s gave rise to the distinctive anti-tax constituency that is characteristic of American politics today.

Chapter 7 sets the story in a broad, comparative perspective. Chapter 7 shows that even in countries with very different political cultures, people have often taken collective action to defend their informal tax privileges, in ways that are strikingly similar to the American property tax revolt. The comparison underlines the central point of the book: the tax revolt was not itself inherently conservative or anti-state.

You may experience déjà vu as you read the narrative that follows. As I write this, voters in at least three states have just considered (and rejected) new and more restrictive tax limitations. If the history of the tax revolt is any guide, failure will not deter the proponents of tax limitation. With the 2001 tax cuts set to expire in 2010, Congress will soon be facing pressure to pass record-breaking income tax cuts once again. The legacy of the tax revolt is still with us. This book aims to illuminate where that legacy came from—and, perhaps, what we can do about it today.

2 A SEEDBED OF TAXPAYER REVOLT

The Modernization of the American Property Tax

TO FIND THE ROOTS of the tax revolt, you need only look at the state tax reforms of the 1960s. One of the most ambitious reforms was outlined in *A Program of Tax Reform for California*, published by the California State Assembly Interim Committee on Revenue and Taxation in July 1965. The committee chair was a liberal Democrat from the San Francisco Bay Area named Nicholas Petris, and this was a frankly liberal program whose purpose was to support increased government spending. In nearly 400 pages of small print, the committee proposed a total overhaul of the state's tax structure. The committee would make it easier to collect personal income taxes by instituting a new system of paycheck withholding. It would raise taxes on business by closing tax loopholes. And it would increase personal income taxes, corporate income taxes, inheritance taxes, sales taxes, and the state excise tax on cigarettes.[1]

You might expect this long list of tax increases to be controversial. But the part of the package that proved most contentious—and the only provision that provoked a minority report from a Republican member of the committee, with the stern warning that it would sow "a seedbed of taxpayer revolt"—was not any of these. It concerned the local property tax—the one tax that the committee was actually proposing to cut. And the most controversial reform to the property tax was a technical provision that the committee dismissed as "without major revenue significance." This was the proposal to modernize property assessment.[2]

Modern tax assessment meant market-oriented tax assessment: the committee proposed to increase the consistency and efficiency with which local authorities estimated the market value of taxable resources. In practice this meant administrative modernization—specifically, the centralization, professionaliza-tion, and standardization of tax administration. The counties would centralize all authority for appraising taxable real estate. The state would administer a stan-dardized test to screen county assessors for competence. Most importantly, the state would enforce a common performance standard. County assessors would henceforth appraise all taxable property uniformly at its market value and assess all property for tax purposes at 25 percent of that value, with no exceptions.[3]

This reform was one of the first of its kind in the United States, and it really did sow a seedbed of taxpayer revolt. The problem was not that it raised taxes too high, but that it reformed taxes too late. The states missed their last great opportunity to modernize local property tax administration during World War II. By the time that they undertook to modernize the tax, after two decades of peacetime economic growth, too many people had developed deeply vested in-terests in the continuation of the old, premodern system. A majority of Ameri-can households enjoyed informal tax privileges under the old system, and those tax privileges were worth more than ever before.

Why did public officials delay the modernization of property assessment? There are two answers to this question. The first answer is simple: some offi-cials did not rush to modernize the property tax because they benefited from traditional tax administration. In particular, the local officials who were in charge of property assessment liked the old system because it gave them the freedom to grant or withhold informal tax privileges at will. They could use those informal tax privileges as a resource to be traded for personal or political gain. Different assessors made different uses of that resource, but one of the ways that they used it most consistently was to lobby against modernization—thereby preserving the system that made them powerful.

The second answer is that even officials who did not benefit from the old system sought to avoid blame for tax increases. The politics of property tax re-form were the politics of blame avoidance. For most of the twentieth century, the state officials responsible for the property tax knew that unfair and ineffi-cient assessment was a serious problem, and they knew that the solution was to modernize the tax: to centralize authority, standardize procedures, and intro-duce new requirements for professional training and certification. They also knew that modernization risked infringing on the traditional tax privileges of homeowners. They failed to act for fear of provoking popular protest.

These answers explain why officials *wanted* to delay modernization. To ex-plain why they were *able* to delay modernization for decades, we must turn to the fragmentation of American government, which provided many opportunities for blame avoidance. The federal government assumed no responsibility for property taxation, and indeed the Constitution implicitly reserved property taxes to the states.[4] Fifty states had fifty different property tax systems, but in most states, the law divided responsibility for the tax between state and local levels of government, and then redivided it among local governments, and then redivided it yet again among multiple officials *within* the same local government. In California, for example, city, county, and school district officials all set property tax rates independently of one another; another group of officials— mainly county officials, but also some city officials, and in special cases some state officials—assessed the value of taxable property; and yet another group of state officials ratified or adjusted those assessments.[5] This fragmented structure made possible a many-sided game of blame avoidance that could and did go on for decades. School board members could blame county assessors for high property taxes, because it was the assessors who decided what to record as the taxable value of a property; county assessors could blame county supervisors, because supervisors set the county tax rate; county supervisors could blame the State Board of Equalization, because the board adjusted the county's tax assessment levels; and the board could blame school districts, cities, or counties, as it chose. Most elected officials were content to play this game indefinitely.

It was the courts that finally undermined the power of local assessors and forced action by reluctant state officials. In the meantime, however, delay had made matters worse. More people were drawing more benefits from the traditional system than ever before. Reform sowed a seedbed of taxpayer revolt.

THE PROBLEMS WITH THE PROPERTY TAX

There were many reasons to modernize property taxation. Local property tax administration had not changed since the nineteenth century. Most assessors were elected officials or political appointees: they typically lacked training in appraisal methods, and even where they were capable of appraising property accurately, the political imperative to avoid blame for tax increases trumped the constitutional imperative to assess property at its full market value. Assessors typically dispensed informal tax privileges by assessing property at a small fraction of its market value. This fraction (the "assessment ratio") varied widely from place to place, although, as Chapter 1 emphasized, the practice of fractional assessment provided a valuable subsidy to homeowners almost everywhere.[6]

There were two main problems with this system. The first was that it was inequitable. The system was unfair to property owners who lived in the wrong neighborhood. It was unfair to most business owners, who paid taxes on a greater fraction of their assets' true market value than homeowners did, although campaign contributors sometimes got off easy. More generally, the system was unfair to any taxpayer who was not lucky or savvy enough to get a good assessment. The system was rife with favoritism. Most homeowners got deep tax breaks, but the exact depth often depended on the caprice or avarice of the local assessor. Some assessors traded informal tax privileges for bribes; most assessors traded them, at least implicitly, for votes.[7]

The traditional methods for dealing with this problem were ineffective. Most states had an elected or appointed body—often called a "Board of Equalization"—that was charged with overseeing the work of local assessors and enforcing the constitutional rule of uniform taxation. If the assessor in one county, for example, was assessing property at too small a fraction of its actual value, then the board had the power to raise the entire county's assessments until the assessment ratio was closer to the state average. Equalization was a blunt instrument for creating uniformity, however, that in some ways actually made the problem worse. Raising all the assessments in a county by a fixed "equalization factor" might bring the county's average assessment ratio closer to the state average, but at the same time it exacerbated inequities *within* the county, multiplying them by the same factor.

The second problem with the system was that it was inadequate to meet the rapidly growing revenue needs of local governments. Schools, cities, and counties all needed a growing tax base to meet the growing demands for public spending over the twentieth century. But most assessors did their best to keep the *measured* tax base small. Not only did they assess most property at a fraction of what it was worth, but they allowed this fraction to decrease over time, for two reasons. First, most assessors copied the assessment rolls from year to year, with little or no effort to adjust for rising property values. Second, the fact that assessors were local officials gave them an additional motive to underassess: they were competing with other local areas to attract people, businesses, and state aid, and one way to compete was to have the lowest assessments. This combination of habitual roll-copying and competitive underassessment exerted a force like gravity. Over time, assessment ratios sank closer and closer to zero, and the value of informal tax privileges grew and grew.[8]

Reformers had complained about these problems for decades, but the Great Depression illustrated them in a way that was impossible to ignore.[9] When the Depression struck, local assessors in many areas continued their practice of copying the assessment rolls from year to year. In better times this custom had given people an informal tax privilege: as their homes and businesses appreciated in value, their tax bills lagged behind. But during the Depression, this same custom imposed an informal tax penalty: as the real values of their homes and businesses sank, their tax bills did not. Property taxes not only failed to sink, they even rose, because more and more poor people were crowding onto the county relief rolls, and more and more students were staying in public schools longer in order to avoid the dismal labor market.[10]

Taxpayers responded to the disappearance of their informal tax privileges with protest. In 1932, property owners' associations throughout the country began to threaten local officials with tax strikes. The most famous of the strikes was in Chicago, where tens of thousands of taxpayers withheld the taxes they owed and held out for several months. The Chicago strikers made headlines around the country, but they were not alone. Taxpayers' groups threatened or carried out property tax strikes in Atlanta, Milwaukee, and New York. In California, associations repeatedly threatened local officials with tax strikes in Los Angeles and the nearby counties of San Bernardino and Imperial.[11] "Unless we can provide some relief for the overburdened owner of real estate," the California State Board of Equalization member and State Controller Ray L. Riley told an audience of Los Angeles voters in 1933, "we are headed for a tax strike and resulting chaos."[12]

California's response made it a leader in modernizing state tax structure, but it did not modernize property tax administration. Instead, Riley and another board member named Fred E. Stewart responded to the protests by drafting a constitutional amendment that limited local government spending, shifted some of the costs of education from local school boards to the state, and authorized new state taxes to substitute for local property taxes. The so-called Riley-Stewart amendment also permitted counties to assess and tax the property owned by public utilities—previously a state responsibility—on the theory that this would let them lower the taxes on homeowners and small business owners. Voters approved the amendment on June 27, 1933.

One thing that the Riley-Stewart amendment did not do, however, was restore homeowners' informal tax privileges, and so tax protests continued sporadically throughout the decade. When an earthquake struck the city of Long Beach in 1933, for example, local officials promised disaster relief in the form of reduced property assessments—a clear illustration of the deliberate use of fractional assessment as social policy. And when the assessor failed to deliver the promised reductions, residents responded with a tax strike. Residents of San Bernardino County threatened a strike when the state equalized assessed valuations in 1935, because the equalization reduced informal tax privileges in rural areas. And rising relief loads repeatedly provoked tax strike threats in Los Angeles, San Diego, and suburban Orange County.[13]

The tax revolt of the Depression years foreshadowed the tax revolt of the 1970s, when the erosion of traditional tax privileges would once again provoke homeowners to protest and thereby inspire sweeping tax reforms, but there was one key difference. In the 1930s, the problem could still have been solved by modernizing property tax administration. Property tax privileges were disappearing during the Depression in part because traditional assessment practice failed to keep pace with the sinking price of homes. The obvious solution was to record current property values more accurately—and, as tax experts of the time pointed out, this meant modernizing the administration of the tax by centralizing, standardizing, and professionalizing assessment.[14] By the time that these reforms were finally enacted in the 1960s and 1970s, however, traditional property assessment was no longer threatening traditional tax privileges. To the contrary, it was providing a valuable form of social protection. Home prices were rising, not falling, and the modernization of the property tax would undermine tax privileges by causing taxes to rise in pace with the price of housing. Modernization would sow the seeds of revolt.

WORLD WAR II: A MISSED OPPORTUNITY TO MODERNIZE

If ever there was a golden opportunity to modernize the property tax, it was World War II, and if any state had an opportunity to modernize property tax administration in wartime, California did. The war created an urgent need for modern tax administration, and it also created new tools to satisfy that need.

The war created a burning need for modern tax administration by making unprecedented demands on local government. Federal orders created hundreds of new naval stations, military bases, and supply depots in California alone. New cities arose overnight, as people from all over the country came to work, building ships and airplanes.[15] These new cities needed new roads, new sewers, new schools, and new police. Local governments needed an elastic source of revenue to meet the demand for infrastructure and services. Modern property tax administration was the obvious solution: with modern assessment procedures in place, tax revenues could grow automatically as real estate values rose. The war thus created a new constituency for modernization among local government officials—chiefly city and school district officials—who saw their resources stretched to the limit.

The war also paved the way for modernization by revealing the inadequacy of the traditional assessment system. The war played havoc with property values, increasing them with astonishing speed in many places, and decreasing them in others. For local assessors with little training and few resources, keeping track of changing property values would have been a challenge at the best of times. It was obvious to everyone that it was impossible in wartime. Because local assessors in different parts of the state did little to standardize their procedures, they had little hope of taxing real estate uniformly. They could not keep pace with the rapid and uneven changes in property values.

In some places, for example, the war increased property values dramatically. The War Department must have seemed like Midas: where it touched the land, property values rose. A young man named Howard Jarvis witnessed this magic firsthand after he moved from Salt Lake City to Los Angeles in 1935. Jarvis used some of the proceeds from the sale of his small-town Utah newspaper business to buy an unprepossessing patch of swampy land in the Los Angeles suburb of Venice. As he later told the story, his bank advised against buying, but he decided that it was a good investment when he saw a roll of linoleum in a shop window: "I thought to myself, 'This linoleum isn't very thick, but it costs two cents a square foot more than that land in Venice. The land goes all the way through to China, and it's close to the beach. To hell with the bank.'" The war boom proved him right. In the words of the historian Roger Lotchin, "From mid-1940 onward, while the skies poured death onto Europe, Africa, and Asia, it rained war contracts in the United States; and Los Angeles leaders insured that much of this downpour would irrigate the arid metropolitan Southland." The flood of federal contracts brought a flood of workers and an acute housing shortage to Los Angeles. Jarvis saw his land double in value.[16]

In other places, the war effort reduced property values. The people streaming into California's cities to build ships and airplanes were streaming out of many rural communities. Like Midas, the federal government could also destroy what it touched: federal orders shut down California's gold mines, emptying mountain communities and leaving ghost towns in their place. Meanwhile, the federal government sought to mobilize the industrial economy for war by freezing prices, requisitioning raw materials, and ordering civilian production converted to military uses—all of which also combined to make some urban property unusable and unsellable. Howard Jarvis experienced this side of the war, too. In addition to speculating in land, he invested in a factory near downtown Los Angeles that manufactured soundproof cork-and-rubber padding. Shortly after Japan bombed Pearl Harbor, the federal government confiscated his entire inventory of latex for the war effort. His taxable business property was suddenly rendered worthless.[17]

As if the turbulent property market was not enough to make the assessors' jobs difficult, the war also took away the information they needed to appraise property accurately. Unless a particular parcel is for sale, the only way to assess its market value is to observe the market price of building or buying a comparable property. The war economy obscured these prices. Federal price controls and limits on private construction made it hard to calculate the replacement cost of existing structures. Federal acquisition of land for bases and warehouses made it hard to estimate the price that real estate would fetch in a private, arms-length sale. In short, the war made it more and more difficult to assess property accurately. A statewide agency might still have the capacity to estimate property values, but dozens of little local governments in California surely did not.[18]

The war also made taxpayers and public officials potentially receptive to the idea of modernization. Civilians saw taxes as a patriotic sacrifice that could help to win the war. Never before in history had so many people so willingly shouldered so many new tax burdens. The Revenue Act of 1942 added the majority of wage earners to the federal income tax rolls for the first time and raised tax rates to levels that had never been seen before—and most people accepted the new burden with minimal complaint. Opinion polls repeatedly showed that overwhelming majorities of 85 percent to 90 percent thought the new tax burden was "fair." Local property taxes might have been less popular, because these taxes did not go directly to pay for bombers, but the line between military and civilian uses was fluid in a war that mobilized the entire economy for victory. A large body of historical scholarship confirms the general rule: wars that mobilize the civilian population increase the public's willingness to pay taxes.[19]

The war also provided officials and the public with examples of successful administrative modernization. The War Production Board took on an enormous burden of economic management that required centralized authority, professional administration, and standardized procedures for collecting and processing information about prices—precisely the tasks that would be required for modern property tax administration. The Treasury Department successfully organized the assessment of income for 90 percent of all economically active adults in the United States and the collection of a mass income tax throughout all forty-eight states. Assessment of all taxable property in a single state would have been a modest undertaking by comparison. It was no longer possible to argue that modernization was technically infeasible.[20]

Some public finance experts drew the obvious conclusion and proposed modernizing the property tax. The Treasury Committee on Intergovernmental Fiscal Relations—a committee of three economists hired in June 1941 to study the relationships among federal, state, and local taxes—reported a proposal to modernize the property tax in 1943. The committee members, Harold Groves, Luther Gulick, and Mabel Newcomer, recommended dozens of reforms to state and local taxation that included reforms to centralize, standardize, and professionalize property assessment. They commented on the combination of political pandering and incompetence that led local assessors "to favor new building and new industry by low assessments, and to freeze assessments in the older and blighted areas, where market values are declining." The Depression had shown that this system was broken. They argued that the way to fix it was to centralize and standardize property tax administration: "Effective State supervision, or State assessment, if such central assistance cannot be developed, is needed to offset the pressure of special local interests."[21]

The best evidence that these reforms were technically feasible is that they were actually enacted in Britain only five years later. Local governments in Britain, like local governments in the United States, relied heavily on real property taxes (called the "rates") to pay for education, road maintenance, health services, and poor relief. In Britain, as in the United States, the job of assessing the value of taxable property had always fallen to local officials, and British assessors, like American assessors, had used their discretion to dole out informal tax privileges in the form of fractional assessments.[22]

The Local Government Act of 1948 modernized British property tax administration along precisely the lines that American reformers had proposed on the other side of the Atlantic. The act centralized authority, integrating all local assessors in England and Wales into a single hierarchy in the Inland Revenue Board, the same bureaucracy that was responsible for assessing and collecting the national income tax. The act standardized the property assessment procedures and forms in use throughout England and Wales. It created new professional qualifications, requiring all local appraisers to be screened for competence before being hired into the Inland Revenue. Finally, it required that all real property in England and Wales be reassessed every five years.[23]

The modernization of property assessment was politically feasible in Britain because Britain, unlike the United States, was a unitary political system. In 1945, voters had elected a Labour Party majority to Parliament for the first time in British history, and Labour was able to use its control of the national government to reform local finance. Labour politicians promised to remake Britain from a warfare state to a welfare state. Labour's proposals included a massive system of central government grants-in-aid to local governments for health care, education, and other social services. The aid formula aimed to reconcile equal social rights with local service delivery by equalizing local finances. It targeted grants to those local governments that had a relatively small tax base of their own.[24] This formula created a new incentive for local assessors to underestimate the worth of property, as the Minister of Health, Aneurin Bevan, pointed out:

> If we are to allow local authorities themselves to value their own property, and if their valuation is going to be the basis for the distribution of central assistance, then they will be determining the size of the spoon with which they will be eating out of the national pool, and there will be a tendency—I say no more than a tendency—to increase the size of the spoon.[25]

Bevan solved this problem by centralizing the distribution of spoons: local governments would still levy the rates, but the value of taxable property would henceforth be determined by the central government.[26]

This centralization of assessment at the national level would have been unconstitutional and even virtually unthinkable in the United States, where policy makers took for granted that property taxation was a state and local function. But the same centralization was not particularly controversial in Britain. There was no written constitution reserving the property tax to subnational governments. Almost all important property tax legislation was national in scope, and most of the debate over the bill concerned the details of the aid formula, not the centralization of authority.[27]

Comparable proposals for modernizing property tax administration at the state level went nowhere in the United States. The 1943 Treasury report had no impact. The economist Robert Murray Haig satirized it in a scholarly journal by narrating a fable about a "conscientious governor" who received the report in the mail, together with a congressional request to evaluate its recommendations. "His first impulse is to ignore the communication," Haig wrote. "By what

authority does the Congress 'request' him to 'transmit . . . his recommendations'? If the legislature of his state were to send such a letter to the President,
would a reply be forthcoming from the White House?"[28] Federalism meant that
state officials were free to ignore federal proposals to modernize the property
tax, and so they did.

Thus it was that officials missed their last opportunity to modernize the
American property tax without sparking massive unrest. For the next twenty
years, pressure to modernize the tax grew, but the fragmented structure of government prevented any modernization of the property tax. Congress left property taxation to the states. State officials assumed no responsibility for
assessment, because they wanted to avoid blame for tax increases. Local officials
were divided, but those who wanted modern property assessment were power-
less next to those who controlled assessment and who derived political power
from their ability to dispense informal tax privileges.

POSTWAR FAILURES TO MODERNIZE
PROPERTY TAX ADMINISTRATION

In the postwar era, public officials lined up for or against modern property tax
administration depending on how it affected their institutional interests in the
context of the fragmented American political system. The institutional nature
of the conflict is nicely illustrated by the example of Dixwell Pierce and Malcolm Davisson. These two men came from virtually identical social back-
grounds. They were born less than a decade apart (Pierce in 1898, Davisson in
1907) and they grew up within fifty miles of each other in Yolo County, just outside the state capital of Sacramento. Both men were raised in Republican
households that embodied the California establishment of the early twentieth
century. Their grandparents were white pioneers who had trekked westward to
California in the middle of the nineteenth century; their parents were affluent
ranchers; and they themselves were graduates of the state's most prestigious
university, the University of California at Berkeley.[29] After graduation, both
Pierce and Davisson dedicated their careers to the cause of fairness in property
tax administration as they saw it. But they saw it very differently because they
occupied different institutional positions. Pierce was the executive secretary of
the California State Board of Equalization, which aligned itself with county officials against modernization. Davisson was a professor of economics at the
University of California and a consultant for the League of California Cities,
which supported modernization.

These two groups of officials took different positions on modernization because they had different interests. County officials saw local discretion in property tax administration as being to their advantage. Counties were the primary assessment authorities in California. County assessors had great discretion to grant or withhold informal tax privileges. This discretion permitted them to trade favors for money or political gain. County supervisors could get in on the action too, by manipulating the equalization of assessments among jurisdictions within the county.[30] Supervisors did not mind that assessors kept the tax base from growing rapidly, because they could raise property tax rates to compensate for low assessments.

The State Board of Equalization sided with counties against modernization because the elected members of the board did not want the blame for doing away with informal tax privileges. For most of the postwar era, the board was a rubber stamp that did nothing to question the authority of county assessors. From 1938 to 1955, it did not even carry out its constitutional duty to equalize assessments. "Since those whose duty it is to effect equalization are answerable directly to the taxpayers, there has been an understandable reluctance to act," Pierce explained. "If it be suggested that the officials are lacking in courage, there is the obvious rejoinder that it takes extraordinary courage to do something that is predestined to be followed by an undesirable development for which you are not responsible but for which you know that you will be blamed."[31]

City officials, by contrast, did not like the old system because they derived no political benefit from fractional assessment. Even though California cities relied on property taxes, the great majority of them did no assessing of their own.[32] Most cities simply copied the county assessment rolls, so they had no power to dispense tax privileges in the form of fractional assessments. City officials also resented fractional assessment because it limited their revenues. California law limited a city's bonded debt to a multiple of the assessed tax base, so the more generous the county assessor was with informal tax privileges, the less money city officials were entitled to borrow. Moreover, unlike California counties, most California cities could not raise property tax rates to compensate for low assessments, because state statutes and city charters imposed limits on municipal property tax rates. Local school officials were subject to similar tax rate caps, and they joined city officials in lobbying for modern property assessment. Davisson spoke for all local officials who had to provide more services in the postwar era and who chafed under the restrictions imposed by fractional assessment.[33]

Different groups of officials had conflicting interests. For most of the post-war era, however, the conflict was unequal: the county assessors' ability to dispense informal tax privileges was a political resource that enabled them to defeat modernization. The story of efforts to modernize the property tax is a story of repeated failure.

The First Failure to Modernize the Property Tax

The first postwar proposal to modernize property tax administration came from municipal governments. Shortly before the end of the war, the directors of the League of California Cities commissioned a study of trends in municipal finance from Davisson and the Bureau of Economic Research at the University of California. Davisson reported back to the league at the annual meeting in San Diego on September 17, 1946. The picture he painted was grim. Tax exemptions were growing, property assessments were lagging, and cities were providing more and more services for people who lived—and paid their property taxes—outside the city limits. The general property tax was not keeping up with the growing demand for government services. "However adequate this tax may have been in an essentially rural economy," Davisson said, "it has failed to meet the requirements of urban communities characterized by rapid industrialization."

Davisson recommended modernization. His proposal included the creation of a new state agency that would centralize the assessment of property for the purposes of local taxation. This agency would hire "specialized technical personnel" to assess all property in California on the basis of "uniform techniques." In short, Davisson's proposal would standardize, centralize, and professionalize property assessment.[34]

The league voted its support. After the speech, one of the delegates proposed a resolution that called for a state constitutional amendment to modernize the property tax along the lines that Davisson recommended. The assembled city officials approved the resolution.[35]

Pierce, on behalf of the State Board of Equalization, rallied the counties against this proposal. He announced the board's opposition to centralization at the annual conference of the State Association of County Assessors of California in October. The league's proposal was the talk of the conference; the general manager of the County Supervisors Association of California even departed from his prepared speech to convey that organization's opposition to the cities. "I don't think the Supervisors are going to stand idly by at the liquidation of county assessors," he said. "I don't think the Supervisors feel that such a proposal is sound or wise or well thought out."[36] Pierce agreed. Before the assembled assessors, he affirmed the possibility of "uniformity without regimentation," and asserted, "There is nothing that needs doing in the property tax field in California that can not be done better and more adequately through the county assessors and the State Board of Equalization than any other way."[37] He later reaffirmed this position in the Board's *Biennial Report* for 1945 and 1946. In place of modernization, Pierce called for increased funding to carry out the existing program of county assessment and state equalization.[38]

Pierce and the county officials won the day. Within six months, they had even persuaded the league's board of directors to disown their resolution. "Since adopting the League assessment resolution," the directors explained to their membership, "responsible organizations and individuals have come forward to express agreement concerning the need for reappraisal and statewide equalization but disagreeing with the method proposed by the League to accomplish this purpose."[39] In place of a program for modern property tax administration, the league's directors substituted Dixwell Pierce's legislative program, which called for "a reappraisal of all property in California within five years" to be conducted by the county assessors, together with increased funding for the State Board of Equalization. As a sop to city officials, the league directors called for municipal representation on all county bodies involved with determining assessments, but they dropped the call for modernization. "No legislation has [been] or will be sponsored turning over to the state responsibility for making all assessments of property for local tax purposes," they announced.[40]

The Second Failure to Modernize the Property Tax

The next proposal for modernization came from California school administrators. Like city officials, school officials wanted modern property tax administration in order to ensure that the assessed property tax base would keep pace with the growing demand for their services. In 1958, the state's school lobby backed an insurgent candidate for the Board of Equalization named Richard Nevins. In exchange for their support, Nevins pledged to do something about property tax administration. Democrats swept the elections, and Nevins and two other challengers defeated incumbent Republican candidates for the Board of Equalization—thereby creating a new board majority. It seemed that modernization might be in the cards.[41]

Nevins introduced his proposal to modernize the property tax in 1960. Rather than assume full responsibility for assessment, however, he argued that the state should assume a regulatory role and permit county assessors to continue their work as long as they met a common performance standard. In an address to the State Association of County Assessors, Nevins proposed legislation to create a single, enforceable, statewide standard for the assessment ratio. He assumed that the standard would be less than 100 percent—"We can start with the assumption that the full value directives of the constitution and the Revenue and Taxation Code are dead letters," he said—but he argued that this did not mean the state had to forgo *any* enforceable standard. "Is there any good reason why the law should not direct assessors to assess and the Boards of Equalization to equalize at 25% of full value or some appropriate figure of that magnitude?" Even this proposal, of course, would take away assessors' power to grant or withhold tax privileges.[42]

The California Association of School Administrators and several other major educational organizations supported the proposal. The Berkeley economist Malcolm Davisson, speaking on his own behalf, argued that the proposal did not go far enough—he still thought that a single state agency should handle all property assessment—but he supported the cause of reform by testifying extensively about the failures of the existing system.[43]

County officials, predictably, opposed modernization. They blasted Nevins's proposal in hearings before the Assembly Interim Committee on Revenue and Taxation in 1961. Nevins reported optimistically to the assembly in February 1962 that "some additional time would be needed to secure a consensus of opinion among county assessors as to a workable formula for establishing uniform ratios of assessed value to full cash value," but additional time did nothing to soften the counties' opposition. In 1963, the committee held hearings again, and the assessors continued to testify against the modernization of the property tax. In October 1964, the State Association of County Assessors voted almost unanimously for a strong resolution in opposition to a standard assessment ratio. Only two of the fifty-eight county assessors in the state—including a young reformer from Los Angeles named Philip Watson—voted to moderate the wording of the resolution.[44]

The county assessors' testimony before the assembly tax committee emphasized the distributive consequences—and, indirectly, the political costs—of modernizing the property tax. Their main spokesperson was Russell Wolden, the assessor of the City and County of San Francisco. Wolden was a socialite and a dandy who was popular in San Francisco and in the State Association of County

Assessors. He cultivated an image as a champion of the taxpayer, in part by routinely granting homeowners fractional assessments that were about 10 percent of the true value of their homes—in effect, a tax privilege worth almost 90 percent of their legal property tax liability.[45] Wolden began his testimony against modernization by reminding legislators that "[t]he assessors of California, the State Board of Equalization and the County Supervisors Association have consistently opposed such legislation." The reason for their opposition, he said, was that a standard assessment ratio of 25 percent would redistribute the tax burden. It would grant a new tax privilege to big businesses, whose property was currently assessed close to its true market value; but it would cut the traditional tax privileges of homeowners and small businesses whose property was already assessed at a much lesser fraction of its true value. Thus, he said, "the victims of this proposal would be homeowners and small businessmen; those least able to pay."[46]

As if the implicit threat of a homeowner backlash was not enough, Wolden also threatened to use informal tax privileges as a political weapon against legislators who supported modernization. As one San Francisco official later recalled the hearings: "They [state legislators] would ask Wolden how he assesses property. Wolden would say: 'Well, let's illustrate with a good example—the [San Francisco] Chronicle building at Fifth and Mission.' Everyone would shut up; they didn't want the Chronicle against them."[47] The implication was clear enough: the beneficiaries of Wolden's informal tax privileges included one of the most influential newspapers in the state. A vote for assessment reform would make powerful enemies.

Committee members moved forward anyway, under pressure from local governments that faced growing demand for public services. The committee commissioned a comprehensive study that would culminate in A Program of Tax Reform in California. The twelve-volume research report placed special emphasis on local property taxation, which it described as "the major defect in the California tax system." Property taxes were the subject of the single largest volume in the series, and they occupied pride of place in the final reform program. The report carefully documented the problems of traditional assessment administration, which it characterized as "outmoded, discriminatory, unfair, economically destructive and regressive."[48] The authors quoted liberally from the testimony of Malcolm Davisson. Although Republican Assemblyman Richard Donovan warned that modernization would sow a "seed-bed of taxpayer revolt," the report dismissed his concern. A chapter by the University of California economist Bruce McKim noted that property tax revenues had risen fourfold since World War II without provoking widespread protest. McKim concluded that there was no reason to think that the tax was approaching a "psychological limit." He thought modernization would actually increase the popularity of the tax—in retrospect, a spectacular misjudgment.[49]

The committee packaged property tax reform with a variety of other tax proposals that aimed to increase the elasticity of the state's revenue structure and reduce the state's reliance on property taxes. Committee chair Petris co-authored the reform, Assembly Bill (A.B.) 2270, with Assembly Speaker Jesse Unruh. They unveiled the bill in January 1965. A.B. 2270 included provisions to exempt business inventories and household furnishings from the property tax; to increase sales taxes as a means of funding schools; to provide property tax rebates for low-income, elderly homeowners; and to increase state income tax rates and collect the tax via withholding. Most importantly, however, the bill included provisions to centralize, standardize, and professionalize assessment—and thereby to establish a single, uniform statewide assessment ratio for the local property tax.[50]

Two things killed the bill. One was the intervention of state officials who wanted to avoid blame for tax increases. Governor Edmund G. "Pat" Brown was anxious not to raise taxes, and he undermined legislative support for the bill by announcing in early 1965 that no major new taxes would be necessary to balance his budget. The second thing that killed the bill was the influence of county officials who wanted to preserve their prerogatives under the old system. Small, rural counties were overrepresented in the Senate under an outdated apportionment formula, and supervisors and assessors in these counties were particularly generous with tax privileges for their farmer constituents. According to Nevins, it was these county officials who prevailed on the Senate Committee on Revenue and Taxation to strip all of the property tax provisions from the bill. A.B. 2270 emerged from the Senate a shadow of its former self, and died in conference committee.[51]

Patterns of Failure

Before continuing to the story of how the proponents of modernization finally succeeded in California, let us pause at this point in the narrative—twenty years after the end of World War II—to notice some patterns in the repeated failures. The first pattern to notice is that supporters and opponents of modernization were representing different groups of local officials. Those who had the power to dispense informal tax privileges generally opposed modernization, because it would undermine their power. Those who lacked that power generally favored modernization, because it would provide them with more revenue. The second pattern to notice is that opponents of modernization won because they used tax privileges as a political resource, and because state officials generally wanted to avoid blame for tax increases.

Both of these patterns were common to other states. Although the details of property tax administration differed in detail from state to state, the general outlines of the conflict did not. A comparison of two other states will suffice to make the point. Both Massachusetts and New York, like California, relied comparatively heavily on property taxes, and both states might therefore have been candidates for early modernization of property tax administration.[52] But in both of these states, local officials who benefited from the ability to grant informal tax privileges were able to block efforts at modernization—even though the particular institutional location of those officials differed from state to state.

In Massachusetts, the opponents of modernization were not county assessors but municipal assessors, because it was municipal assessors who enjoyed the power to dispense informal tax privileges. As in California, these assessors granted privileges to homeowners in exchange for votes, and sometimes also to businesses in exchange for bribes. In Boston, for example, the appointed Commissioner of Assessing regularly reduced business assessments in exchange for contributions to the mayor's re-election campaign. The Massachusetts Assessors Association and the cities of Boston and Cambridge did their best to delay any state efforts to modernize the administration of the property tax. They were reluctant to surrender their discretion over property assessment because it was a valuable political resource.[53]

The supporters of modernization in Massachusetts were also municipal officials—but municipal officials who were denied access to this political resource. In 1961, a court decision forced the City of Springfield to reassess all property uniformly at full market value, and this decision paved the way for similar lawsuits against other towns.[54] Under court orders to assess property at its full value, these towns lost their ability to use informal tax privileges. They also paid a price in state aid, since the state used an equalizing formula that provided more aid to towns with lower property tax revenues. The formula was meant to redistribute tax revenue from rich towns to poor towns, but it actually redistributed revenue from the law-abiding full-value towns to towns that were still granting informal and illegal tax privileges. The full-value towns therefore became a constituency for modernization. By 1973, they included the majority of cities and towns in the state. They began to press for legislation that would direct the State Tax Commission to enforce its uniform assessment standard in all of the other towns as well.[55]

As in California, most state officials in Massachusetts lined up with the opponents of reform because they were anxious to avoid blame for doing away with informal tax privileges. The equivalent of California's Board of Equalization was the Massachusetts State Tax Commission, which was responsible for the intercounty equalization of assessment ratios. Although its head was an appointed tax commissioner rather than an elected board, the commission still obeyed the imperative of blame avoidance. It opposed modernization and turned a blind eye to the illegal local practice of uneven and fractional assessment. Legislators, too, were happy to ignore the issue.[56]

In New York the patterns were the same: assessors and other local officials used their discretion as a political resource and blocked attempts at reform. In contrast to California, the primary assessing units in New York were cities, towns, and villages. Local officials in New York who had responsibility for tax assessment often belonged to local political machines that used assessments to reward party loyalty. For example, one state investigation in the early 1970s found that Mayor John Lindsay of New York City rewarded his stalwart campaign fundraisers with positions on the City's Tax Commission, a quasi-judicial body that had the power to grant lower assessments on appeal from the property owner. The commissioners could manipulate assessments to extort bribes, to coerce further campaign contributions out of businesses, or—as appears to have been the case—for both purposes at once.[57] The political use of assessments was not confined to New York City. In Albany, the board of appeals routinely granted abatements to any homeowner whose application had been forwarded by the local Democratic Party ward boss.[58] Many municipal officials, in short, derived benefit from "home rule" in tax administration, and opposed modernization of the property tax.

New York's counties and schools also levied property taxes, but—with few exceptions—they conducted no assessment of their own, depending instead on the assessment rolls that municipalities provided to them. They typically supported modernization. Under increasing pressure from these local officials, the New York legislature repeatedly tried and failed to reform assessment administration. Partial reforms in 1949 and 1958 did not change local discretion or the practice of fractional assessment.[59] In the 1960s, the Board of Equalization proposed legislation that would have centralized some assessment functions at the county level and would have replaced elected assessors with appointed assessors throughout the state. Opponents in the assembly repeatedly voted this bill down in the name of "home rule" for cities. The bill finally passed in 1970 in a watered-down form that confined the county assessment director to an advisory role and made the appointment of local assessors optional. Most cities and towns chose to continue electing their assessors.[60]

There is one last similarity to notice about all of these cases. It is that the story so far resembles a game of hot potato. Although all of the proposals to modernize the administration of property taxes came from public officials, none of these groups of officials proposed to centralize administration under *their own* control. Each group of officials proposed to shift the responsibility to some other level of government. In California and Massachusetts, municipal officials proposed to shift responsibility for modern property assessment to the state; in both California and New York, state officials proposed to assign responsibility for modern property assessment to the counties. We are used to thinking of big government as a power-hungry leviathan, and public officials as little empire builders—perhaps because our eyes have been trained for so long on the spending side of the budget. But when it comes to modernizing property tax assessment, we see that public officials were scrambling to avoid being put in charge of the empire. No elected official wanted to be in the hot seat when homeowners lost their informal tax privileges. It fell to the courts to modernize the property tax.

THE JUDICIARY MODERNIZES
THE PROPERTY TAX

Judicial intervention was the crucial factor that modernized the property tax. Because most judges were not elected officials, they could challenge assessors' control over informal tax privileges without fear of voter retribution. And because fractional assessment was an informal tax privilege in most states, it would not hold up when it was challenged in court. In most states it was the rising cost of schools and other local services that ultimately underlay the disputes that propelled the issue into the courts. But it was the courts that modernized the property tax.

In California, it was a criminal trial that undermined the power of assessors. In July 1965, a San Francisco tax accountant named Norman Phillips leaked documents to the *San Francisco Chronicle* that provided a detailed picture of corruption in Russell Wolden's office. For decades, it seemed, Wolden had operated a kind of protection racket in San Francisco's business district. First, he would deliberately appraise commercial property at a far higher fraction of its true value than residential property. Then, through a network of private tax consultants, he would offer to reduce business assessments in exchange for campaign contributions and bribes, part of which were kicked back to the consultants. Businesses tolerated the system because it made taxes predictable—Wolden even had a fixed fee schedule for bribes—and because it admitted some flexibility for unprofitable firms. Wolden's racket included, in effect, an unofficial appeals process.[61]

The exposé led to a series of investigations and trials that discredited assessors throughout the state. The California attorney general discovered that Wolden had used his professional ties to secure tax breaks for clients in other counties and that other assessors were running similar scams of their own. A jury convicted Wolden of bribery and conspiracy in May 1966. More convictions followed. Under investigation, San Diego Assessor Donald McQuilken committed suicide. By the end of the year, the county assessors of California were in thorough disrepute. Speaking to the annual meeting of the Western States Association of Tax Administrators in September, Ronald Welch, an assistant secretary at the Board of Equalization, summarized the events in California as follows:

> Two West Coast county assessors and a deputy assessor have gone to prison since we last met. A third assessor is at liberty only because he has appealed his conviction. A fourth is in the grave with a coroner's verdict of suicide. As this is being written, a former acting assessor and two tax agents have been convicted and are awaiting sentencing. The trial of another assessor is in progress. Four more deputy assessors and two more tax agents have been indicted and will presumably be brought to trial. Indictments of two deputies were forestalled or dismissed when they turned state's evidence. At least one more indictment is inevitable, and more can be safely predicted.

In other words, it was a bad year for the opponents of assessment reform.[62]

With the county assessors discredited, modernization suddenly seemed like a viable program. Petris and Unruh had planned to introduce another version of A.B. 2270 in the 1967 legislative session.[63] Instead, sensing an opportunity, Petris quickly revived the portions that pertained to property assessment as a stand-alone bill for a special session in 1966. The new bill, A.B. 80, required all county assessors to reassess property annually at a standard 25 percent of its full cash value. It also prescribed new qualifications for non-elected appraisal staff, tightened rules regarding conflict of interest, and centralized assessment authority at the county level by requiring many cities to give up their independent assessment departments.

At first, it seemed that the bill would meet the same fate as A.B. 2270: namely, a slow death at the hands of the Senate tax committee. Petris and Democratic Assemblyman John Knox introduced the bill on March 1, 1966. After two rounds of amendments in Ways and Means, it passed the assembly, but then it was referred to the Senate Committee on Revenue and Taxation, where it was held up by senators who opposed the bill.[64]

This time, however, the political calculus was different because the courts had undermined the main political resource of county assessors. Governor Brown, who had wavered between hostility and indifference to A.B. 2270, actively supported A.B. 80.[65] He began to pressure the Senate Committee on Revenue and Taxation to report the bill, privately telling Democrats on the committee that assessment reform was going to be an important campaign issue.[66] The most recalcitrant member of the committee, San Francisco Democrat Eugene McAteer, finally relented because his personal ties to Wolden made him vulnerable to charges of corruption. The currency with which Wolden and other assessors had once influenced politics—their power to sway votes by granting tax privileges—was now worthless. A.B. 80 passed the Senate with only one member opposed. From there it returned to the assembly where, on June 30, 1966, it passed unanimously.[67]

Assessment Reform in Other States

The judiciary was crucial in other states as well. In Massachusetts, it was a series of civil trials that undermined the power of assessors. The full value towns, led by the Town of Sudbury, sued for an injunction that would cause the State Tax Commission to enforce uniform assessment. Lawyers for the commissioner denied that he had any enforcement powers. On December 24, 1974, the Supreme Judicial Court of Massachusetts denied the town's request for injunction but affirmed that the commission could and should enforce uniform assessment and held open the possibility of an injunction if it did not begin to do so immediately. The justices declared that "the commissioner has the power and the duty to direct local assessors to take such action as will tend to produce uniformity throughout the Commonwealth in valuation and assessments" and that "the functions of the commissioner and the commission in these respects are to command and not merely to advise or educate, and it is the legal duty of the assessors to obey their lawful commands."[68] The court also suggested that compliance should be achieved within four years.

The lawsuit changed the politics of modernization by bringing the Massachusetts State Tax Commission onto the side of the modernizers. Under judicial compulsion, the commissioner joined the full value towns in pressing the legislature for funding to modernize property tax administration and carry out a comprehensive, statewide program of reassessment at full market value.[69]

Legislators continued to delay modernization. The logic of blame avoidance dictated inaction. Fearing an uproar from homeowners, legislators proposed a constitutional amendment to preserve and formalize the tax privilege of fractional assessment. This required ratification by the voters and enabling legislation. In the meantime, rather than comply with the costly mandate of the *Sudbury* court, local officials decided to put their reappraisal plans on hold until the outcome of the legislation was certain. The statewide program of reassessment stalled.[70]

A second judicial intervention forced the issue. Sudbury went back to court in 1977 over the continuing noncompliance of the state's assessors, and the attorney general began enforcement action against noncompliant towns. A judge enjoined the City of Boston from collecting any property taxes unless it could show evidence that it was moving toward compliance.[71] This action undermined the political resource of the assessors and finally forced state lawmakers into action. They enacted a legislative package in 1979 that combined modernized assessment administration with substantial, formal tax privileges for homeowners. The law permitted fractional assessment for homeowners, but it required uniform assessment *within* the class of owner-occupied homes, and it permitted the state tax commission to take over responsibility for assessment from any local assessors who failed to comply. With this reform, the last local jurisdictions in the state were finally forced to modernize assessment administration.[72]

In New York, too, it was the judiciary that finally undermined the power of local assessors to block reform. The plaintiff in New York was an individual named Pauline Hellerstein who sued the Town of Islip in 1974. Her husband, a law professor and tax reformer named Jerome Hellerstein, wrote the brief. Rather than plead for an abatement on their summer cottage, the Hellersteins asked the court to invalidate the town's entire assessment roll because it violated the statutory requirement that all property be assessed uniformly at "full value." A majority of justices agreed and mandated that Islip reassess all properties on its roll by December 1976. In the words of a dissenting justice, it was "the first case in nearly 200 years in which our State's highest court has been invited to confront the issue head-on and to overturn fractional assessments." It was also the last. The majority decision implicitly overturned fractional assessments throughout the state, thereby invalidating the assessment rolls of every municipality in New York.[73]

The New York State legislature delayed modernization, just as its counter-part in Massachusetts had done. Legislators stalled for time and passed emergency legislation to delay implementation of the court's mandate for five years. In 1977, Democratic Governor Hugh Carey appointed a commission to study the problem and make recommendations for permanent legislation. The Temporary State Commission on the Real Property Tax (the "Gerber Commission") began holding hearings in 1978 and issued its first report in March 1979. In the meantime, some individual municipalities moved toward compliance with the mandate while others delayed.[74]

It was the court's action that compelled modernization of the property tax in New York. The statutory moratorium on the *Hellerstein* decision was due to expire within days when the legislature finally passed a bill to modernize property tax administration. Like the Massachusetts compromise, the new law combined modernization of the property tax with a new, formal tax privilege for homeowners. It required all real property to be assessed uniformly throughout the state at a standard fraction of its market value, but it allowed this standard ratio to vary across categories of real property.[75]

California, Massachusetts, and New York were all high-tax states with a reputation for liberalism. They represented a best-case scenario for the modernization of property taxes. And yet, even here the courts had to intervene. It should be no surprise, then, that the same pattern played out in other states, with differences of timing and detail. The modernization of the property tax took the intervention of the courts.[76]

THE COMING TAX REVOLT

State and local officials delayed the modernization of property assessment for decades into the postwar era. They repeatedly postponed reforms for fear of provoking tax protest. But one of the most striking things about this story is that tax protest mostly did not happen. "As the state has grown," Bruce McKim wrote in 1964, "the 'propensity to protest' assessed valuations has declined."[77] As long as officials preserved homeowners' tax privileges in the face of rising prices, people were content to pay heavy taxes. Assessors provided a valuable kind of informal social protection from the rising price of housing, and they guaranteed income security in retirement.

The great irony is that delaying reforms only made protest inevitable. By the time that states modernized the administration of the property tax, the tax affected more people more directly than ever before. The percentage of homes that were owner occupied increased from 44 percent in 1940 to 63 percent in 1970.[78] As Chapter 1 showed, the value of residential property owners' tax privileges increased, too, from $1.6 billion in 1940 to $39 billion in 1971. On the eve of the tax revolt, a majority of American householders paid tax on a small and declining fraction of the value of their homes—by virtue of fractional assessment.

By the time that Massachusetts and New York passed legislation to modernize the property tax, the property tax revolt had already begun. Local governments in these states and others had begun to assess property at its full market value, thereby depriving homeowners of their traditional tax privileges and provoking an unprecedented rebellion.

3 THE OUTBREAK OF A TAX PROTEST MOVEMENT

ON THE MORNING of Wednesday, April 20, 1977, Roger Sutton and fourteen other senior citizens marched up the steps of the old courthouse in Redwood City, California, with their official assessment notices in hand, to meet with the county assessor. The notices showed that their homes were appreciating in value. For senior citizens who had no intention of selling or moving, this was bad news: it meant their property taxes were about to go up. But they had not come to appeal their assessments. They had come instead to demand that the assessor support state legislation to give property tax relief to all low-income taxpayers in California. To dramatize their plight, they set their assessment notices on fire and burned them to ashes in an upturned hubcap on the steps of the county courthouse.[1]

Roger Sutton's bonfire was a minor episode in the tax revolt, but it illuminates many of the reasons why scholars see the tax revolt as an important episode. This was a social movement: these taxpayers were not individually avoiding or appealing their taxes, but instead acting collectively. Their tactics were decidedly unconventional. The action of burning tax documents has a militant, even revolutionary air: with a little imagination, we might picture a younger Roger Sutton two hundred years before, dumping tea into a harbor or burning a British tax collector in effigy. The protest also shows that this was a new kind of social movement. After a decade of protest by America's have-nots—the young, the black, the dispossessed—this protest of elderly, white homeowners looked like a "revolt of the haves."[2]

The bonfire also defies some common stereotypes of the tax revolt. Notice first of all that this protest does not look like a backlash against big government.

The protesters were not upset about some expensive new piece of social legislation. They were upset because they had received an official notice of the market value of their homes. The protesters approached the government not as an enemy but as a potential ally. The housing market was driving their taxes up; they wanted the assessor's help to hold their taxes down. This was a demand for government protection from the rising price of housing.

Notice, too, that this protest does not really look like a conservative backlash against the liberal 1960s. Anyone who had lived through the Vietnam War era would recognize the burning of official documents as a symbol of the political left: it recalled antiwar protesters who burned their draft cards.[3] Sutton and his fellow protesters belonged to the Citizen Action League (CAL), an organization founded and led by veterans of the civil rights movement and the welfare rights movement who saw tax reform as a way to secure economic justice for all Americans. These fifteen elderly protesters were demanding more government income redistribution, not less.

This chapter explains why local protests began and how they came together in a movement against property taxes that ultimately transformed American politics. It shows that local authorities triggered protest mobilization by reassessing property—thereby infringing on the informal tax privileges that had sheltered homeowners from the rising price of housing. It shows that state officials broadened the scale of these protests by modernizing the property tax. Finally, it shows that these institutional dynamics were powerful enough to bring together protesters who otherwise had very little in common.

The most important conclusion of the chapter is that the tax revolt was a movement for social protection from the market. Traditional tax privileges provided homeowners with informal social protection; when assessment reforms revoked these privileges, taxpayers rebelled and demanded their restoration. The official valuation of property was the event that sparked the protest. In Redwood City, it was literally the fuel that fed the flames.

REASSESSMENT LIGHTS A SPARK

Imagine an aerial view of the United States circa 1960, with a bright point of light representing every collective act of protest against the property tax—not just every bonfire, but every demonstration, rally, and tax strike, every petition and picket line. What would you see? At first, not much. But as years passed, you would notice a scattering of bright flashes here and there: sparks of protest, isolated, unsynchronized, and apparently random. Gradually, you would see the sparks grow more frequent and more synchronized as local protesters began to coordinate their actions into statewide protest campaigns. By the end of the 1970s, you would see a flickering carpet of light spread across much of the country.

In order to explain the origins of this social movement, the two questions we have to answer are where the sparks came from and what kindled them into flames. Let us take the first question first: what triggered the initial, local protests against the property tax? The answer is simple: local protests followed local property reassessments.

This answer might seem puzzling at first. Assessment seems like a routine administrative function—it belongs to the very definition of an *ad valorem* property tax. Local government can only tax property according to its value if local officials measure and record that value. Because prices change, the government needs to reassess property with some frequency. In theory, the assessor merely measures the tax base. He or she does not set the tax rate.

In practice, however, the assessor did more than measure. The property tax was not just a way for local governments to raise money but also a way for them to accomplish social purposes. One of the most important of these purposes was the provision of informal social protection. Homeownership promised income security in old age, and in the meantime it protected homeowners from the vicissitudes of the market. Assessors subsidized homeownership by recording only a fraction of the true value of homes on the tax rolls. They further sheltered homeowners from the rising price of housing by allowing the assessment ratio to diminish over time: the value of housing increased, but local assessors did not record those increases. This customary tax privilege underwrote cheap housing in retirement. But—and this is the crucial point for this chapter—the system of informal social protection only worked because assessors did not record current market values. Reassessment was routine in theory but rare in practice.

When reassessment came at long last, homeowners experienced it as a violation of their customary social rights. Fractional assessment had subsidized homeownership; reassessment cut the subsidy. As one California tax protester said, "My assessment doubled this year. . . . I had hoped that in my retiring years I would be free from anxieties and worries after paying off the mortgage. Now I find I am faced with the situation of having to save my not so heavily mortgaged home." This homeowner—and others like him in California and elsewhere— sought to save his home and his retirement by protesting against reassessment. Demonstrators took collective action to demand that reassessments be rolled back and customary tax privileges restored.[4]

An early tax rebellion in Los Angeles County illustrated and foreshadowed the relationship between reassessment and protest. Philip Watson, the Los Angeles County assessor who would buck his colleagues' opinion in October 1964 to vote in favor of modernizing the property tax, was also one of the first public officials in the country to announce that he intended to arrest the growth of informal tax privileges in his own jurisdiction. Earlier that year, he had implemented a plan to bring property values up to a standard fraction of market value and to keep them there by a regular program of reassessment. The result was a short-lived but intense wave of protest.

Watson's actions were remarkably different from the common pattern of buck-passing and blame avoidance. His motives are difficult to discover, but one of them was probably political ambition. He was an aspiring young politician who saw being assessor as a stepping stone to higher office. While working as a civil servant in the assessor's office in the late 1950s, Watson moonlighted as a private consultant for several shopping center developers who were suing the county to have their assessments reduced. They won with Watson's help, and he parlayed their gratitude into a bid for office. A plaintiff and two lawyers who had worked on the case became the core of his election campaign committee in 1962. They solicited contributions of time and money from other businesspeople and arranged occasions for him to speak around the county. Watson made the most of these opportunities, and he won handily.[5]

Another of Watson's motives was probably the desire to avoid a costly court battle. On taking office in 1963, Watson found himself on the wrong side of several ongoing taxpayer lawsuits. The plaintiffs were business owners like Watson's former clients, who pointed out that their property was assessed at a higher fraction of its value than residential property was, in violation of the uniformity clause in the state constitution. Watson made the best of this bad situation. With great fanfare, he announced a plan to standardize the countywide assessment ratio. He thus began to implement a standard 25 percent assessment ratio in 1964, two years before A.B. 80 imposed this requirement on the rest of the assessors in the state.[6]

At the time, Watson's decision to reassess all property in the county at a uniform fraction of market value probably seemed like a bold gamble. It helped him make his mark in a public office that provided few opportunities for innovative policymaking. Watson became something of a star in the state capital of Sacramento, where legislators celebrated his reforms as a model for the rest of California. The decision to reassess also shored up his support among business owners, whose property was overassessed relative to residential property. But Watson knew that his actions were likely to lead to tax increases for homeowners, who were generally paying tax on much less than 25 percent of the market value of their property. He seems to have anticipated a backlash: even before he reassessed, he was calling on the county supervisors to compensate for rising assessments by lowering the property tax rate. Supervisors were under no obligation to lower tax rates, however, and it is hard to believe that Watson ever actually thought they would. This was probably an exercise in preemptive blame shifting.[7]

The reassessment incited a small rebellion. In the first days of November 1964, Watson mailed the new property tax bills to homeowners in suburban Alhambra. Mike Rubino, the delivery truck driver, began contacting his friends and acquaintances to organize a protest meeting for November 10. Their efforts snowballed, and the meeting exceeded all expectations. A newspaper reporter estimated 2,000 people in attendance. The audience spilled out of the building and jammed traffic for three miles around. The following week, Rubino led approximately 1,000 unruly demonstrators to a meeting of the Los Angeles County Board of Supervisors, where they packed the hall, seized microphones, and heckled Watson and the supervisors.[8]

Watson defused the protest quickly. He expressed sympathy for the protesters. He also invited Rubino to meet with him in his office, where a prominently displayed sign read, "We Don't Make Values. We Follow Them." When Rubino showed up, Watson gave him a lecture about property taxes—involving "a tax graph, the type often seen in school books," according to a reporter for the *Alhambra Post Advocate*—and then paraded him in front of a waiting television crew. The *Post Advocate* headline read, "Rubino, Assessor Agree They 'Agree.'" The Alhambra protests petered out shortly thereafter.[9]

Los Angeles was only the beginning. For the next decade and a half, similar events played out in communities throughout the United States. Newspapers reported tax protests following local reassessments in Boston, Detroit, Pittsburgh, and Prince George's County, Maryland. In New Bedford, Massachusetts, a reassessment started a riot when an unorganized mob of some 4,000 taxpayers descended on the mayor's office, "wrecking the mayor's car and temporarily closing down City Hall," according to Robert Kuttner. In Milwaukee, some 400 taxpayers showed up at city hall to demand a three-year freeze on property assessments.[10]

Many people have described the tax revolt as a suburban movement, but these protests were not confined to cities and suburbs. Local reassessments triggered tax protests in rural Ohio. Wisconsin farmers went on a property tax strike, sending their tax payments to an escrow account instead of to the tax collector. Hundreds of farmers and homeowners in rural Putnam County, New York, took a cue from the proliferation of tax-exempt religious retreat centers in the area: they sent away for mail-order ordination in the Universal Life Church so that their property would be tax exempt.[11]

Nor were the protests confined to the affluent states where tax rates were highest. In the mountains of Fannin County, Georgia, for example, the local Board of Equalization provoked widespread protest when it attempted to bring assessed values into compliance with the state's new standard 40 percent assessment ratio. The county-wide equalization in early 1973 dramatically increased the assessments of homeowners in unincorporated areas. One rural taxpayer whose taxes had tripled put an ad in the local newspaper calling for a community meeting and drew some 400 angry taxpayers to the county courthouse on February 7. They declared themselves the Fannin County Taxpayers Association (FCTA) and agreed to initiate a class-action lawsuit to stop reassessment and roll back all assessments to the old level.[12] There were similar local protests against overassessment in Arkansas, Texas, and Virginia. Hundreds of farmers outside Nashville, Tennessee, formed an organization called Citizens for Lower Taxes to fight against a 1973 reassessment.[13]

The protests were at first purely reactive. Protesters sought only to stop reassessment, to exempt themselves from it, or to have it redone on more favorable terms. They did not demand broader property tax reforms, and in fact they shared little agreement about who or what was to blame for their rising property taxes. The Fannin County protesters provide a good example. Some of them apparently thought welfare might be the problem: at the FCTA's first confrontation with the County Board of Commissioners on February 14, the protesters presented the county board of supervisors with a long list of questions about possible economies in the county budget that included—along with queries about the costs of libraries, jails, and the salary of the county assessor—a suggestion to discourage welfare receipt by publicizing the names of food stamp recipients.[14] Other Fannin County protesters blamed the rich. The radical folksinger Si Kahn, who performed at a benefit for the protesters, thought that tax breaks for the wealthy city dwellers were the reason that government was raising taxes on low- and moderate-income rural residents. Kahn was a veteran of the Student Nonviolent Coordinating Committee (SNCC) and the author of *How People Get Power: Organizing Oppressed Communities for Action*. He pointed out that the largest landowner in Appalachia was the

U.S. Forest Service, whose lands were tax exempt. Kahn argued that this tax exemption left poor mountain folk paying all the property taxes and described it as a subsidy paid by poor rural people to affluent urbanites who used the forests for recreation.[15]

Protesters at first picked local targets. Many of them simply sought to shame the local assessor into rolling back assessments. Local groups in Little Rock and Philadelphia organized "tax avoider tours" that highlighted the disparity between tax breaks for big business and the high tax bills of low-income homeowners.[16] In San Francisco, CAL—the organization that would later sponsor the bonfire of assessment notices in Redwood City—led a "Taxpayers' Tour" of downtown, followed by a mass meeting at which an auditorium full of irate homeowners jeered the San Francisco assessor.[17] In Boston, a community group called Fair Share—which, like CAL, was founded and staffed by former welfare rights organizers—pressured the assessor into releasing the names of big businesses that were delinquent in their property tax payments.[18] In these cities, and in other places from Seattle to Appalachia, tax protest groups sought to highlight biases in assessment that they claimed favored big business and unfairly penalized low-income neighborhoods. Some attributed these inequities to discrimination by the assessor. Others blamed the appeals process, which big businesses generally found easier to navigate.[19]

Other groups targeted local appeals boards or the courts. Groups in Michigan, Connecticut, Missouri, and Pennsylvania established tax clinics or distributed handbooks on how to appeal a property assessment.[20] The liberal consumer advocate Ralph Nader founded an organization called the Tax Reform Research Group and distributed a manual entitled *Property Tax Reappraisals* with instructions about how to protest reassessments. It urged homeowners to use the appeals process if reassessment increased their taxes. Where the ordinary grievance procedure was inadequate, it encouraged protesters to turn to the courts. Above all, it counseled collective action.[21]

These local protests did not stop the erosion of homeowners' tax privileges. The tactic of shaming the assessor assumed that the assessor could be held responsible for the rapid increase in property taxes. But this was not the case. Taxes were rising because land prices were rising. Assessors were increasingly constrained by state courts and legislatures to follow prices. To target the local assessor, as the progressive tax lobbyist and former welfare rights organizer Jonathan Kaufman pointed out angrily to the leaders of San Francisco CAL, was to make him or her "culpable for simply obeying the law."[22]

Nor was it adequate to insist on taxpayers' legal rights. Although there were particular cases of discrimination in assessment that helped particular businesses or hurt particular residential neighborhoods, the most general pattern was actually the opposite. Assessors had traditionally treated homes more favorably than businesses. Reforms that increased fairness in property tax administration also increased homeowners' taxes. By making it harder for assessors to discriminate, the reformers also made it harder for assessors to grant informal tax privileges.[23]

As long as the erosion of tax privileges continued, protests continued episodically. Small neighborhood protest associations flickered in and out of existence as local reassessments came and went. The local protests were scattered across the United States and spread out over decades. By 1973, however, the protests had become more frequent, and protesters in different parts of the country were starting to learn from each other. The flames were beginning to spread.

MODERNIZATION FEEDS THE FLAMES

Sparks alone do not make a fire. Local reassessments continued to incite new local rebellions, but by the early 1970s something had begun to fuel a broader movement. Protesters began to coordinate their actions across local areas, to string them together into sustained sequences of collective action, and to articulate demands that went beyond their parochial interests in stopping their own most recent reassessment. The property tax revolt was undergoing a process that social movement scholars have called a "scale shift": it was becoming a social movement.[24]

If our first task was to explain where the sparks came from, our second task is to explain what kindled the flames. How did this scale shift happen? How, in other words, did these isolated, episodic, and reactive protests become a sustained sequence of collective action? The answer is simple. The underlying condition that caused the movement to spread—the fuel that turned the first sparks of protest into a raging fire—was the modernization of the property tax.

Modernization, as in Chapter 2, refers to the centralization, professionalization, and standardization of property assessment. Modernization caused the spread of the movement in three ways. First, it allowed protesters to form coalitions across the county lines by giving them a common target. Modernization took property taxation out of the hands of the local assessor. Protesters consequently began to realize that the assessors were simply functionaries and that they were carrying out rules decided at the state level. Instead of directing their protests at local assessors, protesters in different communities began to make common cause with one another and began to direct their protests at state government.

Second, modernization made it easier for protesters from different local areas to coordinate their protests. Modernizing reforms typically included requirements for periodic reassessment that meant local reassessments were increasingly synchronized with one another. Many states even initiated coordinated, statewide programs of reassessment, with the consequence that homeowners in many different jurisdictions found themselves confronted with the same threat at the same time. This made it easier to mobilize protests in many places at once.

Third, modernization drew new protesters into the movement by increasing the intensity of the threat. Under the old rules, a single, local reassessment was only a one-time income shock, a temporary infringement on homeowners' traditional tax privileges. The assessor might raise your taxes by recording the true market value of your home, but soon enough that assessment would be out of date, and the assessor would go back to dumbly copying the assessment roll from year to year. The assessment ratio would once again begin to fall; the value of informal tax privileges would once again begin to rise. Modernization, by contrast, meant more than a one-time cut in your informal benefits. It meant that the rules had changed for good. The assessor would henceforth be required to keep values current. Taxes would rise in lockstep with the housing market. Homeowners, in short, saw that their tax privileges might be permanently reduced or altogether revoked. Homeowners mobilized in proportion to the threat they faced.

The case of California illustrates the process and prefigures developments that came somewhat later in other states. The movement spread throughout the state of California in the late 1960s and early 1970s following the statewide modernization of assessment. In 1965, the state legislature followed Philip Watson's example and required all assessors to implement computerized assessment at 25 percent of market value. In response, homeowners founded new protest groups in cities, towns, and suburbs throughout California. They also began to knit together broad protest coalitions from unlikely combinations of existing civic groups. CAL, for example, had begun as a San Francisco community organization focused on utility rate reform. The core of the property tax revolt in Sacramento was a neighborhood crime watch organization called the People's Advocate. When reassessment came to the Bay Area suburb of Fremont, a local union of the United Auto Workers (UAW) canvassed door-to-door with a sound truck to recruit tax protesters.[25] Almost any organization, no matter what its ideology, could be turned into a vehicle for tax protest. The founders of CAL included a former welfare rights organizer named Tim Sampson and an organizer named Mike Miller, who was a veteran of Students for a Democratic Society (SDS) and SNCC and who had also worked with the legendary progressive organizer Saul Alinsky.[26] The founder of the People's Advocate was a conservative former car salesman and real estate agent named Paul Gann.[27]

Modernization led all of these protesters to shift their attention from the local assessor to the statehouse. By 1965, Mike Rubino had raised his sights beyond Alhambra and joined forces with a greater Los Angeles area coalition of homeowners' associations called the United Organizations of Taxpayers (UO). In 1968, this coalition finally quit heckling the local assessor, Philip Watson, and began instead circulating a petition for state legislation that would eliminate the property tax altogether. In 1976, CAL gave up on shaming the San Francisco assessor and began lobbying the California legislature for "Fair Share Taxes" that would restore tax privileges for low-income homeowners.[28] By 1977, most of the local tax protest groups in the state had joined one of two competing coalitions that were working for state legislation to restore homeowners' tax privileges. One coalition, led by CAL, was organizing coordinated protests in assessors' offices in far-flung cities. Another, led by the People's Advocate and UO, mobilized local groups to circulate identical petitions in communities 600 miles apart. The local tax protests, in short, had come together to form a statewide movement.

Modernization and Protest: Comparing States

California is illustrative, but the true test of the theory that modernization caused the scale shift is comparative. If modernization caused the emergence of the movement, then the states that did the most to modernize the property tax should be the places where sustained, statewide protest campaigns emerged; and conversely, the states that did the least to modernize the property tax should be places *without* statewide protest campaigns.

How can we test this hypothesis? For evidence of a scale shift, we can use a simple indicator: the presence of a voter-initiated petition to provide any kind of real property tax relief that appeared on the ballot from 1964 to 1978.[29] This fifteen-year window captures the period from the first state reforms to the year when the conflict over the property tax effectively went national, spilling over all state boundaries and fundamentally transforming the dynamics of the movement (as we shall see in Chapter 5). A qualifying petition is a simple criterion for identifying the presence of a movement. If a state certified an initiative petition to appear on the ballot, we can be pretty sure that there was a sustained, statewide, and programmatic mobilization behind it. The presence of a qualifying petition is not a perfect indicator, because it is not perfectly comparable across states—different states had different thresholds for the number of petition signatures required—but systematic data on protest are otherwise hard to come by. Until 1978, property tax protest was seen as a parochial issue, and protests rarely made it into national newspapers of record. Most property tax protests were peaceful indoor meetings of a few hundred people and not the large, violent clashes with authority in public places that the media are most likely to cover.[30]

For a comparative test of the hypothesis, we also need criteria to distinguish the states that most thoroughly and effectively modernized the property tax from the states that did not. The most advanced states implemented three reforms in particular. First, they established statewide standards for the training and certification of local assessing officers. Second, they required assessors to use standard property ownership maps, or else they implemented new standards for parcel mapping. Third, they implemented some form of computer-assisted appraisal—whether by supplying a common computer system to all local assessors or by monitoring or regulating the use of computer systems for conformity to state standards. We can assign each state a score from zero to three to represent the number of these reforms it implemented between 1964 and 1978.[31]

The comparison shows that the movement against the property tax was indeed concentrated in states that did the most to modernize property tax administration. Table 3.1 reports the presence of a qualifying petition and the extent of modernization among all states that permitted the ballot initiative. Three of the five states that scored the highest for modernization—California, Idaho, and Oregon—all had one or more petition campaigns for property tax relief. (The other two, Arizona and Utah, had petition drives underway in 1978 that simply did not qualify for the ballot until later.)[32] Petition drives were also present in most of the states that implemented two out of the three modernizing reforms. By contrast, the states that implemented none or only one of the

Table 3.1. Modernization and Mobilization: Assessment Reforms Caused Petitions for Property Tax Relief in Initiative States, 1963–1978

	Statewide mobilization for property tax relief?						
Number of reforms	No qualifying petitions			One or more petitions			
	States	N	%		States	N	%
3	AZ, UT	2	40		CA, ID, OR	3	60
2	AR, ME, MO, SD	4	36	CO, IL,[†] MI, MT, NE, NV, WA		7	64
1	ND	1	50		MA	1	50
0	AK, OH, OK	3	100		. . .	0	0

[†]Advisory measure (not a binding initiative).
See endnotes for sources.

reforms generally did not have any statewide petition qualify for the ballot. There is one exception, Massachusetts, which will be discussed in more detail below; even there, as we will see, it was the threat of impending modernization that mobilized taxpayers.

The comparison tells us that modernization and the movement went hand in hand. It does not tell us anything about the process by which modernization caused mobilization, however. In order to answer this question and in order to uncover *how* modernization contributed to the spread of the movement, the next part of this chapter will zero in on property tax protest in two otherwise typical states: Illinois and Missouri.

FROM MODERNIZATION TO MASS MOBILIZATION IN ILLINOIS AND MISSOURI

If you were to resume your imaginary bird's-eye view of the spreading tax revolt, you would find Missouri and Illinois directly below you at the geographic center of the U.S. population. If you wanted to follow the course of the spreading tax revolt in an average state, either of these two would have made a fine choice. Missouri was as close to an average state as you could find in 1970—one out of every ten people was black, seven out of every ten lived in an urban area, seven out of every ten homes were owner occupied, and property taxes consumed just under four cents of every dollar generated in the state, just as in the United States as a whole. Illinois was a bit more urbanized but otherwise not much different.[33]

Which state's residents would be the first to join the growing movement against the property tax? It would have been hard to predict in advance. On one hand, the property tax burden—property tax as a percentage of personal income—was slightly heavier in Illinois. On the other hand, the concentration of homeowners was slightly greater in St. Louis. Both were close to average. If you chose to measure the presence of the movement, as Table 3.1 does, by observing the presence of a grassroots initiative on the state ballot, then you would probably have favored Missouri. Both states permitted the ballot initiative, but the rules in Missouri made it substantially easier to get a petition certified for presentation to the voters. The state constitution in Missouri required petitioners to collect a number of signatures equivalent to one of every twenty votes cast in the last gubernatorial election. In Illinois, the requirement was one of every ten; the denominator was not just voters, but the larger pool of everyone who was *registered* to vote; and—since it was a larger state—the pool of registered voters was twice as big to begin with. To top it off, the Illinois constitution permitted only advisory ballot initiatives that the legislature was free to ignore even after voters approved them. You might expect angry taxpayers in Illinois to conclude that a statewide petition was not worth the trouble.

Yet Illinois was the state where property taxpayers mobilized first. In Missouri they did not mobilize until much later—after the period described in Table 3.1. As the following case studies show, it was modernization that made the difference. Although Table 3.1 scores both states as partial modernizers—both states passed two out of three modernizing reforms in the period from 1964 to 1978—Missouri was a relative latecomer that modernized the property tax only at the end of that period. Early attempts to mobilize taxpayers in Missouri foundered because the state had not yet modernized the property tax. Illinois was quicker to centralize, professionalize, and standardize the administration of property taxes, and Illinois taxpayers were therefore quicker to rise up together in protest.

Illinois: Modernization Makes the Movement

Before the 1970s, property tax administration in Illinois was traditional, highly politicized, and notoriously corrupt. Every county and every township had its own elected assessor. Local assessors were subject to little state supervision, and they used fractional assessment as a political resource. The most notorious assessor in the state was P. J. "Parky" Cullerton of Cook County. Cullerton, assessor since 1958, was also a ward boss in the Chicago Democratic Party and a close associate of Chicago Mayor Richard J. Daley. His control over assessments gave him an important role as the unofficial "banker" of Daley's political machine. "In theory, there are standardized criteria for determining property tax assessments," a local journalist wrote. "In practice, the property tax break has often been proportional to the size of the real estate owner's contribution to the party's campaign fund."[34] Cullerton kept homeowners in the party fold by assessing their property far below the legal standard of fair cash value. By the mid-1960s, he was assessing the average parcel at about 30 percent of its market value. This practice of buying votes by granting unofficial tax privileges was blatantly illegal, but it was common practice throughout the state. The average assessment ratios in other Illinois counties varied from 8 percent to 53 percent of market value.[35]

The threat of litigation compelled the state to modernize the property tax. In 1969, state legislators voted to create a new Department of Local Government Affairs to centralize supervision of the local assessment function. They also centralized assessing functions at the county level, requiring all township assessors to submit their work to the county assessor for approval. They required counties to appoint new assessors who met certain minimum qualifications— including two years of experience and competitive performance on a standardized exam administered by the new Department of Local Government Affairs. Finally, they attempted to make it easier for county assessors to standardize their practices without committing political suicide, by permitting fractional assessment as long as it was granted uniformly and not just according to the whim or favoritism of the assessor. In 1970, legislators adopted a new state constitution that lowered the legal standard for property assessments to 50 percent of fair cash value, and that permitted large counties to authorize even lower standards for residential or agricultural property.[36]

Modernization was at first only partial. The Department of Local Government Affairs published a manual for assessors and required all assessors to use standardized parcel maps in their work, but fewer than 20 percent of county assessors used computers to assist in record-keeping or in the standardization of appraisals. The biggest gap in the modernizing reforms, however, was a loophole for Chicago: the new constitution specifically permitted Cook County to retain an elected assessor who did not meet the minimum qualifications for appointed assessors in other counties.[37] Cullerton continued to practice favoritism in assessment. He also continued to protect homeowners with low assessments.

In this context, Chicago homeowners had comparatively little to complain about. There were protests against the assessor's office, but these were not actually protests against taxation at all, and they had nothing in common with the growing tax revolt in California. The Chicago protesters were more concerned about air pollution. The air was said to be so laden with corrosive chemicals in the summer of 1969 that it could peel paint off the houses in some Chicago neighborhoods, and one of the worst polluters was U.S. Steel's South Works plant. A community-based organization called the Citizens' Action Program (CAP) challenged Cullerton's assessment of the plant as a way to get the company to the bargaining table. CAP's staff researcher combed through various public records in an effort to dig up incriminating information about the company, and he happened to hit paydirt at the assessor's office: a search of the assessment rolls showed that South Works was scandalously underassessed. CAP leaked the information to a local newspaper and demanded that Cullerton reassess the property. The tactic persuaded U.S. Steel to bargain with CAP and the city over its emissions and incidentally netted local governments some $5 million in additional tax revenues.[38]

The initial antipollution protest of CAP may have contributed to increasing the pace of modernization in Chicago. It created political ammunition for Republicans in the statehouse, who sought further assessment reforms in order to deprive Chicago's Democratic machine of a key patronage resource. Cullerton tried to stave off state action with modernizing reforms of his own. He commissioned an outside study of assessment practices by a private appraisal firm. He also hired a young assistant state's attorney named Thomas Tully to clean house. Tully replaced several patronage appointees with qualified appraisers in 1970 and 1971. In 1972—inspired by Philip Watson in Los Angeles—Tully began to implement a new, computer-assisted system to standardize the appraisal of residential structures.[39]

Modernization in turn fueled much more protest against the local assessor—and this time, the protests were actually directed against the property tax. Shortly after Tully's reforms began, homeowners in unincorporated areas of the county formed the Taxpayers Protest Committee of Cook County and demanded that the state limit the county's taxing powers.[40] After the new assessments were sent out in the spring of 1972, a group of 120 apartment owners voted to support a tax strike.[41] Even CAP turned its attention from pollution to the property tax. In February 1972, CAP began contemplating a campaign to stop property taxes.[42] In May, CAP demonstrated before the County Board to demand a temporary "freeze" that would ban all property tax increases for two years. In June, 200 CAP members demonstrated in Mayor Daley's office to demand that he use his clout on behalf of statewide legislation to freeze the tax.[43]

Indeed, CAP quickly became one of the most militant and successful property tax protest organizations in the country. CAP does not fit the stereotype of the tax revolt as a movement of affluent conservatives in the suburbs. Its members were low- and moderate-income homeowners in the city. They had first come together in a "Campaign Against Pollution" initiated by the progressive organizer Saul Alinsky in 1969. The co-chairs of the organization were quintessential 1960s radicals. One was a priest named Leonard Dubi, a self-described "liberal do-gooder" whose activism was inspired by the civil rights movement. The other was a former union organizer and student activist named Paul Booth, who was a member of SDS—who was, in fact, one of the original signers of the Port Huron Statement that famously called for a "new left" that would unite liberals and socialists to transform America.[44]

The organization turned its attention from pollution to taxes because its elderly members saw rising property assessments as a threat to their income security. A recently retired CAP member named Margaret Person learned in late 1971 or early 1972 that rising taxes were about to force her elderly neighbors from their home. She was appalled. "They thought they could live there till they died," she told the writer Harry Boyte. "I just thought it was so terrible." Person joined the board of CAP and began lobbying other board members to start a campaign for property tax relief.[45] In the winter of 1972, the *Chicago Tribune* ran interviews with other elderly people who found themselves forced to sell their homes to pay their property taxes. The co-chair of CAP, Dubi, denounced the property tax as an unfair burden on the elderly and announced a grassroots campaign for state legislation that would protect them from rising property taxes.[46]

The campaign for property tax relief united CAP with liberal taxpayers' groups and senior citizen organizations from around the state.[47] The coalition had some initial successes that encouraged it to set even more ambitious goals. In July, the legislature passed a refundable tax credit for low-income elderly people. The taxpayers' groups responded by broadening their demands for property tax relief. CAP called for a general freeze on property tax increases. In February 1973, the group bused its members to Springfield to join a 700-person rally in support of the proposed Property Tax Freeze Act of 1972. Although the bill failed, demonstrators told reporters, "We're going to raise hell until they stop raising our property taxes."[48]

More modernizing reforms the following year fueled the further growth of the movement. Cullerton stepped down following a bribery scandal in 1973. Cook County voters elected Tully to succeed him as the assessor. Tully made a clean sweep of the assessor's office. He implemented new training requirements for all of the staff, replaced the 1932 appraisal manual that Cullerton had used, and replaced the old bricks-and-mortar appraisal formula with his new computer-assisted method of estimating current market value from the sales prices of comparable homes in the county.[49] Other Illinois officials knew from their conversations with assessors in Arizona and California that "jurisdictions which have instituted computer-assisted assessment systems have discovered an initial high level of protests," and Tully probably knew this, too. He went ahead anyway.[50]

Suburban homeowners rebelled when the new assessment notices arrived in the northeast part of the county in July 1977. A young bank auditor named James Tobin and a handful of his friends, mostly members of the Libertarian Party and a libertarian group called the National Taxpayers United of Illinois, met in a living room in suburban Evanston to plan a protest meeting. Within a week they had formed a new organization called the Taxpayers Protest Committee, and they pulled together a public meeting that drew 150 homeowners who voted to support a tax strike. News of the strike spread rapidly. In the next two weeks, several more hastily convened meetings drew hundreds more protesters. By the end of the summer, more than 1,500 taxpayers had met to demonstrate against high taxes and vote their support for the strike.[51]

The protests continued to spread the following year. Taxpayers packed into protest meetings in suburban Lake, Du Page, and Will Counties.[52] Tobin's group began to circulate petitions for binding referenda to cap the property tax rate in Du Page County.[53] Meanwhile, a grassroots lobbying group called the Illinois Public Action Council began lobbying for a property tax freeze and rebate for all low-income taxpayers. Another statewide group, the Coalition for Political Honesty, led by a notoriously abrasive politician named Pat Quinn, began circulating a statewide petition for an advisory ballot measure that would call on the legislature to approve similar legislation.[54] The Democratic candidate for governor, Michael Bakolis, began circulating a similar petition. Not to be outdone, campaign volunteers for the Republican governor, William Thompson, responded with a petition of their own for an advisory referendum on limiting the property tax.[55] Thompson's petition was the first such advisory initiative to qualify for the ballot in Illinois history.[56]

The property tax revolt had become a social movement—and the fuel that kindled this statewide movement was modernization. Modernization united homeowners across county lines. It drew their attention away from local assessors, who no longer had free rein to dispense tax privileges, and focused their anger on the state. It enabled them to act in common across local boundaries. And it drove them to mobilize on an unprecedented scale.

Missouri: Traditional Tax Administration and Failed Mobilization

By contrast, tax protest groups had little success mobilizing taxpayers in places like Missouri where traditional tax administration still held sway. Of course, it is hard to know for sure that protest was missing in these states: even the most vigorous property tax protests sometimes left little trace in the newspaper. The best evidence for Missouri comes from the papers of the St. Louis Tax Reform Group, a small group of activists in a bastion of traditional tax assessment who were trying to start a property tax revolt in the early 1970s—and failing.

Mary Ann Fiske and a small group of other progressive activists founded the St. Louis Tax Reform Group in November of 1972, inspired by the example of CAP in Chicago. They hoped to use the issue of local property tax inequities to motivate a broader movement for economic justice.[57] Their first public action was a "Tax Hearing" in April 1973 that gave neighbors an opportunity to grill local officials about state and local taxes, including the local property tax. It was just the sort of accountability session that attracted thousands of angry homeowners in Los Angeles and Chicago, cities that were undergoing mass reappraisals. Fiske and her friends mounted a serious organizing drive:

> We offered every incentive we could think of, short of paying people to attend: free transportation, free child care, free professional income tax service.
>
> We distributed over 7,000 "stop-sign" leaflets, plus some 4,000 [newsletters titled] *Beyond Just Gripes*, in the previous three weeks. Twelve volunteers spent over 150 hours talking with people (doorknocking) in neighborhoods near the nine transportation centers. Packets were delivered to 50 supportive community groups and churches in St. Louis with follow-up telephone calls which indicated that the literature had been distributed. Days were spent telephoning many of the local unions and PTA's. UAW mailed flyers to its 50 local unions urging people to attend. Teamsters circulated 400 flyers with agendas at their Council Meeting. 43 organizations which had seen our slide show, plus miscellaneous individuals were notified by mail of the Hearing.[58]

Only three new people showed up. Fiske estimated total attendance at forty-five, of whom forty-two were the volunteers who had organized the hearing and their friends.[59] The small turnout was a crushing disappointment. "[I]t turned out to be a real waste of energy as we were unable to overcome the apathy/cynicism of the working and low-income communities in St. Louis," Fiske wrote. "Many people are ready to gripe about taxes but few are willing to try to do anything about changing them."[60]

The apathy of homeowners in St. Louis was not due to any shortage of injustice. The Tax Reform Group went on to publish reports exposing the unfairness of traditional assessment practices in the city. In November 1973, for example, the group released *The Case for Property Tax Reform*, which presented side-by-side comparisons of "the wealthiest homes in the City of St. Louis as well as some very deteriorated slum dwellings," all in the city's 25th Ward. The comparison showed surprisingly similar assessed values for both categories of housing: in the eyes of the assessor, the rich were poor, and the poor rich. It was a vivid illustration of the inequities that followed traditional tax assessment. It was also a scathing indictment. The assessor was an unqualified political appointee, and the assessments reflected his deference to the status and power of wealthy property owners rather than his evaluation of the actual market values of their homes. There was no regular program of appraisal. Homes were reassessed "piecemeal" when their owners appealed to a board consisting of political appointees who were not trained appraisers; wealthy homeowners appealed frequently and successfully, while poor homeowners did not.[61]

It was all grossly unjust, but injustice did not make a social movement; only modernization did. Fiske opened a storefront tax clinic staffed by VISTA volunteers to help low-income homeowners appeal their property assessments. It was a useful service, and it increased the number of individual appeals to the City Board of Equalization, but it did not jump-start the property tax revolt. The next year, the St. Louis Tax Reform Group turned its attention away from local property taxes to lobby instead for reform of the state's regressive sales tax.[62] The property tax revolt would have to wait for the modernization of property assessment.

Missourians would finally mobilize in 1980. By this time the state had modernized the property tax. The property tax revolt had also begun to spill into Missouri from other states. The organization spearheading the drive was the Taxpayers' Survival Association, which had been founded in the early 1970s by the same Pat Quinn who later campaigned for property tax relief in Illinois. The author of the petition was a St. Louis businessman named Mel Hancock, who simply copied a grassroots initiative petition that had succeeded in Michigan two years before. And the petition was part of a wave of tax limitation that had begun to spread outward from California after 1978.[63]

The lesson of the comparison is clear. In Illinois, the gradual modernization of the property tax fed the growth of a statewide protest movement. In Missouri, the persistence of traditional assessment hindered the best efforts of local activists. Nothing like CAP got off the ground until the end of the 1970s. Where there was no modernization, there was no movement.

Massachusetts: Movement Without Modernization?

Massachusetts appears to be an exception to this rule. As Table 3.1 shows, the state of Massachusetts had not yet modernized the property tax by the end of the 1970s. It had not implemented computerized appraisal methods by 1978. It did not even require assessors to be certified by examination. Yet Massachusetts indisputably had a statewide protest movement against the property tax that included several grassroots ballot initiative campaigns for property tax relief. Does this case refute the argument that modernization caused mass mobilization against the property tax?

No. In fact, it provides further confirmation. It was the looming threat of modernization that drove the movement in Massachusetts. Although the state had not yet implemented a computerized mass appraisal system or new system of certification for assessors by 1978, many local governments had already begun to modernize property assessment under legal pressure in the early 1970s. After the *Sudbury* decision in 1974, it was only a matter of time before the state's courts forced the legislature to modernize the property tax throughout the state. Homeowners were aware of the looming threat to their tax privileges and mobilized to prevent it.

One of the most active social movement organizations was Massachusetts Fair Share. A former welfare rights organizer named Mark Splain organized the first chapter of this organization in the working-class suburb of Chelsea in 1973. Residents were outraged about their high and rising property taxes.[64] Fair Share waged a campaign to reduce property taxes on homeowners by shifting the taxes onto businesses: in particular, Fair Share sought to reduce property tax abatements for local oil storage companies.[65] In 1975, Fair Share successfully shamed the Boston assessor into collecting property taxes from delinquent business owners.[66]

Fair Share expanded its campaign for property tax relief to the state level in 1977. By this time, the state attorney general was taking action against cities and towns that continued to delay reassessment, and statewide modernization was clearly in the offing. Fair Share was also poised to organize a statewide tax revolt, with twenty-eight chapters and some 7,000 members throughout the state.[67] They waged a creative campaign of protest to preserve homeowners' traditional tax privileges. Fair Share first proposed a bill to restore and formalize tax relief for low-income homeowners and renters. Organizers bused hundreds of homeowners and renters from around the state to the capitol to testify before the legislature and demonstrate in favor of the Fair Share tax relief bill. After both houses of the legislature approved the bill, Fair Share mobilized more than 1,000 people to a demonstration demanding that the Democratic Governor Michael Dukakis sign it.[68]

When Governor Dukakis vetoed their bill, the organizers of Fair Share then turned to the ballot initiative. In 1978, they began circulating petitions for a constitutional amendment that would restore traditional tax privileges. Campaign mailings warned voters that "We are all faced with the threat of 100% valuation." Members put up lawn signs that read "For Sale—Unless We Stop 100%." The campaign literature quoted members who feared for their income security in retirement: "I've lived in this house for 46 years. I have two couples renting upstairs, they're old like me. If 100% goes through, I'll have to raise their rent or sell my home. What will they do upstairs? Who would buy my house with taxes at 100%?" The petition, Fair Share explained, would overturn the basis of the *Sudbury* judgment and allow fractional assessment for homes. The petition qualified for the ballot in 1978.[69]

Fair Share was not the only group campaigning for property tax relief. In May 1978, the president of the Greater Boston Real Estate Board, Margaret C. Carlson, founded a group called Citizens for Guaranteed Property Tax Relief. Together with the realtor Jack Conway, she drafted a petition that they called the "Conway-Carlson tax cap." It was a nonbinding ballot initiative that encouraged state legislators to approve a limit on the local property tax levy. Conway and Carlson persuaded the Associated Industries of Massachusetts to contribute funds, but the campaign relied almost entirely on volunteers—almost all of whom were real estate brokers. Campaign records show that Conway and Carlson had volunteers in every state senatorial district in the state. They easily gathered enough signatures to place their petition on the ballot. Conway and Carlson followed up with a "giant realtor tax relief rally" that drew real estate professionals from around the state to Boston's Faneuil Hall to demonstrate in favor of the initiative.[70]

In short, the modernization of the property tax was responsible for the growth of a social movement against the property tax. Even where mobilization preceded modernization, it was the threat of impending modernization that fueled the movement.

AMERICAN POLITICAL INSTITUTIONS AND THE SPREAD OF PROPERTY TAX REVOLT

By the time Roger Sutton lit his assessment notice on fire, he was adding only one more point of light to a flickering carpet of protest that already had spread across much of the United States. But it was still a patchwork carpet. One state might be brightly lit, while another was yet dark; the progress of the American tax revolt remained unsynchronized, reflecting the decentralized character of the American property tax. The pattern of property tax revolt, in short, followed the geography of American political institutions. Mobilization did not take place on a nation-wide basis because the modernization of the property tax did not take place on a nationwide basis. A brief comparison to Britain will test this argument. The tax revolts that swept Britain in the 1970s show that a national reassessment could spark a national protest. And the close fit between the geography of property as-sessment and the geography of protest provides one last, additional test of the hypothesis that modern property assessment fueled the flames of tax revolt.

The Local Government Act of 1948 had modernized British property tax ad-ministration on paper, but in practice, the central government repeatedly de-layed reassessment. The government postponed the first reassessment until 1956, and then directed the Inland Revenue to dampen the shock by appraising homes at the values they would have had before the war rather than at their cur-rent values. The next reassessment, which took place in Scotland in 1961 and in England and Wales two years later, was therefore the first time that homeown-ers were taxed on the current value of their property. Reassessment revoked homeowners' traditional tax privileges. The sudden income shock provoked a sudden outpouring of protest, just as Philip Watson's reassessment would in Los Angeles the following year.[71]

The national reassessment of 1974 in England and Wales triggered a second wave of protest—just as local reassessments were doing across the Atlantic, in American states from Washington to Georgia. British ratepayers, like American property taxpayers, saw the revaluation as an assault on their retirement security. "There are a lot of retired people around here and they are just flabbergasted," said one activist in Newcastle. "It seems to me that the only way we can fight is to unite."[72] Taxpayers founded new protest groups with names like the North Tyne-side Rates Action Group and the Greater London Rate Revolt Committee. Protest meetings throughout the country drew thousands of militant taxpayers who resorted to unconventional collective action, including demonstrations and tax strikes. "If you act sensibly and reasonably—having meetings and quietly lobbying—they don't want to know," the taxpayer activist Ian Scott said. "If, however, you march on London with banners etc., then everyone listens."[73]

The modernization of assessment administration made it easy for the new protest groups to form alliances across parochial boundaries. Assessment administration was now national, so protest was national, too. In 1974, under Scott's leadership, the new protest organizations came together to form the National Association of Ratepayers Action Groups (NARAG).

Just as in the United States, the protest movement was not only geographically but also politically diverse; some members of NARAG were conservatives who wanted to reduce government spending, while others were socialists and social liberals who merely wanted to replace the rates with national or local income taxes. The Conservative Party attempted to co-opt the movement—a rising MP named Margaret Thatcher drafted a plank for the Conservative Party's 1974 election manifesto that pledged to abolish the rates and replace them with "taxes more broadly based and related to people's ability to pay"—but the movement as a whole remained nonpartisan and ideologically pluralistic. The efforts of a few protest leaders to get NARAG to endorse Conservative policy positions provoked a series of bitter splits and resignations within the organization in 1975.[74]

The protest that flared in response to the English and Welsh reassessment of 1974 died away rapidly, much as the first local reassessment protests in the United States had done, and for the same reason: the reassessment was a one-time income shock, not a permanent revocation of ratepayers' privileges. Although modernization was supposed to enable the government to update assessments continuously, blame-averse MPs regularly intervened to postpone or cancel scheduled revaluations. Each delay temporarily restored informal tax privileges by holding assessments stock still while home values continued to climb. Protest calmed. By 1978, a close study of the ratepayers' revolt concluded that most of the protest groups founded in 1974 had "withered" and that NARAG itself was only a paper organization without its former ability to mobilize a membership base.[75] When the next five-year revaluation came due in England and Wales in 1979, the incoming Tory government—now under Prime Minister Thatcher—simply canceled it, thereby putting paid to the ratepayers' protests once and for all. (This was a transparent exercise in blame avoidance. The Environment Secretary Michael Heseltine reportedly warned the prime minister of the political problem posed by the impending deadline for reassessment. "There's no problem," Thatcher is supposed to have replied. "We're not doing it.")[76]

In Scotland, however, modern assessment was implemented more consistently, and taxpayers built a sustained protest movement. Assessment in Scotland was not the responsibility of the Inland Revenue but of an independently appointed assessor under the Scottish secretary. This organization insulated Parliament somewhat from the political consequences of reassessment. As a result of this insulation, reassessment proceeded every five years in Scotland with minimal political interference, and protesters were able to sustain organized campaigns for rate relief from one assessment to the next.[77] In 1975, after an act of Parliament reorganized Scottish local government, Scottish ratepayers' organizations coalesced in the Federation of Scottish Ratepayers (FSR). The new coalition organized protests against the reassessment of 1978. Its constituency continued to swell as the privatization of public housing increased homeownership rates in the late 1970s. When the next reassessment came due in 1984 and 1985, all of Scotland erupted in protest. FSR organized protest meetings throughout the country and mobbed Conservative party meetings to heckle members of Parliament. Protesters also deluged the Scottish secretary with letters and protest delegations, demanding the abolition of the rates.[78]

Events in Britain thus provide additional confirmation of the story that this chapter has told about America. Protests occurred where and when reassessment eroded traditional tax privileges. The modernization of the property tax made it possible for protesters to form coalitions that could act across local boundaries and sustain campaigns of protest over time. In both countries, the pattern of protest followed the geography and the timing of property assessment.

The outcomes of protest in the United States and the United Kingdom, however, would be very different indeed. The next chapter tells the story of how American political institutions shaped the outcome of the property tax revolt. The same federal structure that delayed the reform of American property taxes, and that dictated the state-by-state checkerboard pattern of the American property tax rebellion, also blocked the efforts of the government in Washington to provide property tax relief. Federalism, in short, was an obstacle. But federalism had another face as well. It enabled different states to experiment with different solutions to the property tax crisis, and it ultimately paved the way for a new form of property tax relief that would change the face of American politics.

4 THE TWO FACES OF FEDERALISM

IT GRADUALLY BECAME CLEAR to many activists in the movement that the property tax crisis could not be solved by protest or litigation. It was a structural crisis that required a policy solution. But what policy? By the mid-1970s, many activists on the right and the left had arrived at the same radical answer: abolish the property tax.

In Chicago, the left-leaning community organization CAP favored the wholesale abolition of the property tax, which the group's board described as a regressive tax that unjustly let the wealthy off scot-free.[1] In the neighboring suburb of Evanston, the right-leaning Taxpayers Protest Committee agreed that the tax should be abolished, but for very different reasons. Its leader, the libertarian bank auditor James Tobin, proclaimed before audiences of elderly homeowners that property taxes were "immoral" precisely *because* they taxed wealth. Whatever differences these two groups had—and they had many—they agreed on one thing. The property tax should be abolished to protect the elderly.[2]

This chapter shows how the growing movement to abolish the property tax splintered on the rocks of American federalism. The Constitution gives state officials an effective veto over any program for property tax reform. They used their veto to stop a federal proposal for the elimination of local property taxes. The fragmented structure of American government blocked efforts to abolish the property tax, just as it had previously blocked efforts to modernize property tax administration.

This chapter also shows that federalism has another face. Federalism can block innovative policy at the national level, but it can also facilitate policy innovation at the state level. The autonomy and political diversity of the states in the American federal system allows policy alternatives to flourish, and flourish they did. Although no state granted protesters' wish by abolishing the property tax, many states experimented with alternative policies to provide protesters with property tax relief. These tax relief laws spanned the political spectrum, from liberal policies that provided tax relief to low-income people, to conservative policies that limited the government's power to tax property. The sheer variety of property tax relief policies revealed the ideological diversity that underlay the common demand to abolish the property tax.

THE DEMAND TO ABOLISH THE LOCAL PROPERTY TAX

The demand to abolish local property taxation came from all over the United States and from all over the political spectrum. Protesters framed the problem with the property tax in different ways. From the right, some complained that it was a tax on property, and therefore punished those who worked hard and saved money. From the left, others complained that it was regressive and that poor communities had to charge high tax rates to pay for the same public services that wealthy communities could get more cheaply. But almost everyone could agree that the tax fell too heavily on homeowners who were not able to pay and on the elderly in particular. The convergence of right and left illustrates an important point about the property tax revolt: homeowners were reacting to a shared threat, but they were not necessarily advancing a shared ideology.

It would be hard to find stranger ideological bedfellows, for example, than George Wiley and Howard Jarvis. These two men would emerge as important leaders of the property tax revolt, but they otherwise had almost nothing in common.

Wiley was a former chemistry professor at Berkeley, an African American civil rights organizer, and the executive director of the National Welfare Rights Organization (NWRO). He was also the country's most well-known and militant spokesperson for the poor. In 1970, he became notorious as the man who claimed credit for killing the Nixon administration's Family Assistance Plan—a proposal to provide a guaranteed annual income for all Americans—on the grounds that it was not generous enough. ("$5,500 or Fight" was the NWRO slogan, and the administration was only offering $1,600.) Most liberals found him too extreme.[3]

Jarvis, by contrast, described himself as "to the right of Barry Goldwater."[4] If no welfare program in existence was generous enough to satisfy Wiley, any welfare program at all was too much as far as Jarvis was concerned. He thought the

New Deal was a mistake. He even claimed with a kind of perverse pride to have been Herbert Hoover's press man in the 1932 election campaign. ("It was a real bitch," he later wrote. "There would be people out there waiting for Hoover, and they would throw rotten eggs and tomatoes.")[5] Jarvis was a blunt speaker who had nothing kind to say about intellectuals, Berkeley radicals, or welfare. He distanced himself from openly racist conservatives, but some of his comments about California's public employees—many of whom were black—sounded to liberals like thinly veiled racial slurs.[6] We can only guess what he would have said about Wiley.

There is no evidence that these men ever met. Nonetheless, for a brief period in the late 1960s and early 1970s, they, and the protest groups they represented, advocated a common position in favor of abolishing the local property tax.

Jarvis wanted to abolish the property tax because it was a first step toward lowering all taxes. Like many conservatives, Jarvis objected to heavy taxes on principle and especially to taxes that redistributed income from rich to poor. In 1961, he called for a constitutional amendment to repeal the federal income tax. Progressive income taxation, in his view, was "un-American and illegal."[7]

The growing movement against the local property tax persuaded Jarvis that property taxes were even worse than income taxes. In 1962, his neighbors recruited him to join a nascent coalition of homeowners' associations in the Los Angeles area that opposed property tax increases. The coalition began to grow rapidly two years later when Watson's office implemented modern assessment procedures, and in 1965, it incorporated as the United Organizations of Taxpayers (UO). Jarvis helped to write the bylaws for the UO. He became the first head of the organization after Mike Rubino turned down the position.[8]

In early 1968, Jarvis drafted a petition for an amendment to the state constitution that would eliminate all state and local property taxes in California. "Property taxes must be phased out of California or the economic base of the state will be destroyed," he told a reporter in February. Even income taxes would be preferable, he said, because they at least bore some relation to the taxpayer's ability to pay. "At the present time the California property tax is based on the inability-to-pay principle, and we've got to have one system or the other," he explained. Abolishing all property taxes was an extreme remedy, but Jarvis warned voters that the modernization of the property tax was an extreme crisis. He quoted the assessor, Philip Watson: rising property values would force property taxes to quadruple before long. The petition drive failed, but not before Jarvis and other UO volunteers collected 55,000 signatures.[9]

Jarvis remained committed to abolishing the property tax. His autobiography, written ten years later, included a list of suggestions "for improving this country" that began, "1. Eliminate All Property Taxes." He argued that property taxes should be eliminated because they bore no relation to the taxpayer's ability to pay. Income taxes were a lesser evil, and sales taxes were the least evil of all. Still, all taxes should be reduced. Government needed to shrink. In particular, he thought, it should shed inessential functions like Social Security and public assistance for the poor. Government should confine itself to protecting truly basic rights: " 'Life, Liberty, and the Pursuit of Happiness,' " he groused— "not 'Life, Liberty, and Welfare or Food Stamps.' "[10]

George Wiley agreed that the property tax should be abolished, but for very different reasons. "Life, Liberty, and Welfare or Food Stamps" was a recognizable caricature of Wiley's political philosophy: he thought that a guaranteed annual income was a fundamental human right. In February 1968, while Jarvis was launching his campaign to end the property tax, Wiley was meeting with Dr. Martin Luther King Jr. to discuss plans for a "Poor People's Campaign" that would demand increased government spending on aid for the poor.[11] Nevertheless, four and a half years later, on December 16, 1972, Wiley announced that he was leaving his job in the welfare rights movement to join what he described as a growing tax revolt around the country. "[T]he new movement in the suburbs among the middle class on abolishing property taxes is just a few short steps from realizing the need for over-all tax reform," he told a reporter for the *New York Times*. "That's what the welfare rights movement has been talking about, with the idea of income redistribution."[12]

For Wiley, the property tax issue was appealing because it promised to unite the poor and the middle classes. The NWRO lost the fight for a guaranteed adequate income early in 1972, and the re-election of President Richard Nixon— who ran in part on an anti-welfare platform—convinced Wiley that the NWRO's strategy had been flawed. Poor people on public assistance were a small and unpopular minority who would never win on their own. The only way to win substantial income redistribution was to build an electoral majority, and that meant designing a redistributive program that would benefit the majority. In December 1972, Wiley founded a new organization called the Movement for Economic Justice (MEJ) that would embrace a constituency he defined as all low- and moderate-income Americans. For the next eight months, until his tragic death in a boating accident, Wiley devoted all of his time, energy, and fund-raising clout to the MEJ and the search for a "majority strategy." Organizing taxpayers was at the top of his agenda.[13]

Wiley, like Jarvis, focused on the federal income tax until the growing grassroots movement against the property tax changed his priorities. His initial goal was to finance tax relief for the poor and middle classes by eliminating income tax loopholes that favored the rich. In April 1973, the MEJ invited grassroots progressive organizations from around the country to a "tax seminar," with the goal of building a grassroots activist network that could be used to promote federal income tax reform. The local organizations were apparently more interested in sharing information about how to protest rising property taxes.[14] Wiley deputized his staff to keep abreast of the growing movement against the property tax. A staff person named Julia Mark became a sort of one-person clearinghouse for the movement. In July and August she compiled much of what she had learned from local tax protest groups into a *Property Tax Organizing Manual* that would give resources and guidance to other groups around the country.[15]

The manual presented readers with a menu of possible progressive reforms to the property tax that included as the final item on the list—in effect, the ultimate reform—abolishing the tax altogether. The MEJ manual did not exactly recommend abolition, but it did not exactly *not* recommend it, either. Instead, it presented the case for abolition as a sympathetic summary of other people's views: "Some opponents of property tax argue that it cannot be reformed enough to become progressive and equitable. Therefore, it should be abandoned altogether in favor of a progressive income tax with few exceptions and loopholes. Of course, current income tax laws would have to be completely reformed to achieve progressiveness and equity—a goal worthwhile by itself."[16] Wiley died before this was written, but it was probably a fair description of his views. The property tax should be abolished to make way for a better and more equitable tax.

The demand to abolish property taxes was unorthodox. Academic experts on public finance agreed almost unanimously that the tax should be retained, as George Wiley learned in the spring of 1973. At Harvard on a two-month fellowship from the Institute of Politics, he convened several meetings with liberal professors to discuss strategy for his new MEJ. One of these meetings was devoted to tax policy. At that meeting, prominent liberal economists—apparently alarmed by Wiley's sympathy for the cause of abolishing the property tax—urged him to step back from the brink. According to notes from the meeting,

"[Lester] Thurow made an urgent plea not to work towards the elimination of the property tax. He argued (and everyone agreed) that an across-the-board reduction would result primarily in gains for large real estate owners, with little relief for those with incomes under $15,000."[17] Public finance experts also tended to agree that real property, being immobile, was the most efficient tax base for local government. Although imperfections remained, one scholar noted in a textbook on the subject, "it would be far better to strengthen this levy than to plan for its eradication."[18] Some property tax rebels agreed with the experts. Jonathan Rowe, the spokesperson for the liberal Tax Reform Research Group, took the position that the property tax should not be abolished. Instead, Rowe argued, existing laws should be enforced to make large property owners pay their fair share.[19]

Jarvis and Wiley nevertheless spoke for a substantial grassroots constituency. All across the country, homeowners who were angry about their property taxes were willing to entertain extreme remedies—up to and including abolition of the tax. In Rochester, New York, a community-based civil rights organization issued a position paper in 1971 calling for the "replacement of the real property tax in Monroe county by a county-wide income tax."[20] In San Bernardino County, California, an organization called Americans Nonpartisan for Tax Equity (ANTE) also called for property taxes to be eliminated.[21] In local tax protest groups around the country, liberals and conservatives set aside their differences and called for the abolition of local property taxes.

FEDERALISM AND THE FAILURE OF ABOLITION

Abolition of the property tax looked like a viable political program. For a brief period in the early 1970s, the movement enjoyed a set of particularly favorable political opportunities. Three factors in particular seemed to make the time right for the movement: it had elite allies, those elites perceived the property tax to be in crisis, and they were competing for election.[22]

First, the movement had a powerful ally in Republican President Richard Nixon. The president knew Howard Jarvis personally from their early days together in the California Republican Party. He may have begun paying attention to the tax revolt as early as 1968, when it is likely that homeowners in his old congressional district signed Jarvis's petition to abolish property taxes.[23] Nixon saw tax-conscious suburban homeowners as an important part of his political base, and he began to respond to their protests. In 1970, Nixon appointed a Commission on School Finance to recommend alternatives to local property taxation.[24] In December 1971, he announced that he would seek "a complete overhaul of our property taxes and of our whole system for financing public education."[25] He made this announcement at a White House Conference on Aging, signaling his special concern with protecting senior citizens from rising property taxes. In his State of the Union address a month later, he announced a plan for "Federal action to cope with the gathering crisis of school finance and property taxes."[26]

Nixon's announcement suggested the protesters' second advantage: policy elites perceived the property tax to be in crisis. In the mid-1960s, civil rights attorneys had begun to challenge the constitutional basis for the local financing of public education. The ideal of equal educational opportunity articulated in *Brown v. Board of Education* and championed by the civil rights movement seemed to many advocates to imply more than desegregation: even schools that were not legally segregated by race might nevertheless fail to provide equal educational opportunity if they allocated opportunity according to wealth. This critique implied that the local property tax was an unfair basis for funding public schools, for as long as school revenues came from local property taxes, students who attended school in an area of high property values could expect to have greater access to educational resources than their peers who attended school in an area where property values were low. By the mid-1960s, activists had articulated a number of legal theories under which such inequalities were unconstitutional. At the time that Nixon appointed his Commission on School Finance, civil rights attorneys had already initiated challenges to local property tax financing of public schools in Michigan, Illinois, Virginia, Texas, and California.[27]

The President's Commission on School Finance clearly saw this challenge as a crisis in the making. Although the outcome was not yet clear, the threat was that equalizing property taxes among school districts would increase property taxation in some areas—and thereby contribute to the spread of the tax rebellion. Events were coming to a head in California. In 1968, while Jarvis was circulating his petition to abolish the California property tax, a group of Los Angeles legal aid attorneys were suing the state on behalf of a plaintiff named John Serrano to overturn California's property tax–based system of school financing. In 1971, the California Supreme Court ruled in their favor in *Serrano v. Priest*. Although the justices remanded the case to the lower courts, they affirmed that there was an issue to be tried. If the local property tax was as unequal as the plaintiffs alleged, then it was indeed an unconstitutional basis for school finance. The *Serrano* decision seemed to require a redistribution of property tax revenues that would further increase taxes in some wealthy districts. The decision thereby put the courts on a collision course with the property tax revolt. It seemed only a matter of time before the issue was taken up in the U.S. Supreme Court.[28]

The third temporary factor that worked to the movement's advantage was electoral competition. Nixon's strategy for re-election in 1972 hinged on appeals to suburban voters for whom property taxes were a potent issue. The candidates for the Democratic nomination in the 1972 presidential race were putting forward plans of their own to reduce local property taxes. Senator George McGovern (D-South Dakota) argued that the federal government should assume much more of the financing of public schools. Under public pressure from Ralph Nader's Tax Reform Research Group, Senator Edmund Muskie (D-Maine) announced a plan for federally subsidized property tax relief targeted to the elderly.[29] Nixon could not ignore the issue.

These three strategic advantages were enough to get the movement's demands onto the policy agenda. In February 1972, the President's Commission on School Finance unveiled a proposal to abolish property taxes as a means of funding public schools. With one blow, this proposal would have abolished almost half of all local property taxes in the country, and thereby wiped out almost half of local school district budgets. The public schools would make up for the lost revenue with the proceeds from a national Value Added Tax (VAT). The federal government would levy this new tax on businesses—in particular, on the difference between their sales receipts and their purchases —and businesses would pass the cost along to consumers in their prices, much like a sales tax. The commission proposed to set aside some of the proceeds from the VAT to pay for a federal income tax credit that would offset the regressivity of the new tax. The rest would go to the states to pay for education. In exchange for a share of VAT revenues, a state would be required to abolish all local school district property taxes and to forswear all state taxes on residential property.[30]

The proposal ran aground on American federalism. The Constitution precluded the federal government from making property tax policy directly. Any federal initiative to abolish local property taxes would therefore require the consent of state governments. This feature of American government explains the structure of Nixon's proposal: rather than requiring states to abolish property taxes, he merely encouraged them to do so with the incentive of new federal aid.

This feature of American federalism also explains why Nixon sought the consent of state officials before putting his proposal before Congress. The plan was worth proposing only if it would work, and it would work only if the state officials would play along.

State officials would not play along. A 1971 survey of state and local officials responsible for public education that was conducted for the President's Commission on School Finance found that large majorities of officials in virtually every category—state governors, state legislators, state school officers, state school board members, representatives from state associations of local school boards, and even public school teachers, as represented by state PTA presidents and teachers' union officials—opposed abolishing local property taxes.[31] As long as they were able to avoid the blame for rising property taxes, state and local officials were happy to keep the tax. Organizations of state and local officials loudly condemned the plan in public. In early 1972, Nixon asked the U.S. Advisory Commission on Intergovernmental Relations (ACIR), a body made up largely of state and local elected officials, to evaluate the proposal. The ACIR responded in December 1972 with a negative recommendation backed up by a 250-page report that was pointedly titled *Financing Schools and Property Tax Relief—A State Responsibility*. The ACIR also released the results of a poll showing that the public opposed plans for a new VAT. The National Association of Governors denounced Nixon's plan to replace property taxes with the VAT, since they saw the VAT as a sales tax and sales taxation as a state prerogative.[32]

The chorus of state and local opposition killed the proposal to abolish school district property taxes. Nixon quietly scrapped plans for a VAT and abandoned his plan to earmark federal funds for property tax relief. He limited himself to pushing for a program of "general revenue sharing" that states could use for virtually any purpose. This program permitted but did not mandate that the funds be used to offset property tax cuts—though Nixon continued to describe it as a program for property tax relief.[33] By the end of 1973, the window of opportunity had closed. Nixon remained sympathetic to the movement, but the urgency of the issue had passed. He was re-elected. The legal crisis had abated since the Supreme Court upheld the constitutionality of local school finance in *Rodriguez v. San Antonio Independent School District* (1973). A few property tax rebels continued to push for abolition of the local property tax, but their demands never returned to the federal agenda.

Was federalism really to blame for this failure? The opposition of state and local officials seems telling, but there were other obstacles too. For one thing, the abolition of the property tax went against more than two hundred years of tradition. For another, public opinion was unfavorable toward Nixon's plan for a VAT. Maybe the protesters would have failed even if the U.S. Constitution did not give state officials an effective veto over national property tax legislation.

The best way to tell whether federalism was to blame, of course, would be to conduct an experiment: to observe an identical protest movement in a different constitutional environment—a unitary system where authority was *not* divided between the central government and state officials—and to record whether it succeeded or failed. A perfect natural experiment would require a perfectly identical movement; it would require, in fact, that everything but the constitutional structure were the same. History rarely obliges social scientists with a perfect copy. But happily for us, the Scottish property tax rebellion of 1985 comes close.

UNITARY GOVERNMENT AND THE ABOLITION OF THE RATES

The Scottish tax rebels had a lot in common with their American counterparts. They too were mainly homeowners who were rebelling against the loss of their traditional tax privileges. Their rebellion was also sparked by a reassessment, in this case a revaluation of all taxable property in Scotland that was completed in 1985. Most important for the purposes of this chapter, they also demanded the abolition of local property taxation.

The FSR, the umbrella organization for the Scottish protesters, called for "a fundamental and far-reaching reform of the rating system; [and] if possible its abolition and replacement by a fairer system of raising finance for local government." FSR publications offered a grab bag of objections to local property taxation that sounded very much like the arguments of Howard Jarvis. The rates were objectionable because they bore "no relation to the ability of the ratepayer to pay them." The rates were also objectionable because it was wrong to tax property owners for services enjoyed by everyone—a complaint that was somewhat inconsistent with the idea that taxes should be based on the ability to pay. Finally, rates were objectionable because their burden fell on a minority of voters and therefore encouraged local governments to spend too freely.[34]

As in the United States, the protesters raised their demand at the right time. Several conditions seemed to create a favorable political opportunity for abolishing the rates in the mid-1980s. Like the American protesters, the Scottish protesters had elite allies, a perception of crisis, and electoral competition all working in their favor.

First, the protesters had a strong ally in Prime Minister Margaret Thatcher, whose antipathy to the rates was sincere and well known. Like President Nixon, Prime Minister Thatcher thought of suburban homeowners as her core constituency. She had long regarded a tax on property as "manifestly unfair and unConservative" because it penalized hard work and saving. When she ran for Parliament in 1974, she had even made an election promise on behalf of her party to reform or abolish the local property tax on homeowners, the so-called domestic rates. The party manifesto in 1979 backtracked somewhat, but it implied a commitment to reform or abolish the rates eventually.[35]

Second, as in the United States, the government faced an impending crisis that threatened to expand the conflict. A reassessment of property was long overdue in England and Wales, where the last revaluation had taken place in 1973. The government had canceled reassessments of residential property in 1978 and 1983, but it could not postpone action indefinitely. A reassessment was anticipated for the late 1980s. Thatcher and her cabinet took the Scottish rebellion as a sign of the backlash that would come to England and Wales if they went ahead with reassessment. As Scottish Secretary George Younger later recalled, "Mrs. Thatcher was keenly aware of what would happen if her old ladies in Finchley"—the London suburb that was her home constituency—"suddenly found themselves facing a ten-times increase in their rates bills."[36]

Third, the Thatcher administration, like the Nixon administration, faced significant electoral competition over the issue of local property taxes. After the reassessment notices went out in the spring of 1985, the Scottish Nationalist Party and the Labour Party in Scotland began campaigning for the abolition of the rates. Opinion polls and county election results showed that they were gaining ground even in formerly safe Tory constituencies. Conservative MPs from Scotland felt the heat and urged their colleagues from England and Wales to take the rating issue seriously. When Thatcher called the next general election for 1987, her Scottish party colleagues began pushing for immediate action to abolish the rates.[37]

Thatcher, like Nixon, obliged the protesters with a proposal to abolish the local property tax and replace it with another tax. In January 1986, her Department of the Environment issued a "Green Paper" called *Paying for Local Government* that outlined the government's plan. Local governments would not levy any property taxes. They would make up the lost revenues from two sources. First, the central government would tax nonresidential real estate and redistribute the revenues to local governments on a per-capita basis. Second, local governments would replace residential property taxes with the "community charge," which was a new per-capita tax on all adult residents, or poll tax. The plan also included a vague proposal for tax exemptions to make up for the regressivity of the new tax.[38]

The fate of this proposal differed from the fate of Nixon's proposal to abolish local property taxes because the British political system differed from the American political system. Britain was a unitary political system without any written constitution to reserve particular taxing powers to state or local governments. The central government had the power to create and destroy local governments at will or to remake them as it wished. The local governments levied property taxes only at the pleasure of Parliament. It was therefore possible and surprisingly easy for Parliament to abolish local property taxation.

In practice, the unitary structure of the British state meant that Thatcher, unlike Nixon, had no need to consult with subnational government officials about her plans for the local property tax. The relationship between the Thatcher administration and local government was anything but cooperative. It was actively hostile. Thatcher set the tone shortly after she took office. In 1980, her administration proposed to restrain local government spending by replacing need-based central government grants with a new system of block grants that would be fixed in advance. The government pushed this new granting system through Parliament over the objections of all of the major local government associations, including the Association of County Councils, the Association of Metropolitan Authorities, and the Association of District Councils. The conflict escalated in 1983, when Thatcher obtained parliamentary authority to cap the property tax rates of a handful of local governments that she thought were spending too freely. Some Labour-controlled local authorities responded by refusing to set tax rates at all, in defiance of the law. The central government answered by prosecuting local officials and by tightening the rules governing local property tax rates. The climactic confrontation between central and local governments came in 1985 when Thatcher persuaded Parliament to dissolve the Greater London Council, a Labour-dominated local government that was often at loggerheads with her policies.[39]

The unitary structure of British government explains why Thatcher ignored local government objections to the abolition of the local property tax. There were no local officials present at the crucial meeting at the Prime Minister's country residence in March 1985 when her cabinet decided on abolition. ("It didn't seem at all odd to us not to have any local government people there," one participant later told a political scientist who interviewed him about the meeting. "After all, they were the problem.") During 1986, hundreds of local governments submitted written objections to the plan outlined in the Green Paper. The local governments were nearly unanimous: do not abolish the rates, and whatever you do, do not enact a poll tax. In the United States, this was precisely the kind of opposition that had killed the Nixon plan to abolish local property taxes. In the United Kingdom, it was simply ignored.[40]

So it was that the Scottish tax revolt succeeded in abolishing the local property tax. Pressure from the FSR, and from Scottish MPs who feared for their political careers, persuaded the government to abolish the rates, starting in Scotland. The Scottish MPs all but begged their colleagues to schedule a vote on abolition before the 1987 general election. The administration obliged with a bill in December 1986 to replace the Scottish rates with a poll tax. Parliament approved it the following spring.[41] Most MPs voted along party lines. The following year, Parliament approved the abolition of the domestic rates for England and Wales. As we will see in the next chapter, it was a disastrous mistake; the crucial point for the present chapter is simply that it happened at all.

The results of our comparison are in: a property tax revolt in a unitary state abolished local property taxes. To be sure, this comparison of the American and Scottish tax revolts is not a true experiment, because the two movements were not exactly identical and because the United States and Britain differ in many ways other than the presence or absence of federalism. Still, the comparison does allow us to rule out many other possible explanations for why the American tax revolt failed to abolish property taxes. For example, the crucial difference between the two tax revolts was not the breadth of public support. The Scottish tax rebellion was an isolated regional movement, while the American tax rebellion was already widespread by the early 1970s. Public opinion polls suggest that the substitution of a new tax for local property taxation was if anything slightly *less* popular in Britain than it was in the United States.[42] The tradition of local property taxation was even older in Britain— scholars usually trace its genealogy to the Elizabethan Poor Law of 1601—so if sheer inertia counted for anything, the outcome should have gone the other way.

In short, the variable that made the difference was constitutional structure. Federalism foiled the American tax rebels.

THE OTHER FACE OF FEDERALISM:
POLICY EXPERIMENTATION

If this were a book about presidents and prime ministers, the story might end there. It would be a familiar story to students of British and American political economy. The fragmented American political system has many veto points, so proposals that start in the cabinet often hit an obstacle somewhere on the long road to becoming policy. The unitary British political system has few veto points, so cabinet proposals, even radical ones, hit fewer road blocks. Many excellent comparative studies of the United States and Britain have made precisely this point.[43]

But this is a book about social movements, and the story does not end there because the American tax rebels did not stop there. The failure to abolish the property tax was only a prelude. Thwarted at the federal level, the tax rebels turned to the states. They continued to demand policies that would restore their traditional tax privileges and protect them from the rising price of housing. And federalism provided them with at least as many political opportunities as political obstacles.

Federalism provided political opportunities because it allowed the states to act independently of the national government. This observation should not be surprising, because it is implied in one common definition of the term: federalism is a constitutional system that reserves some policy responsibilities exclusively for subnational governments. The point is worth emphasizing, however, because studies of taxation and social policy too often make a contrary assumption: that policy making in federal states requires the cooperation of national and subnational governments. In the metaphor of the political scientist Ellen Immergut, federalism lengthens the "chain of decisions" necessary for a policy proposal to become law, with each level of government another link in the chain—and the longer the chain, the greater the chance that at least one link will break.[44] But in fact, the chain of decisions is not necessarily any longer in a federal state than in a unitary state. President Nixon could not act on the issue of property taxes without consulting the states, but the states could and did act without consulting President Nixon.

Federalism also provided political opportunities because of the political diversity of the states. In the famous metaphor of Justice Brandeis, this diversity enabled states to function as laboratories of democracy: American federalism established fifty different political environments with fifty slightly different property tax systems—and fifty slightly different sets of social interests pushing on the property tax.[45] The property tax rebels took advantage of this political diversity, by forging different alliances in different states. The political diversity of the American states permitted an extraordinary range of innovative policy experiments. The movement actually consisted of dozens of different state-level movements, each with its own mix of ideas about how to restore tax privileges.

State legislators tried almost everything short of abolishing the property tax in their efforts to appease the protesters. Policies on the table included, among others, providing state aid earmarked for the reduction of local property taxes; lowering the tax rate by expanding the tax base to include previously exempt property such as churches; replacing the flat tax rate with a rate that was graduated according to the value of property; exempting all buildings, so that the tax fell most heavily on large landowners; imposing legal limits on the property tax levy; creating targeted tax credits; and permitting property owners in distress to delay payment, sometimes indefinitely. Each of these types of property tax relief in turn encompassed countless variants. Tax credits, for example, might be targeted to all homeowners, or more specifically to veterans, the elderly, the disabled, farmers, the poor, business owners, or some combination of these; the amount of the credit might be fixed as a dollar amount, as a percentage of assessed value, as a percentage of tax payments, or as a function of the taxpayer's income; and the credit might be funded by state or by local government.[46] Most states tried two or more different approaches to providing property tax relief. Almost every conceivable variation was represented by a policy somewhere in the United States.

I will illustrate this diversity by considering three strategies that eventually emerged from this hothouse as the strongest strains of property tax relief, and as the strains most warmly embraced by the protesters themselves. These were *circuit-breaker* laws, *classification* laws, and *tax limitation* laws. Schematically, we can think of them as the remedies favored by the left, the right, and the center, respectively. Although they were not logically incompatible, each of the three implied a different understanding of the problem with the property tax, and each proposed a different solution.

Circuit Breakers: Property Tax Relief
for Low-Income People

Progressives generally argued that taxes should be allocated according to the ability to pay. The problem with the property tax, in their view, was that it violated this principle. Low-income people faced tax bills that exceeded what they could afford. The logical solution was to provide a formal tax privilege for low-income people. And the principal strategy to this end was to graduate the property tax liability according to the income of the taxpayer—much as a progressive income tax is graduated.

A state law that graduated the property tax was called a "circuit breaker," because, one analyst said, "Its advocates compare it to its electrical namesake—when there is an overload relative to income, the circuit breaker shuts off the property tax system." Circuit-breaker laws were diverse. Some took the form of a property tax exemption that could be claimed by any homeowner or renter below a fixed income threshold. Others were targeted to low-income homeowners or the low-income elderly in particular. Still others permitted local governments to graduate the property tax more finely according to the income of the taxpayer.[47]

Circuit-breaker laws predated the outbreak of tax protest. In fact, state legislators often packaged legislation to modernize the property tax together with a circuit-breaker program in an attempt to preempt the protests against modernization. (Richard Nevins, the California Board of Equalization member who had proposed modernizing the property tax as early as 1958, characterized the thinking behind California's 1966 circuit breaker in exactly these terms: for a small price, he said, school officials thought they could buy off opposition to modernizing the property tax.) The proponents of circuit breakers thus included school officials who wanted to forestall protest against the property tax, along with labor unions and other liberal groups that favored progressive taxation.[48]

Many homeowners' groups nevertheless seized on the circuit-breaker idea as their own. CAP in Chicago and Fair Share in Massachusetts both waged grassroots campaigns for circuit-breaker tax relief. In 1973, a grassroots taxpayers' organization representing low- and middle-income homeowners in Rhode Island also drafted a circuit-breaker law and lobbied aggressively to get it enacted.[49] In other states where circuit breakers already existed, taxpayers' groups fought to expand them. CAL's 1976 campaign for "Fair Share Taxation" in California, for example, was based on a plan to expand the existing Senior Citizens' Property Tax Assistance Program into a super-circuit-breaker that would apply to "all homeowners and renters with incomes under $20,000."[50]

Circuit breakers did not, however, have unanimous support among protesters on the left. Some objected to their complexity. Writing in 1973, Mary Ann Fiske of the St. Louis Tax Reform Group took this view of a new circuit breaker in Missouri:

The form is horrendous. As one law professor told us, he would rather figure out ten income tax forms for Anheuser-Busch than figure out one senior city property tax credit form. Renters must get the signature of their landlords (imagine the problem of this in slum areas); city owners must get the assessor's signature (won't the assessor love that) [and] in rural areas, not one but three signatures are required, the assessor, county clerk and one other! We sure have quality administrative draftsmen in Jefferson City!!![51]

The problem, in other words, was not the redistributive principle, but the fact that it was implemented in a way that imposed burdensome administrative obligations on the poor, and that could even expose them to coercion. This objection mirrored the radical critique of welfare advanced by George Wiley and the NWRO: income redistribution was just in principle, but punitive and stigmatizing in practice. The solution was to simplify the program and make it more generous.[52]

Other progressives thought that circuit-breaker policies were unjust in principle. Jonathan Rowe of the Tax Reform Research Group, for example, argued that "A property owner, even an elderly property owner, burdened by high property taxes is not really 'poor' . . . . Owning valuable property is not a trait of the poor." A circuit breaker targeted to the elderly, he pointed out, would merely shift the tax burden from the cash-strapped elderly onto other taxpayers, many of whom— although temporarily richer in income—might be even poorer in wealth. Instead of shifting the tax onto these people, Rowe argued, elderly taxpayers should be permitted to defer payment indefinitely until their property was sold.[53]

Nevertheless, circuit breakers were high on any list of progressive solutions to the property tax crisis. The MEJ's *Property Tax Organizing Manual* listed circuit breakers first on its menu of possible reforms. "Unlike 'across the board' relief plans like the *homestead exemptions*," the manual read, "the circuit breakers limit relief to those who most need it—to those whose incomes are relatively low and whose property taxes are high compared to their income."[54]

This approach proved especially popular with liberal legislators. By the end of 1976, a majority of states had enacted some form of property tax circuit breaker.

Tax Limitation: A Permanent Tax Privilege
for Long-Term Property Owners

Conservatives in the movement typically saw the problem with the property tax differently. To them, the most important problem with the tax was not that it was regressive. It was that it infringed on private property rights. The solution was therefore to limit the infringement, and the simplest means to this end was to impose a legal limit on the amount of tax that could be levied. As one conservative taxpayers' group put it, "The only alternative to tax limitation is unlimited taxation."[55]

Tax limitation laws aimed to limit the annual growth of the property tax levy. The nature of the limit might vary: some proposals imposed a fixed maximum, such as 2 percent per year, while others imposed a variable cap that was indexed to some other quantity, such as annual population increase, or the growth of total personal income in the state. Some property tax limits were written into state constitutions, while others were imposed by statute. The limits also varied in how they were applied. In most cases, the tax limitation applied to the total property tax revenues collected by any local government. But in some states, the limit also applied to the assessed value of every *individual* property. The latter strategy most closely approximated the old informal custom of fractional assessment.[56]

Property tax limitation was not a new idea. Several states had constitutional limits on the property tax rate that dated from the late nineteenth or early twentieth century, although only Arizona and Colorado had laws from that era limiting the growth of property tax revenues. Tax limits caught on more widely in the early 1970s as the tax revolt spread. Real estate professionals in particular embraced this strategy, although it was also popular with other business groups.

Many homeowners' organizations also began to demand property tax limitation as a second-best alternative to abolishing the tax. After the UO failed to abolish the property tax in 1968, for example, its members began circulating petitions for a property tax limit. Improbably enough, UO members allied themselves with the assessor, Philip Watson, who was trying to stay in office by positioning himself as a champion of property tax relief for the overburdened homeowner. In 1968, while volunteers circulated Jarvis's amendment, Watson paid a professional firm to circulate a constitutional amendment of his own. This was Proposition 9, the so-called Watson Amendment. It would cap the property tax levy at 1 percent of full market value and earmark all local property tax revenues for "property-related" services such as fire protection, sewers, and road repair. "People-related" services such as education and welfare would have to be funded from the state budget. In a few months, the petition gathered 745,000 signatures statewide, more than enough to qualify for the ballot.

Jarvis and his allies did their best to drum up support for the Watson Amendment once their own had failed. The opposition, however, was overwhelming. California's Republican Governor Ronald Reagan opposed the amendment, as did other conservatives and business spokespeople who feared that limiting the property tax would only lead to increasing the income tax. Liberals opposed it on the grounds that public school funding would suffer and that most of the tax relief would go to businesses and wealthy landowners. At the last minute, the Democratic legislature put forward an alternative ballot measure that exempted the first $750 of the assessed value of owner-occupied housing from tax. Two weeks before the election, opinion polls found that the legislature's alternative had only a slight edge, with substantial minorities still undecided on both propositions. The Watson Amendment lost badly in the end, however, with only 32 percent of the vote. The legislature's alternative passed with 53 percent.[57]

For a decade after 1968, Southern California tax rebels petitioned again and again for tax limitation, as Jarvis and Watson continued to put forward competing ballot proposals. In 1971, Jarvis copied Watson's proposal for a 1 percent limit on the property tax rate. Watson countered with another slightly more moderate petition of his own that set a higher limit on the local property tax and that earmarked state cigarette and sales taxes to make up the lost revenues. The campaign was a virtual replay of 1968. Once again, Jarvis failed to secure enough signatures, and he threw his support behind the Watson plan. Once again, the governor and the legislature countered by raising the homeowners' exemption. Once again, Watson lost at the ballot box.[58] In 1976, Jarvis and Watson tried yet again—Watson this time with the support of the Sacramento activist and former car salesman Paul Gann and his group, the People's Advocate. Both camps failed to win a place on the ballot.[59]

Just as some liberals and radicals remained skeptical of circuit breakers, some conservatives and libertarians remained skeptical of property tax limits. Ideological purists who preferred an income-indexed limit on *all* taxation ridiculed Jarvis's proposal for a fixed 2 percent limit on property tax increases as a "blunderbuss approach" to limiting the growth of government.[60]

But tax limitation remained a popular approach at the grassroots, even if few states passed property tax limits. By the spring of 1978, eight states had limited the growth of at least some local property taxes. Jarvis was still trying to limit the property tax in California, and homeowners' groups in at least two

other states had copied his latest petition and begun to circulate it themselves.[61]

Classification: A Categorical Tax Privilege for Homeowners

Some pragmatic protesters took yet a third view of the property tax crisis. On
this view, the problem with the tax was not a matter of principle—whether the
principle at issue was progressive taxation or private property rights—so much
as it was a matter of politics. Recent assessment reforms had shifted the burden
of the tax from some groups onto others. The way to pacify angry taxpayers was
to shift it back.

In practice, this meant restoring the traditional tax privilege for homeowners. This strategy was called "classification." A classification law would permit
local authorities to tax business and residential property at different rates.
Some laws applied the principle of classification directly to the property tax
rate, while others retained a single tax rate but permitted assessors to assess
different classes of property at different fractions of their true market value.
All classification laws distinguished between residential and commercial property, but some established other classes as well, including agricultural property, industrial property, and various subcategories of these.[62] Classification
typically required a constitutional amendment, because most state constitutions required local governments to tax property uniformly according to its
value.[63]

Classification was a compromise policy. Although it had a populist, anti-
big-business ring to it, even many conservative business owners embraced it
when they thought the alternatives were worse. In California, the state Chamber of Commerce—which opposed Jarvis's tax limitation amendment but did
not want a broad-based circuit breaker put forward as an alternative—
endorsed classification in 1978.[64] Labor unions and other liberal groups in California, chastened by the failure of CAL's circuit-breaker proposal the year
before, also endorsed classification as an alternative to property tax limitation.
The resulting proposal was embodied in a bill authored by state senator Pete
Behr (D) that would have lowered the tax rate on residential property, limited
the revenues of local government, and reduced homeowners' property taxes by
30 percent. It also included a modest expansion of the state's existing senior citizen circuit breaker. The whole package was conditional on the passage of a
constitutional amendment, called Proposition 8, that authorized the nonuniform
taxation of residential and commercial property. Proposition 8 was endorsed

with some reluctance by what the journalist Robert Kuttner called "the entire spectrum of California's power elite":

> the state association of manufacturers and the AFL-CIO; the liberal California Tax Reform Association and the conservative California Taxpayers Association; every good government group from the venerable League of Women Voters to the upstart Common Cause, as well as consumer, environmental, police, fire, schoolteacher, feminist, minority, and senior citizens organizations.

As you might imagine, the result was an uneasy compromise.[65]

The left typically embraced classification only when it became clear that more progressive reforms were off the table. The MEJ's change of heart on classification illustrates the path followed by many progressives. The MEJ *Property Tax Organizing Manual*, written in 1973, did not include classification among its recommended reforms to the property tax.[66] But five years later, Massachusetts Fair Share—which had begun as a pilot organizing project of the MEJ, with funding and guidance from George Wiley—began to campaign for a classification amendment to the state constitution. What had changed in the meantime was the political feasibility of MEJ's first choice, a circuit breaker.

Fair Share first tried to win a circuit breaker. Like other homeowners, many Fair Share members faced the loss of their traditional tax privileges because of the *Sudbury* decision that invalidated fractional assessment. They sought a circuit breaker as a way to restore tax privileges for low- and moderate-income people. The way appeared to be blocked at the ballot box. Massachusetts voters had rejected an initiative for a progressive or "graduated" income tax rate by a large majority in 1976, so it seemed unlikely that a circuit breaker, which was in effect a graduated property tax rate, would do any better.[67] Fair Share therefore tried to push a circuit breaker through the legislature. Fair Share organizers bused hundreds of homeowners from around the state to the capitol for a demonstration in which they symbolized their demands by presenting legislators with a pile of blown fuses. The results of this protest campaign were described briefly in Chapter 3: the legislature passed the bill, Governor Dukakis vetoed it, and Fair Share went back to the ballot box with a new policy.[68]

The important point for the present chapter is that when the activists of Fair Share turned to the ballot box, they also turned to a new form of tax relief: classification. It was plainly not the organization's first choice, but it appeared to be the only politically viable strategy left. Fair Share's campaign portrayed classification as a defensive return to tradition rather than as the progressive tax reform that Wiley had envisioned. "It will allow all Massachusetts cities and towns to continue their historical practice of giving lower assessments to homeowners than to profit-making businesses," one Fair Share flyer explained.[69] The classification bill passed, as part of the same legislative package that finally modernized property tax administration throughout Massachusetts.

Classification may have been no one's first choice, but it was popular enough as a second choice. Massachusetts voters approved the Fair Share initiative by a wide margin. Voters in other states seemed favorably disposed toward classification as well. By 1978, seven states had classification laws in place. Five of them had passed their classification laws since 1968.[70]

THE TWO FACES OF FEDERALISM

By the late 1970s, the American property tax revolt looked like anything but a failure. Although protesters' most radical demands had been thwarted in 1972, the protesters themselves had not been deterred. They continued to press for the restoration of their tax privileges. In state after state, they won new tax privileges. The 1970s saw a burst of innovative policy making to provide homeowners with security from rising taxes and rising prices.

Federalism was clearly what enabled this proliferation of policies. British policy makers, by contrast, seriously considered only one policy response to the movement: the abolition of the rates. There were many other options—increasing tax credits for homeowners, limiting property taxes, or replacing the rates with a local income tax, to name a few that were debated at the time—but the Green Paper *Paying for Local Government* dismissed every alternative except the poll tax.[71] Because the British political system was unitary, this was the only policy to make it onto the policy agenda. This was a dramatic contrast to the United States, where protesters could press their demands in multiple arenas, and almost every option short of abolishing the property tax became law somewhere.

Federalism may enable outsiders to win. This view of federalism will sound familiar to some students of state politics, but it is different from the usual view taken by comparative scholars of taxation and social policy.[72] Most recent studies of federalism and fiscal policy have assumed that federalism blocks policy innovation by multiplying veto points. On this view, the more subnational governments there are, the more authorities have to agree before any new policy can become law. Each subnational authority is a potential obstacle; the more such obstacles, the less new policy of any kind we should expect.[73]

The veto points view of federalism is not wrong, but it is partial. It is the view from the Oval Office. President Nixon depended on the states to implement any program of property tax relief; from his seat, the states looked like fifty separate veto points. Federalism lengthened the road that Nixon's proposal had to travel before it could become law and the number of obstacles that it had to pass along the way.

The view from the states was different. For a state legislator considering property tax limitation, the national government was not a veto point. From the point of view of an outsider like Howard Jarvis, the long road from the Oval Office through the states looked, in fact, like an unnecessary detour. It was much simpler to press for state legislation. The more that federalism dispersed authority, the *more* opportunities outsiders like Jarvis had to change public policy. Although Jarvis failed repeatedly to limit the property tax in California, for example, protesters could and did take his tax limit proposal to Idaho and Michigan.[74] As we will see in the next chapter, once Jarvis was successful, his policy experiment spilled across all state boundaries.

The positive point of this chapter, then, is that federalism has two faces. It appears as a structure of veto points that block policy innovation by the central government. But it also appears as a structure of access points that encourage policy proposals from political outsiders. Both faces are important to explaining the fate of the property tax revolt. Federalism blocked the president's plan to abolish the property tax—but it encouraged the proliferation of other property tax relief policies.

The chapter has a negative point, too, and that is that the movement to abolish the property tax was not an inherently conservative movement for limited government. It was simply a demand to protect taxpayers from the rising price of housing by taxing them on something else instead. Even a libertarian like Jarvis acknowledged that abolition of the property tax was mainly a way to shift the tax burden: "[W]hile total tax levels should be reduced," he wrote, "the property tax burden should be shifted to income, sales, and other forms of taxes."[75] The specific alternatives that the protesters demanded spanned the political spectrum—some were conservative policies that favored the wealthy and limited government, but others were liberal policies that protected social spending and redistributed income from rich to poor. The true ideological diversity of the movement was revealed only after the abolition of the property tax failed, and protesters were thrown back on their second choices. There were many ways to design tax privileges that would provide social insurance for homeowners.

How, then, did we come to think of the tax revolt as a conservative movement—as a backlash against big government, a rebellion against the welfare state, and even a mandate for free-market conservatism? That is the story narrated in the next chapter. It is the story of how the tax revolt turned right.

5 A NEW BALL GAME

How the Tax Revolt Turned Right

"I BELIEVE today we need a taxpayer's revolt," George Wiley told an audience at a March 1973 conference sponsored by the National Council of the Churches of Christ,

> a taxpayer's revolt that is shaped and directed not against welfare mothers but a taxpayer's revolt that is shaped against the real welfare recipients who are chiseling billions and billions of dollars out of the federal treasury. I believe we need a real taxpayer's revolt today against the real welfare program that takes care of the welfare of the corporations, of the corporate farmers, of the oil industry, of the millionaires and of the people who live off the public dole—who live at the public trough.[1]

In this speech, and in other speeches and writings of this period, Wiley used the phrase "taxpayers' revolt" to describe an emerging progressive movement for income redistribution.

Many others in the 1970s also spoke of a growing tax revolt.[2] But not everyone agreed with Wiley that it would grow into a populist rebellion against big business. To the contrary, some conservatives welcomed it as a populist rebellion against big government on behalf of the market. As Howard Jarvis put it, "We have a new revolution. We are telling the government, 'Screw you!' "[3] Both progressive and conservative interpretations of the movement at first seemed plausible enough: beyond the immediate demand for property tax relief, the protesters' goals were multiple, sometimes conflicting, and often unclear. As Wiley's remarks suggested, the ultimate political significance of the taxpayers' revolt would depend on how it was "shaped and directed."

Today, most people who remember the tax revolt probably remember Howard Jarvis as its leader and do not think of George Wiley as part of the same movement at all. From the vantage point of 1973, however, it would have been just as natural to conclude that Wiley was the true leader of the property tax rebels. Wiley was a household name. He was the first to proclaim the existence of a property tax revolt in the national media when he announced his resignation from the NWRO in 1972. He was the first to sponsor a national conference of grassroots tax protest organizations in April 1973, which gave local groups from all around the country the chance to share strategies for protesting the property tax. He had traveled around the country for the express purpose of forging connections with property tax protesters. He had even helped to found and finance grassroots campaigns for property tax relief in Massachusetts and California by providing seed money and staff for Fair Share and CAL.[4]

Jarvis, by comparison, was unknown outside Los Angeles. Most locals knew him, if they noticed him at all, as a crank who showed up occasionally to city council meetings to deliver a harangue, or as a no-hope candidate for the State Senate in 1962 and the State Board of Equalization in 1971. The famous verdict of one liberal activist of the time was that "Nobody here takes Jarvis seriously."[5]

History is filled with reversals: by 1980, Wiley was gone and Jarvis was triumphant. The phrases "taxpayers' revolt" and "tax revolt" had come to be used as synonyms for a wave of conservative legislation that copied a blueprint drawn by Jarvis. The new laws constrained state and local governments' ability to raise revenue, curtailed spending on education and social programs, and created windfall tax breaks for the corporations and millionaires whom Wiley had lampooned as welfare chiselers.[6] This wave of tax limitation was said to have helped to propel the conservative Ronald Reagan into the presidency. By the 1990s, many scholars looked back on the tax revolt as the death knell of the New Deal order.[7]

This chapter argues that the tax revolt turned right suddenly, and in response to a symbolic event. That event was the passage of a constitutional amendment called Proposition 13 in the California primary election of June 6, 1978. Before the election, liberal solutions to the property tax crisis were more popular and more successful. After the election, protesters and politicians alike embraced conservative solutions to the crisis. "Proposition 13 fever" swept the country.

Why did this event turn the tax revolt right? The key to explaining Proposition 13 fever is not only the content of the amendment, but also—and more importantly—the way in which it came about. There were many other popular ways to restore homeowners' tax privileges, and there were many other ways to distribute tax relief. Protesters and politicians in other states elevated Proposition 13 above all the alternatives not because they preferred its details, but because it alone had become law by a vote of the people. Direct democracy turned the tax revolt right.

How did direct democracy turn the tax revolt right? Not, as you might suppose, by allowing voters to dictate the policy that they wanted most. The institution of the ballot initiative did not screen for the proposal that voters thought best, but instead for the first proposal that they thought was good enough. There were many policies that might have won majority approval; even as late as May 1978, the public expressed willingness to vote for a more progressive alternative. What the ballot initiative did was simply to guarantee that whichever of these policies was enacted first would be consequential. When a proposal won the approval of a majority of voters, both protesters and politicians in other states revised their opinions of it. Previously hostile politicians endorsed it as a tried and true vote-getter; previously skeptical protesters embraced it as a winnable demand. It did not have to be the best understood or even the most popular policy. It only had to be the first plausible solution that had proven it was popular enough to get 50 percent of the vote.

Finally, direct democracy turned the tax revolt right because of how the California ballot initiative fit into the framework of other American political institutions. Not every ballot initiative starts a national landslide. Proposition 13 was unusual because of California's place in the federal system and the electoral college. California was the most populous state—the state that would decide the next presidential election—and the victory of the conservative Proposition 13 seemed to defy the California electorate's reputation for liberalism. California was also an influential and innovative state to which politicians and activists in other states routinely looked for guidance. Observers saw the California initiative as a bellwether for national political trends. They took Proposition 13 as the sign of a conservative turn in the tax revolt—and this prediction became a self-fulfilling prophecy.

THE TRIUMPH OF TAX LIMITATION IN CALIFORNIA

The right turn in the tax revolt could not have been foreseen before 1978. The most widely available opinion polls at the national level simply asked whether people thought property taxes were fair, not what they thought should be done about unfair taxes.[8] What little evidence there was suggested that more people preferred liberal remedies. Few states had tax limits, compared to circuit break-ers. Californians had voted on tax limits twice and rejected them both times. As Chapter 4 noted, they had approved more liberal forms of tax relief, such as a homeowners' property tax exemption.[9] Circuit breakers, classification, and tax limitation were all live options.

Even as late as 1976, conservatives in California seemed unable to get their act together. Early that year, Jarvis and the UO entered into talks with Los Angeles assessor Philip Watson and the Sacramento activist Paul Gann to see if they could coordinate their efforts on behalf of property tax limitation.[10] The first round of talks broke down quickly. Jarvis thought Watson's name should not ap-pear on the initiative petition because he was under investigation for possible campaign finance violations.[11] Gann thought Jarvis was a foul-mouthed buf-foon who was impossible to work with. As Jarvis later told the story, the three men came to an initial agreement, but Watson persuaded Gann to renege.[12] Re-gardless of who was to blame, the talks fell apart. The result was a pair of com-peting initiative petitions, one signed by Gann that was co-written with Watson and one that was written and signed by Jarvis.

The conservative wing of the tax revolt began to pick up momentum later that year. Both the Jarvis petition and the Watson-Gann petition failed. But each se-cured more than half of the signatures that were necessary for ballot access—Jarvis was only 1,400 signatures short—and activists in both camps recognized that a coalition effort could secure access to the ballot. Watson removed the great-est obstacle to unity by resigning. In May 1977, Gann contacted a UO board member to arrange another meeting with Jarvis. The two agreed to sign and cir-culate a common initiative petition, as long as they could divide up the state so that they did not need to deal with each other for the duration of the campaign.[13]

The new Jarvis-Gann proposal effectively formalized the assessor's old tradi-tion of copying the tax rolls from year to year with minimal adjustment for mar-ket prices. It established a 1 percent limit on the property tax rate. It rolled back assessed values to their 1975 levels, and it permitted assessments to increase no more than 2 percent a year from that baseline, regardless of how much the price of housing increased. Property could be reassessed to reflect its new market value only when it changed hands. The proposal provided homeowners with a valuable form of social protection against the rising price of housing. It had a distinctively conservative cast, however, because it provided this protection to business owners as well as homeowners and because it benefited the rich even more than the poor. And it was especially conservative because it packaged this protection with provisions that limited government's ability to raise other taxes. Certain local tax increases required a vote of the people, and a state tax increase required a two-thirds vote of both legislative houses.[14]

In July 1977, Jarvis and Gann mounted the biggest petition drive in the history of California. UO's network of homeowners' associations fanned out through Southern California. Gann contacted chambers of commerce and local real estate boards throughout the state. Real estate agents everywhere in California carried the petition with them while they were showing houses. Jarvis acquired a regular talk radio spot and a newspaper column, both of which he used to plug the initiative. He also took a position with the Los Angeles Apartment Owners' Association and began to use the association's mailing lists to promote the initiative. Both Jarvis and Gann drove up and down the state organizing groups of volunteers to collect signatures. They even took a page from Watson's playbook and hired a public relations firm to publicize the petition, although signature collection itself remained mostly a volunteer effort.[15]

The left wing of the tax revolt was gaining momentum at the same time. CAL's grassroots campaign for a circuit breaker began in November 1976, when the group announced its campaign for " 'Lifeline' tax relief for those who cannot afford to pay." In January, CAL unveiled the Tax Justice Act of 1977, drafted in consultation with the labor-backed California Tax Reform Association and introduced by Senator Nicholas Petris. The bill would expand the state's existing circuit breaker into one of the most ambitious programs of property tax relief in the country. Instead of a modest tax break for low-income senior citizens, the program would cut property taxes in half for all California households with incomes below $30,000 a year. The bill would protect taxpayers from inflation by adjusting the tax credit annually for the rise in consumer prices, and it would finance this tax relief by increasing the state income tax rates on the top income brackets and eliminating the capital gains deduction in the state income tax. It was endorsed by labor unions, senior citizens' groups, antipoverty groups, and the liberal California Democratic Council.[16]

CAL launched a massive grassroots campaign. The group organized protest actions throughout the state in the spring of 1977, including Roger Sutton's April 20 bonfire on the steps of the San Mateo County courthouse. On April 27, while the Tax Justice Act was bottled up in the Senate Finance Committee, CAL brought almost 2,000 protesters to Sacramento for a demonstration in support of the bill. They swarmed the capitol, buttonholed legislators, and rallied on the capitol lawn.[17] CAL focused its attention on Finance Committee members who had previously voted against the bill and claimed credit when the committee voted to report the bill to the full senate on May 9.[18]

The circuit-breaker bill almost passed. After a summer of heated negotiations—in which successive conference committees stripped some progressive provisions from the bill in order to please business lobbyists and then partially restored them in order to please labor—the bill came up for a final senate vote on September 15. It got twenty-one votes, just six votes shy of the two-thirds majority it needed under the California constitution. All of the Republicans opposed it. Four Democrats abstained but pledged to vote for the bill if the last two votes could be found on the Republican side of the aisle. There were two likely candidates: Senators John Nejedly and Milton Marks, both Republicans representing liberal districts in the San Francisco Bay Area, both of whom had voted for the bill in its early stages. Dean Tipps, a lobbyist for the CTRA, thought in retrospect that just a little more effort might have swayed Nejedly and Marks to vote for the final bill.[19]

CAL kept the pressure on. It began protests targeted at senators and assembly members who had voted against the bill. Activists threatened to deliver a "hill of beans" to Senator Marks, who had allegedly said that his signed pledge to support property tax relief was not worth a hill of beans. Protesters swamped other legislators with letters and mobbed them in unruly crowds.[20] CAL also began a series of protests that aimed to pressure Governor Jerry Brown into recalling the legislature into special session. On November 20, CAL members began a three-week vigil in front of the governor's Los Angeles office, demanding that he meet with them and that he promise to recall the legislature in order to secure property tax relief by the end of the year. On December 9, the night before property tax bills were due around the state, CAL members 350 miles away packed the Alameda County Assessor's office with a rally to "Save Our Shirts" (flyers asked, "Are property taxes taking the shirt off your back?"). The next day they held a rally in Los Angeles County to announce the end of the three-week vigil and unveiled a hastily assembled petition from 150,000 Los Angeles–area residents demanding property tax relief before the end of the year.[21]

Meanwhile, on December 2, the conservative Jarvis-Gann initiative qualified for the June primary ballot with over a million signatures. This was many times more signatures than the progressives of CAL presented to Governor Brown, but in this case the numbers may be misleading: Jarvis and Gann had simply been at it for many more months and had even hired paid signature collectors. Now their task was to persuade the voters. Jarvis hired a pair of campaign consultants who began to arrange speaking engagements and media appearances for him.[22] He traveled around Southern California at a hectic pace to campaign for the initiative that was now officially designated Proposition 13. Jarvis regaled audiences with earthy and frequently outrageous diatribes. He variously characterized the critics of Proposition 13 as communists, "horses' asses," and "marinated bureaucrats and over-animated popcorn balls." He excoriated public officials in particular for their cowardice and greed; one reporter quoted Jarvis as saying that victory would make his last days sweet, because "I'll die knowing I really put the hot rod up the butts of those goddamned stupid politicians."[23] Most of all, however, Jarvis hammered on the threat of rising property assessments. His warnings grew more and more outlandish as the campaign progressed. If voters did not approve Proposition 13, he predicted, their tax bills might go up 100 percent within three years; then he predicted that their taxes would go up 100 percent a year "or more," perhaps even 200 percent.[24]

In early 1978, with CAL's broad-based circuit breaker off the table, legislators from both parties agreed to counter Proposition 13 with a classification amendment. The coalition supporting classification included all the groups that had opposed the Watson amendments in 1968 and 1972. Conservative organizations, including the business-backed California Taxpayers' Association, opposed Jarvis-Gann on the grounds that it was fiscally irresponsible and would ultimately cause the state to raise taxes on business. Liberal organizations, including labor unions and the CTRA, opposed it because it would hurt schools and public services. The compromise counterproposal had two parts. The first was an amendment to the state constitution that would permit classification. The legislature approved this amendment in February 1978, and it became Proposition 8 on the June ballot. The second part was the Behr bill, described in Chapter 4, which would reduce homeowners' property taxes by 30 percent and expand the senior citizens' circuit-breaker program on the condition that Proposition 8 passed. The Behr bill would not cut homeowners' taxes as deeply as Proposition 13. But it would cut them more deeply than ever before, and it promised lasting protection against tax increases. This bill was a substantial program of property tax relief and a serious alternative to Proposition 13.

The Assessor Tips the Scales

The center might have held. Several opinion polls from early 1978 indicated that the majority of Californians held favorable opinions of classification. As late as

April, Proposition 13 was running neck and neck in opinion polls with Proposition 8, and Proposition 13 appeared to be losing popularity.[25]

Then the assessor struck. The Los Angeles Board of Supervisors had appointed a young Democratic reformer named Alexander Pope to replace Watson. Like his predecessor, Pope nursed ambitions to run for statewide office. By April 1978, Pope had completed his first annual reassessment, which encompassed one-third of the property in the county. Ordinarily, the new increases would not have been announced until July, and most homeowners would not have been notified until their tax bills were sent out in October. Pope, however, was running for election in November, and he presumably did not relish the thought of voters getting the news of the tax increase on the eve of the vote. On May 16, he held a fundraising dinner at the Beverly Wilshire Hotel, at which he announced to the press that the assessment rolls were going to be opened for public viewing. Property owners could come to the assessors' branch offices throughout the county and see their new assessments.[26]

The result was pandemonium. Thousands of panicked and angry homeowners besieged Pope's office. Jarvis's most outlandish predictions had come true: the average increase in assessed value was well over 100 percent. The news media carried story after story featuring people who announced they would have to take second jobs or sell their homes to pay their property taxes.[27] Governor Jerry Brown, desperate to undo the damage, ordered Pope to roll back the assessments. When Richard Nevins at the Board of Equalization pointed out that this move was illegal, Brown scrambled to get the legislature to rewrite the law. It was too late. The City of Los Angeles had already budgeted for the increase, and city officials announced that if assessments were rolled back, they would have to raise the municipal property tax rate to compensate.[28] Almost overnight, public opinion in California—and especially Los Angeles—shifted from the moderate Proposition 8 to the more extreme Proposition 13.[29]

There is little evidence that the shift reflected a newfound preference for tax limitation over classification. Polls showed that Californians still liked classification in principle. The preference for Proposition 13 seems instead to have reflected a preference for the policy that would provide the greater immediate tax cut. A series of opinion polls asked Californians whether they thought the Behr bill offered enough tax relief, and the answer shifted dramatically in the wake of the Los Angeles reassessment. In April, a substantial majority of those with an opinion said the Behr bill provided just enough or more than enough relief (59 percent). By the end of May, a majority thought it did not (51 percent).[30]

Voters were also drawn to Proposition 13 because it seemed to express their displeasure most forcefully. Polls that presented people with arguments for and against the measure found that the most popular reason for supporting it had nothing to do with the details of the policy itself. It was simply that Proposition 13 was "the only way of sending a strong message to government officials that people are fed up with high taxes and too much government spending."[31] Although Proposition 8 and Proposition 13 proposed conflicting amendments to the state constitution, a voter who wanted to be sure of getting some property tax relief might reasonably have voted in favor of both.[32] Supporters of Proposition 13 nevertheless campaigned against Proposition 8. They particularly resented the efforts of state and local government to "blackmail" voters by threatening reductions in services if Proposition 13 passed. As one campaign jingle had it:

> We pay for education, police, and fire protection too
> And we place these three priority one and not priority two
> Like those bureaucrats who hide the truth and use scare tactics too
> Let's show them how we feel—
> No on Eight and Yes on Thirteen—
> No on Eight and Yes on Thirteen—
> No on Eight and Yes on Thirteen—
> Three cheers for Jarvis-Gann![33]

Presumably, voters reasoned that a vote for Proposition 8—the option that had been placed on the ballot by the California legislature and endorsed by most government officials—would not have sent those officials a very strong message. A surge of hostility toward incumbent politicians contributed to the momentum for Proposition 13.[34]

On June 6, 1978, California voters approved Proposition 13 by a vote of 65 percent to 35 percent. They rejected Proposition 8 by 53 percent to 47 percent. People whose property tax bills were increasing the most rapidly—especially residents of Los Angeles County—were the most likely to vote for tax limitation. Support for tax limitation also ran especially high among traditionally conservative constituencies, such as men, the affluent, Republicans, white people, and the elderly. But a majority of almost every group voted in favor of tax limitation. The only exceptions were African Americans, public employees, and renters, all liberal constituencies that also had little to gain from tax limitation. Most people in these groups preferred Proposition 8. And almost everyone who voted cast a ballot for one or the other form of property tax relief.[35]

A Preventable Proposition?

In retrospect, some commentators presented the triumph of tax limitation as inevitable. The economist Milton Friedman, for example, told anyone who would listen that the vote showed taxpayers were finally ready to launch a broad-based movement for a constitutional limit on *all* taxes, as he had long predicted. "The movement is gaining steam much faster than I thought it would," he said.[36]

Other commentators pointed to the many missed opportunities to avert tax limitation. It was easy to think of alternative scenarios. Philip Watson had been warning California politicians since 1966 that some sort of policy was necessary to protect homeowners from rising property taxes. The state had a large budget surplus that it could have spent on property tax relief. Had the legislature acted sooner, the tax limit might never have been proposed. Had two Republican senators agreed to vote for CAL's circuit-breaker bill in 1977, Proposition 13 might never have qualified for the ballot. Had Pope stuck with the regular schedule for releasing assessments, Proposition 13 might have gone down to defeat at the ballot box.[37]

All of these arguments rest on the same untested assumption: that a successful circuit breaker or a classification law could have preempted Proposition 13. Is this assumption correct? The best way to answer this question would be an experiment: to compare two otherwise identical states, introduce a circuit breaker or a classification law into one, and examine whether they subsequently pass property tax limits. No two states are identical in practice, but we can approximate the experimental situation by comparing the actual chances of property tax limitation in states with and without these more liberal forms of property tax relief. We can use statistical models to adjust for the differences among states and to control for the effects of other variables—from the tax rate to the homeownership rate—that might distort the comparison. Appendix 2 reports the results from a model like this that is designed to estimate the annual probability that a state would pass a property tax limit like Proposition 13.

Figure 5.1 shows how passing a circuit breaker or a classification law affected the annual probability that a state would subsequently pass a tax limitation law. Figure 5.1 shows adjusted probabilities for an average state in 1978. They are based on the statistical model in Appendix 2, which attempts to control for factors such as the rate of homeownership, the property tax burden, and the party in control of the state legislature. Figure 5.1 suggests that either form of tax relief

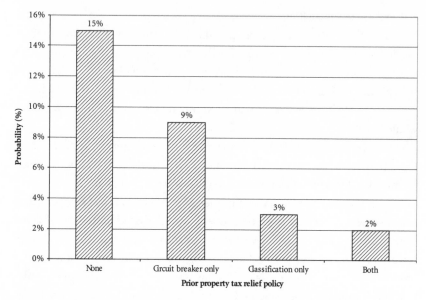

Figure 5.1. Adjusted annual probability of passing a property tax limit in an average state, 1978
SOURCE: Calculated from Table A2.1.

might have inoculated a state against Proposition 13 fever, although it was not possible to measure the effect of circuit-breaker laws with much certainty, and the analysis suggests that they were not very effective at preventing tax limits. But classification laws were strong medicine indeed.[38]

In short, timely legislative action could have prevented Proposition 13. The failure to preempt this law was fateful for the American tax revolt. Within weeks, protesters and legislators around the country had Proposition 13 fever. Tax limits began to spread.

THE TAX REVOLT TURNS RIGHT

Proposition 13 was headline news across the country. *Newsweek*'s cover was a colorful photo of a crowd of Californians, smiling and surrounded with Proposition 13 campaign paraphernalia, while *Time* went with a photo of Jarvis, fist upraised. The *U.S. News and World Report* ran the story inside, under the title, "Nationwide Cry: 'Cut Our Taxes!' "[39] Coverage of Proposition 13 saturated local and regional media throughout the country, to the point that a national public opinion poll six months later indicated that 76 percent of adults in the United States claimed to have "heard or read" of Proposition 13. (By comparison, only

40 percent claimed to remember the name of the candidate their district had just elected to Congress.)[40]

People liked what they heard about Proposition 13. A majority of people surveyed across the United States (54 percent) said they would vote for "a measure similar to Proposition 13" if given the opportunity. But it is not clear what they thought this meant. The survey described Proposition 13 only as a large tax cut, rather than as a constitutional limitation of the government's power to tax: "In June California voters passed Proposition 13, which reduced property taxes by more than half. Opponents of the measure said that the tax cut would force local communities to reduce services. Have you heard or read anything about this California property tax vote?"[41] This wording suggested that *any* big tax cut might qualify as "a measure similar to Proposition 13." By this standard, even CAL's original circuit-breaker proposal was similar to Proposition 13: it would also have reduced property taxes by half for low- and middle-income taxpayers.[42]

Nonetheless, politicians and protesters alike seized on Proposition 13 as a sign of property tax rebellion. In newsletters, demonstrations, letters to the editor, and testimony before public officials, protesters claimed Proposition 13 as their own and invoked the threat of another Proposition 13 to support their own plans for tax relief. Public support for "a measure similar to Proposition 13" came from across the political spectrum and from every sociodemographic group.[43]

Why was this event so contagious? Proposition 13 was not the first policy victory for the property tax rebels, nor even the first tax limitation law. But it was the first and most conspicuous to pass by the ballot initiative.

Jonathan Kaufman, the director of CTRA, pointed out in a 1974 grant proposal that the ballot initiative gave struggles over tax policy in California national significance. The argument was self-interested—Kaufman was trying to persuade a national foundation to make a grant to his organization—but it was still true. Unlike tax protesters in many other states, Kaufman argued, protesters in California had access to the ballot initiative, potentially enabling them to write their demands into law even over the objections of their elected representatives. California was also the nation's largest state, so a victory at the ballot box in California might resonate elsewhere. And, Kaufman argued, the alignment of forces seemed to favor progressive tax reform:

We think the time is ripe for a major new breakthrough for tax justice in California—a breakthrough that could have national implications. The final court decision in *Serrano v. Priest* has mandated a new tax structure for financing public education. Numerous political candidates have lately been on the hustings calling for tax reform. And the success of two major citizens' initiatives— Proposition 9 (political reform) and Proposition 20 (coastal protection)—and the defeat of Governor Reagan's regressive Proposition 1 show that popular state reforms can be enacted in the face of all-out opposition from well-heeled special interests.[44]

Kaufman was right. It was precisely these three factors—California's ballot initiative process, its size, and its liberalism—that would make Proposition 13 so contagious.

First, the fact that Proposition 13 passed at the ballot box is clearly important to explaining its appeal outside California. A simple comparison makes the point: in the decade prior to 1978, six state legislatures enacted new property tax limitation without sparking anything like the wildfire of interest that followed Proposition 13. By 1988, sixteen more states had followed suit, most of them within the three years immediately after the passage of Proposition 13. Unlike early property tax limits, Proposition 13 was contagious because it showed protesters and legislators in other states that tax limitation had popular support.

Still, not every ballot initiative sparks imitators. The second factor, as Kaufman pointed out, was that California was the largest state. These were not just any voters: they were the voters who might decide the next presidential election. By contrast, no one paid attention when voters in the state of Washington approved a constitutional amendment in 1972 that tightened their state's existing, statutory property tax limit. Washington, like California, was a comparatively liberal state with a reputation for innovative policy.[45] But California had six times the population of Washington—and, more important, five times the electoral votes. The Washington tax limit amendment of 1972 attracted virtually no attention in the national media.

Third, California's liberalism was important, although not in the way that Kaufman thought. It magnified the impact of a conservative policy by making the victory of Proposition 13 stand out as an especially interesting piece of news. When Californians voted in 1968 to establish a homeowner's property tax exemption, they attracted little national attention. This vote was unsurprising. By contrast, editors must have found "Californians vote to limit taxes" an irresistibly shocking reversal almost on par with "Man bites dog." The editors of the *Wall Street Journal* thought the headline was surprising enough to be worth a meta-headline of its own: "California Votes to Slash Property Taxes, Stealing Headlines from the Candidates."[46]

Finally, the fact that the vote took place in a liberal state confirmed the sense of politicians and protesters elsewhere that tax limitation was a politically viable solution to the property tax crisis. If conservative tax limitation was popular in liberal California, surely it would pass in conservative Idaho. And in liberal Massachusetts. And in moderate Missouri. And so it *did* pass, at the ballot box and in the statehouse, in these states and others, again and again—until, by 1990, the majority of states had property tax limitations of their own.

A WAVE OF LEGISLATION

The only certain conclusion to be drawn from the California election was that voters might be willing to vote for property tax limitation. In the long run, however, even this lesson was enough to give tax limitation policies a significant advantage over other forms of property tax relief. No one knew whether a circuit breaker or a classification law would satisfy the protesters. But everyone knew that voters would go for tax limitation.

Politicians and activists did not need to know which solution voters preferred most. They only needed to find one solution that voters would settle for. To property tax rebels, the lesson of the California election was that tax limitation was a politically viable way to restore their tax privileges. To state legislators, the lesson of the California election was that a tax limit could mollify angry taxpayers and even yield an electoral payoff. Maybe another policy would satisfy the public as well—but why risk it? Tax limitation was a proven winner.

The rightward turn is clearly visible in the record of state legislation. Table 5.1 illustrates the shift by listing the states that adopted each form of tax relief— circuit breakers, classification, and tax limitation—in each year. Before 1978, states were most likely to adopt circuit breakers. After 1978, states were most likely to adopt tax limits. The rightward shift was sudden. Moreover, the statistical analysis described in Appendix 2 shows that the shift cannot be explained away by any of the other structural trends that affected property tax legislation in this period, such as increasing rates of homeownership, rising school expenditures, economic growth, or the changing political party composition of state legislatures. Some of these factors also mattered—richer states, for example, were

Table 5.1. States Adopting Property Tax Relief Policies Favored by the Left, the Center, and the Right

Year	Circuit breaker	Classification	Tax limit
1964	WI		
1965			
1966			
1967	CA, MN		
1968		AZ	
1969	ND, VT		
1970	KS		KS
1971	CO, ME, OH, OR, PA		WA
1972	IL, WV	AL	AK, DE
1973	AZ, AR, IA, MI, MO, NV, TN	IL, TN	IN
1974	CT, ID, OK		
1975	MD, WY		
1976	SD	SC	OH
1977	HI, NM, RI, UT		
1978	NY	IA, LA	CA, IA, LA, MI
1979		MA, OH	KY, NM
1980			MA, MS, MO, NJ
1981	MT	NY, ND	AR, ND, NY*
1982		MS	TX
1983		GA, UT	NV
1984			
1985	IN	CO, MO	RI
1986		KS	
1987			MT
1988		WY	
1989			
1990	NJ		NE, WV

The table includes only the first policy of each type passed by a respective state. The right-hand column includes all limitations on the growth of assessed values or limitations on the growth of the total property tax levy that apply to general purpose local governments. See endnotes for sources.

* Property tax limitation applied to New York City and environs only.

less likely to pass property tax limitations, all else being equal. But Proposition 13 had an even greater effect, and that effect is evident in the data even if we restrict our comparison to states at comparable levels of personal income. The right turn in the tax revolt was due to Proposition 13.

Three brief case studies of similar, high-income states will show *how* Proposition 13 altered the politics of property taxation. Massachusetts, Michigan, and New York were all confronting property tax crises of their own in 1978. In all three states, Proposition 13 altered the balance of power. Conservative interest groups that had previously sat out the protest began to see that it was possible to limit taxation—if they were willing to focus on the property tax. Moderate politicians embraced property tax limits as a proven vote-winner. Even liberals began to rethink their opposition to tax limitation, since it seemed to be a politically viable way to get property tax relief.

Massachusetts: Conservatives Enter the Fray

The electoral victory of Proposition 13 inspired conservative groups that had previously sat out the property tax revolt to take an interest in the property tax issue. Capitalizing on the popularity of property tax limitation, they began to craft policies that grafted property tax limits onto more conservative antigovernment programs. Massachusetts illustrates this process clearly.

Grassroots efforts to limit the property tax were already underway in Massachusetts when the passage of Proposition 13 gave them a significant boost. The Citizens for Guaranteed Property Tax Relief, founded by the realtors Jack Conway and Margaret C. Carlson, was only two weeks old when Proposition 13 became national news. Suddenly victory seemed more likely. The Associated Industries of Massachusetts (AIM), an organization of the state's manufacturers, called a meeting to get its members involved in the Conway-Carlson campaign. The headline item on the agenda announced, "Proposition 13—It's a New Ball Game . . . And We're At Bat!"[47] In press releases and public statements, the realtors and manufacturers referred to their tax cap initiative as "Massachusetts' version of 'Proposition 13.' "[48] In a speech two weeks before the election, one of the campaign managers credited Proposition 13 with the success of the petition drive: "Our efforts, which were planned and implemented in the pre-Jarvis days, I think now clearly dramatize a case of positioning oneself in the right place and at the right time, as is evidenced by the Proposition 13 fever which has captured the nation."[49] Voters approved the Conway-Carlson tax cap by a three-to-one margin.[50]

Proposition 13 also encouraged other conservatives to get involved in the movement. One of them was a Republican activist named Edward F. King, who had founded an organization called Citizens for Limited Taxation (CLT) in 1973. For years, King had campaigned unsuccessfully for a constitutional amendment to limit the growth of the state budget. This was a conservative policy that aimed to restrain the growth of state spending on social programs in particular. At first it had nothing to do with the property tax revolt. But after Proposition 13, King and other CLT leaders decided to jump on the bandwagon and repackage some of their proposals together with a limit on the local property tax.

On June 6, 1978, the day that California voters passed Proposition 13, the Massachusetts legislature was preparing to vote on a constitutional amendment drafted by King that would limit the annual growth of state taxes. That morning, the *Wall Street Journal* reported that the executive director of CLT, a libertarian activist named Don Feder, claimed to have seventy-four votes lined up in favor of the King amendment. The next day, the passage of Proposition 13 in California was headline news in Massachusetts, and it immediately shifted the political calculus. Feder did not get seventy-four votes. He got 222 votes. To his frustration, however, the legislature introduced a loophole that permitted state tax increases that were earmarked for aid to local governments. This change was a logical response to the property tax revolt—state aid to local governments would reduce pressure on the local property tax—but King and Feder were not trying to cut local property taxes. They were ideological conservatives who wanted to limit the *state* budget. They, and CLT, repudiated the resulting amendment.[51]

If you can't beat them, join them: Feder and King went back to the drawing board, and this time they decided to link their cause to the property tax revolt. According to Feder, CLT had been "watching Proposition 13 very carefully through the spring of 1978. . . . We were thinking that if this goes over well in California—which is a fairly liberal state—perhaps we should try it in Massachusetts."[52] They drafted the policy in consultation with some Republican legislators and with Howard Jarvis. At the suggestion of conservative newspaper columnist Warren Brookes, the proposal was dubbed "Proposition 2½." This was an unconventional name in Massachusetts, where the state traditionally labels ballot initiatives with letters rather than numbers and calls them "questions" rather than propositions. The name was a direct homage to California's Proposition 13 and a reference to the proposed 2.5 percent maximum tax rate.[53]

Proposition 13 became a major campaign issue in the governor's race later that year. A Democrat named Edward J. King—who was not related to the CLT's Edward F. King—decided to make the property tax a central issue in his campaign. It was a long shot: King was the executive director of the state airport authority, and his opponent in the Democratic primary was the incumbent governor, Michael Dukakis. King's campaign was floundering until he seized on the property tax as his main issue. He promised voters a particularly restrictive limit on the property tax, which he called "Massachusetts Thirteen" or the "Zero Cap." The strategy worked. King came from behind to beat Dukakis in the September primary.[54]

King went on to win the general election with the help of Howard Jarvis, who recorded a television ad for his campaign ("If Ed King cannot do it in

Massachusetts, my name is not Howard Jarvis"). After the election, King kept his promise to introduce the zero cap legislation. In 1979, the legislature passed a more lenient version that established a 4 percent limit on the annual growth of local taxes, but exempted all school districts and any other local governments that voted to override the cap.[55]

In 1979, all three conservative camps—the business backers of the Conway-Carlson campaign, the conservatives of CLT, and Governor King—finally came together. The previous legislative session had ended with no action on the Conway-Carlson tax cap; although voters approved it, the initiative was not binding on legislators, who ignored it. The manufacturers of AIM promptly began drafting a binding tax limit initiative, which, like CLT's proposal, was also modeled after Proposition 13 and also called Proposition 2½. Rather than compete with each other for signatures, CLT and AIM met to negotiate a compromise. They circulated the CLT version of Proposition 2½ as a statute and the AIM version as a constitutional amendment. Both versions easily gathered the necessary number of signatures to qualify for the ballot, pending review by the legislature.[56]

Governor King was instrumental in putting the tax limit before voters. The legislature attempted to adjourn its regular session without voting on Proposition 2½, but the governor recalled the legislators into special session. They finally voted to put the initiatives on the ballot, and voters approved the statutory version of Proposition 2½ in November 1980.[57]

Proposition 13, in short, brought conservatives into the Massachusetts movement and pushed them to the fore. It had the same effect in other states.

Michigan: Moderates Join the Bandwagon

A similar story played out in Michigan. But the case of Michigan also illustrates a second crucial mechanism by which tax limitation spread through the states: moderate politicians who had previously opposed tax limits rethought their political calculations in light of the California election returns.

As in Massachusetts, conservatives in Michigan began to take a new interest in limiting the local property tax after Proposition 13. Until then, conservative taxpayers' groups had focused mainly on limiting state taxes. The most influential was a group called Taxpayers United for Tax Limitation (or "Taxpayers United"), founded in the early 1970s by an industrial engineer named Bill Shaker with help from a California conservative activist named Lewis Uhler. Like the Massachusetts group CLT, the Michigan group Taxpayers United at first ignored the local property tax and focused on limiting the state budget. And as in Massachusetts, conservatives in Michigan initially met with failure. In 1974, the group's first petition drive fell hundreds of thousands of signatures short. In 1976, with support from the Michigan Chamber of Commerce and the Michigan Association of Realtors, the activists of Taxpayers United qualified a petition for the ballot, only to see it rejected by voters. But in 1977, the growing momentum of the tax limit campaign in California convinced Shaker and Uhler that the property tax revolt was the key to victory in Michigan, too.

These conservatives made a calculated decision to ride the coattails of the movement by packaging their issue, which was a limitation on the state budget, together with a more popular issue, which was a limit on the local property tax. When Shaker passed the reins of Taxpayers United to a young insurance executive named Dick Headlee, he offered this advice: "Politically, I believe that the Tax Limit language for '78 must include voter control over local taxes, as well as the state limit. I am rapidly reaching the conclusion that there is no way that Constitutional Tax Limitation can succeed at the polls in '78 if it doesn't." The limitation of the local property tax, Shaker wrote to Headlee, "tends to capture the essence of todays' [sic] tax protest."[58] Lew Uhler agreed: "My cumulative experience has led me to revise the tax limitation model, retitling it 'Property Tax and State Tax Limitation Amendment,' and placing the property tax reduction and limitation sections right up front. With the nationwide hue and cry over property tax bill increases due to dramatic increases in assessed valuation, the need for framing the amendment in this way is underscored."[59] The new idea, Uhler wrote to Headlee, was "to deal head on with control over property tax assessments and local spending so as to both eliminate those as issues and ride the political momentum occasioned by the property tax revolt which grips Michigan, California and many other states."[60] The new tax limit proposal limited the state budget to a fixed percentage of total state personal income. It also limited the growth of property taxes. If assessed values grew faster than the general rate of consumer inflation, then local governments would be forced to lower their tax rates.[61]

Michigan also had another tax protest campaign that was modeled on Proposition 13. A rural drain commissioner named Robert Tisch copied his tax limit petition and his abrasive personal style from Howard Jarvis. In June 1978, he began collecting signatures for a constitutional amendment that would limit annual property tax increases to 2.5 percent per year and cap the state income tax rate for good measure. After California voters approved Proposition 13,

Tisch arranged for both Jarvis and Gann to take separate trips to Michigan to campaign for the so-called Tisch Amendment and against the Headlee Amendment.[62] Tisch spared no kind words for Headlee, whose comparatively lax tax limitation proposal Tisch saw as a sellout. When a reporter asked Tisch whether his tax limitation petition would result in teachers losing their jobs, Tisch replied that 15 percent of the state's teachers were incompetent anyhow, and he suggested that they might be better off selling insurance for Dick Headlee.[63] "Without the Jarvis victory in California, Headlee would still be scrounging for signatures," Tisch told another reporter.[64]

It is at this point that the story of the tax revolt in Michigan diverges from the story of the tax revolt in Massachusetts—and reveals the new calculations of political moderates. Unlike Massachusetts Governor Michael Dukakis, who had allowed himself to be outflanked on the property tax issue, Michigan Governor William G. Milliken read the handwriting on the wall. Milliken was a moderate Republican who had opposed the Taxpayers United campaign for tax limitation in 1976. According to one press account, he had even dispatched state employees to campaign for the defeat of the initiative on work time.[65] But Milliken did not think he could oppose tax limitation again in 1978. The developer John Rapanos—a friend and supporter of Milliken's—wrote to him less than a week after the California election to outline the political considerations:

> I am firmly convinced that such a strong position in support of the tax limit proposal of Taxpayers United is the *only* way that you will be elected to another term as governor. The Democrats are already jumping on in support of this issue, and I feel that the Republicans will wait until the train leaves. As Senator Howard Baker said on June 7, Republicans will be idiots if they don't run with tax limitation. Jeffrey Bell won the senate nomination in "liberal" New Jersey because of his strong support for the concept of tax limitation.
>
> Secondly, if the reasonable tax limitation proposal of Taxpayers United is not enacted, Michigan will be faced with an extreme cut-back in tax revenues, such as California's Proposition 13. As you may know, a "Jarvis" group has already started circulating petitions in Michigan. I doubt if they have time to qualify by the cut-off date of July 11, but if the Taxpayers United proposal is not passed this year, 1980 will bring approval of a much more drastic approach.[66]

Governor Milliken waffled for another two months and then wrote back to announce his decision. He would take Rapanos's advice and endorse the Headlee Amendment. To his erstwhile allies on the Michigan Association of School

Boards, he wrote apologetically that at least the Headlee Amendment was not as bad as its predecessor of 1976. "It would not cripple the operation of current state government programs and services in any important way," he wrote, in a carefully qualified statement.[67] Milliken was not an enthusiastic convert, but he was a calculating politician, and Proposition 13 changed his calculations.

New York: Liberals Rethink Their Opposition

New York State illustrates a third mechanism by which Proposition 13 spread tax limitations throughout the states. Proposition 13 persuaded liberals to re-think their opposition to property tax limitation, by demonstrating that tax limitation was a popular and therefore a politically viable form of property tax relief. Even the most progressive circuit breaker was no use to anyone if it did not have the political support to get through the legislature. A property tax limit might provide benefits to the rich—but it provided tax relief to the middle class and even to many poor people, too. Many liberals followed this reasoning and reluctantly embraced property tax limitation.

By coincidence, June 6, 1978, the day that Californians were voting on Proposition 13, was also the day that the Gerber Commission held the first of its hearings on New York State's own property tax crisis. The minutes from that meeting record no mention of the California initiative. In the hearings of the coming weeks, however, Proposition 13 became a common reference point in the testimony of homeowners, realtors, public officials, political candidates, and protesters who appeared before the commission.

Many people called for a similar tax limitation in New York. On July 23, a re-altor named Philip Pagliarulo submitted testimony calling for "Our Own 'Propo-sition 13,' " including a 3 percent annual growth limit on property assessments.[68] A conservative candidate for state senate appeared before the commission in or-der to announce his support for "a Proposition 13 type of Constitutional Amend-ment and a temporary freeze and then reduction of real property tax rates."[69] The Senior Homeowners' Association of Spring Valley called for a "1% Maximum Property Tax Amendment to the State Constitution (Proposition 13)."[70]

Even people who supported other policies invoked the threat of Proposition 13. The chairman of the Nassau County Board of Assessors described Proposi-tion 13 as "a spectre haunting all of us who are involved in the business of as-sessing real property for taxation" and argued that the way to exorcise it was with a circuit breaker.[71] A spokesperson for the North Shore Council of Home Owners Associations invoked "the overwhelming mandate of Proposition 13" to support the repeal of the state's uniform assessment requirement—that is, to support a classification law.[72] The mayor of Albany argued that Proposition 13 was a mandate to abolish the local property tax altogether.[73] A public school administrator thought that greater state aid to school districts was the way to remedy "the inequities taxpayers complain about through Proposition 13 actions."[74] The California vote clearly dominated the imagination of protesters and property tax professionals alike.

When the commission met to discuss and draft its recommendations in March 1979, the members of the commission considered recommending a constitutional limit on the property tax levy. The members, who were mostly representatives of the real estate industry and lawyers who specialized in property tax appeals, were generally unsympathetic to homeowners' traditional tax privileges, but they represented business interests that would benefit from tax limitation.[75] The staff of the commission prepared two alternative drafts of a chapter on tax limits for discussion, motivated by the observation that "At every hearing held by the Commission, witnesses have called for the enactment of some form of 'Proposition 13' in New York State." One of these drafts called for a Proposition 13–like limit on the real property tax levy.[76] An apparently later, more polished draft rejected this approach as probably unworkable and called instead for a "full disclosure law" that would require local government to hold public hearings before increasing the property tax rate.[77] Even this reduced version did not make it into the final report, however, which was conspicuously silent on the question of tax limits.[78]

The commission held back because the speaker of the assembly, a liberal Democrat named Stanley Fink, threatened to dissolve it. Fink's staff regarded the commission as "an embarrassment" that "continue[s] to write memos in opposition to our tax bills."[79] The temporary state commission had another year to serve, and its membership served at Fink's pleasure. Aware of Fink's hostility, and apparently anxious to retain his position, the commission chair, George S. Gerber, met with the secretary of Fink's Task Force on School Finance and Real Property Taxation in early March. "Mr. Gerber was concerned with what he perceived as the hostility of the Assembly to the Commission, evidenced at the [prior] meeting we held with him in your office," the secretary reported to Fink. The secretary's report continued: "I reiterated that you felt it was beyond their mandate for them to make recommendations of a Proposition 13 type for 'levy limitations' applicable to local governments. Further you doubted that they had the competence [sic], in terms of staffing, research capacity, hearings held, and so forth, to justify strong recommendations on so fundamental and broad-range a revision of our governmental structure." This was a clear message to Gerber to back off or else risk losing the chair of the commission. He backed off.[80]

Fink nevertheless found himself supporting a property tax limit the following year, because it was the only politically possible way to provide property tax relief. He and his Democratic allies proposed a classification bill, but he was unable to get it through the Senate, where Republicans held the majority. A handful of Republicans aligned with the Conservative Party were backing a quixotic bill that would preserve informal tax privileges for homeowners by repealing the requirement to modernize the property tax. The bill that finally passed both houses of the legislature was an intricate compromise between classification and tax limitation. It authorized local governments to assess homes at a smaller fraction of value than businesses. But in New York City and suburban Nassau County, where conservative homeowners were particularly well organized, the bill also included a property tax limit. The assessed value of homes could rise no faster than 6 percent per year. Democratic Governor Hugh Carey vetoed the bill. The assembly, led by Fink, voted to override his veto, and the tax limit became law.[81]

How Direct Democracy Mattered

These three stories illustrate that Proposition 13 was a turning point in the tax revolt, and the institution of direct democracy is the key to explaining why. Proposition 13 fever caught on, not because the details of the legislation were especially popular or even very widely understood, but because of the fact that it had passed by ballot initiative. The popular vote ratified it as a politically winnable goal.

Would the tax revolt have turned right without direct democracy? It is certainly likely that some states would have acted to limit taxes. Six states had already passed property tax limits in the decade before Proposition 13. But many more states had also passed liberal forms of property tax relief. The distinctive change after 1978 was that the movement as a whole united behind a single, conservative solution to the crisis—and this would not have happened without Proposition 13.

The true test is comparative. Britain once again provides an excellent test case. Unlike the California tax revolt, the Scottish ratepayers' rebellion of 1985 and 1986 did not have direct access to the ballot. And there the movement did not unite behind a demand for any particular tax policy, even when it spread beyond Scotland's borders into England and Wales. Instead of turning right, the British taxpayers' rebellion turned left.

BRITAIN: THE TAX REVOLT THAT NEVER TURNED RIGHT

The Scottish tax revolt, like the American tax revolt, was at first ideologically pluralistic. The FSR's eclectic list of arguments against the rates was broad enough to appeal both to progressives, who thought taxes should be levied on those who had the most ability to pay, and to conservatives, who thought taxes should be levied instead on those who consumed the most government services. Virtually every political party in Scotland joined in the protests against the 1985 revaluation. Conservatives, who were most influential in FSR, argued for abolishing the rates and replacing them with a poll tax. Labour Party and Scottish Nationalist Party members argued for abolishing the rates and replacing them with a local income tax. Almost everyone opposed the rates. The only question was how to design tax relief.

You might expect that the Act of Parliament that abolished the rates in Scotland would have settled the question. It might even have inspired tax rebels to demand a similar solution in England and Wales—just as property tax limitation in California had inspired tax rebels to demand similar policies in New York and Massachusetts. It did not.

The Abolition of Domestic Rates Etc. (Scotland) Act failed to quell the protests because, unlike Proposition 13, it failed to restore traditional tax privileges. By replacing the rates with a poll tax, it actually burdened more people than it benefited. The poll tax fell on many adults who had previously been entirely exempt from local taxation. Despite temporary rebates that were designed to ease the transition for the poorest taxpayers, the transition from a property tax to a flat per-capita tax increased the tax burden most dramatically where large numbers of adults shared inexpensive quarters—that is, in low-income households that were least able to pay. Roughly half of all households paid more tax under the new system than the old. But these were households with comparatively large numbers of adults, so the losing half of all households included far more than half of all taxpayers. Most people were hit harder by the poll tax than by the rates revaluation.[82]

Underlying this fatal flaw in the poll tax was another, more fundamental reason why it did not catch on. Unlike Proposition 13, the poll tax policy was made without consulting the voters. Prime Minister Thatcher might have avoided this disastrous policy if she had submitted the poll tax to a referendum. One opinion poll in the fall of 1987 found that 68 percent of Scots were convinced the poll tax would be less fair than the rates.[83] Later polls confirmed that all of Britain thought the poll tax was an unfair burden. The hostility that Britons expressed toward the poll tax was comparable to the hostility that Americans had expressed toward property taxation at the peak of the American tax revolt. In 1990, for example, 71 percent of British adults surveyed said the local poll tax was "too high," a verdict that only 64 percent of Americans had delivered against the local property tax in 1978, at the height of Proposition 13 fever.[84] A majority of the British public would almost certainly have voted against the poll tax if given the opportunity. They were not given the opportunity because the British constitution did not provide for initiative or referendum on matters of local finance.

In the absence of any direct democracy, election returns provided little information about the content or strength of voters' policy preferences. Thatcher discounted opinion polls, assuming mistakenly that the voters would come around to the poll tax, given enough time. The closest thing to a referendum on Thatcher's local tax policy was the general election of June 1987 that immediately followed Parliament's decision to abolish the rates in Scotland. The Scottish Tories did disastrously at the polls, losing eleven of their twenty-one seats. But even observers who saw the 1987 election as a referendum on local taxation could not agree on what these losses meant. Did voters identify the Tories with the rates, or the poll tax? With hindsight, political scientists today see the Scottish election returns as a rejection of the new poll tax. Others at the time, however, including most of the defeated Conservative MPs, saw the same election returns as a rejection of the old rating system and a confirmation that the poll tax was the right policy. They concluded that the replacement of the rates with a poll tax had simply come too late in the election campaign to restore the party's credibility. "We would have done worse still if we'd tried to ride the revaluation wave," one said.[85]

Instead of uniting in support of a particular policy of tax relief—as the American tax rebels had united behind Proposition 13—the Scottish tax rebels united *against* the poll tax. The Labour Party in Scotland, which had previously campaigned to replace the rates with a local income tax, now began a campaign of resistance to the poll tax. Labour urged taxpayers to delay registering for the new tax and urged local authorities to slow down implementation. The Scottish Nationalist Party, which had also campaigned against the rates, now urged Scots to refuse payment of the poll tax altogether. A small left-wing group within the Labour Party also began to organize a national tax strike, led by a group of 100 prominent Scots who pledged that they would not pay the tax.

Some Labour-led local authorities announced that they planned to introduce new informal tax privileges in defiance of the law, by simply refusing to collect the tax from elderly, poor, or disabled people.[86]

Taxpayers formed a dizzying array of new protest organizations and campaigns that had little in common save their rejection of the poll tax. One group, called Citizens Against the Poll Tax, petitioned for the repeal of the new tax. Another, the radical Anti-Poll Tax Federation, organized perhaps as many as 100 local Anti-Poll Tax Unions in communities throughout Scotland to encourage civil disobedience. These groups turned out thousands of protesters to demonstrations against the tax in Glasgow and elsewhere. On April 1, 1989, the day the new tax was due, the Scottish Trades Union Congress organized a march and demonstration of 30,000 people in Edinburgh to demand its repeal.[87]

The tax revolt expanded into England and Wales following the introduction of the poll tax in the winter of 1990. Thousands of demonstrators converged on town halls in Plymouth, Devon, Exeter, Bath, Barnstable, Taunton, Norwich, Bradford, Maidenhead, Birmingham, Reading, Gillingham, Thamesdown, Ealing, Hillingdon, Haringey, Newcastle, Lambeth, Southampton, and Southwark—among other places. In Bristol, protesters burned their poll tax notices in public trash cans, much as California protesters had burned their property assessment notices in the 1970s. Demonstrations in Bristol and Hackney devolved into riots, with angry taxpayers smashing windows and throwing bottles at the police.[88]

The movement culminated in the notorious poll tax riots of March 31, 1990. The left-wing All-Britain Anti–Poll Tax Federation had organized simultaneous demonstrations in Edinburgh and London to mark the one-year anniversary of the tax in Scotland. In Edinburgh, some 40,000 demonstrators marched peacefully and dispersed without violence. The London demonstration began peacefully as well. Credible estimates of participation range from 50,000 to 100,000 marchers. As the demonstrators passed the prime minister's residence on Downing Street, several hundred of them sat down and blocked a major intersection. The police attempted to arrest the sitting demonstrators and used force to redirect the rest of the crowd toward the main rally at Trafalgar Square. Demonstrators fought back with rocks and bottles. Skirmishes continued for the rest of the afternoon, and after the speeches had ended a full-fledged mêlée broke out between police and the remaining demonstrators. Protesters threw bottles, burned cars, built barricades from trash bins, and bashed in windows with bricks. The next morning much of Westminster was a wasteland.[89]

Because there was no Proposition 13 that provided a road-tested vehicle for tax relief, lawmakers continued to experiment with different proposals to quiet the growing rebellion. The government first tried raising the income threshold for exemption from the poll tax. Then, at Thatcher's insistence, Parliament passed a temporary expenditure limitation that capped the growth of all local government budgets for 1991. Unlike Proposition 13, this budget limitation did not attract much public support because it did nothing to lower tax bills immediately. Labour meanwhile proposed a return to the old rates, with a system of rebates for the poor—in American terms, a property tax with a circuit breaker.[90]

The comparison between the British and American tax revolts shows that direct democracy turned the American tax revolt right. Without the ballot initiative or referendum to screen policies for their popularity, the British government did not know what policy the protesters would settle for. Nor did protesters know or agree among themselves. The solution that finally quieted the movement was the restoration of the rates—combined with a tax limitation. In March 1991, a new Conservative government under Prime Minister John Major abolished the poll tax. Local governments made up some of the revenue with a new local property tax. The rest of the local revenue came from a small increase in the national VAT—the solution that Richard Nixon had proposed for the United States in 1972. The government also instituted new tax privileges, including a system of approximate or "banded" property assessment that provided some protection from rapidly rising housing prices, particularly for the affluent; the top band effectively capped assessment increases, much as Proposition 13 did in California.[91]

THE HINGE OF HISTORY

In a study of prerevolutionary France, the sociologists Edgar Kiser and April Linton argue that successful tax revolts can be turning points, "hinges of history" that open up new paths of historical development and close off others. Tax revolts alter the course of future conflicts by changing the behavior of taxpayers and government officials. Revolts teach public officials new lessons (though not necessarily true lessons) about how and how much they can tax without provoking rebellion. They also teach taxpayers what combination of risks and rewards they can expect from collective action in the future. Successful tax rebellions, then, alter the long-run course of tax policy and the likelihood of future tax rebellions.[92]

That is the story of Proposition 13. But the reason that this law was so influential was not only how much it cut taxes. It was how it cut taxes. The ballot initiative showed that tax limitation could win a popular vote in a large state. It thereby persuaded conservatives to join the property tax revolt, which they did by packaging other conservative policies together with property tax limits. It persuaded moderate politicians to embrace property tax limitation for political gain. And it persuaded even liberals that property tax limitation, as a politically viable solution to the property tax crisis, might be better than nothing.

By 1980, the transformation was complete—and the movement had generated momentum for a new, more conservative wave of tax limitation policies that went beyond the property tax to limit the taxing and spending powers of state and local governments in general. In the decade before Proposition 13, for example, only two states had passed statutory or constitutional limitations on the growth of *state* budgets, of the kind that the Massachusetts Citizens for Tax Limitation and the Michigan Taxpayers United had sought; but in the decade after Proposition 13, eighteen states did so. As the case of the Headlee Amendment showed, the success of these state budget limits was due in part to the symbolic influence of Proposition 13.[93] And the spread of tax and expenditure limitations—no longer just limitations on the local property tax, but limitations on the growth of state and local budgets in general—would contribute to a far-reaching transformation of American politics.

6 WELCOME TO THE TAX CUTTING PARTY
How the Tax Revolt Transformed Republican Politics

"I THINK THE PASSAGE of Proposition 13 has sent a shock wave through the consciousness of every public servant—presidents, governors, mayors, state legislators, [and] members of Congress," President Jimmy Carter told the press on July 28, 1978. "I do believe that Proposition 13 is an accurate expression of, first of all, the distrust of government."[1]

Ronald Reagan agreed. The former governor of California described Proposition 13 as a rebellion against "costly, overpowering government" and urged Republicans to adopt Proposition 13 as their mascot in the 1980 presidential race. Reagan was already positioning himself to run against Carter. His audience was a small crowd of people who had supported his ill-fated 1976 campaign to win the Republican nomination away from the incumbent president, Gerald Ford, and his old running mate from that race, Senator Richard Schweiker of Pennsylvania, predicted that "Proposition 13 is the cause that will propel Governor Ronald Reagan all the way to the White House in 1980."[2]

Many commentators today think that the tax revolt did that and more. Thomas Byrne Edsall and Mary D. Edsall, in their influential book *Chain Reaction*, described the tax revolt as "a major turning point in American politics" that "provided conservatism with a powerful internal coherence, shaping an antigovernment ethic, and firmly establishing new grounds for the disaffection of white working- and middle-class voters from their traditional Democratic roots." The California journalist Peter Schrag did them one better: Proposition 13, in his account, "set the stage for the Reagan era, and became both fact and symbol of a radical shift in governmental priorities, public attitudes, and social relationships that is as nearly fundamental in American politics as the change brought by the New Deal." Acclaimed historians have echoed the judgment of these commentators that the tax revolt transformed American political culture.[3]

In this chapter, I assess the legacy of the tax revolt for American politics. The evidence presented here deflates some of the most grandiose claims that have been made for the property tax revolt. It was not the New Deal in reverse. It did not cause a radical shift in public attitudes. Nor did it spell the doom of the American welfare state. But dispensing with the most exaggerated claims allows us to appreciate what the tax revolt actually did. Although it did not change what most people thought about taxes, it *did* change how much the major parties paid attention to taxes. The tax revolt elevated taxes to prominence as an issue of partisan competition. Entrepreneurial Republican politicians began to distinguish themselves from their Democratic opponents by their opposition to high taxes and big government. The result was that taxes took center stage after 1978.

The tax revolt also changed *how* tax policy entered the public sphere. Politicians had previously treated taxation as an instrument for achieving other policy ends. When they argued taxes, they argued specifics: tax cuts were for some people, for some purposes, for some occasions, and the political debates concerned who, and what, and when. Since the tax revolt, some politicians have begun to treat tax cutting instead as a general principle: either you stand for tax cuts, or you stand for tax increases. In practice, it is the Republican Party that has claimed the anti-tax ground. As one congressional staffer recently told the tax scholars Michael Graetz and Ian Shapiro, "Democrats were put on earth to raise taxes; Republicans were put here to stop them." It is an effective partisan rhetoric because it opens a one-sided argument: no Democrat will respond with an endorsement of indiscriminate tax increases.[4]

This chapter thus tells the story of how an ideological debate over tax cuts came to occupy a central place in American politics. It thereby sheds new light on the general question of how social movements can have a lasting impact on public policy. Scholarship on social movement impacts is plentiful, but most of this work emphasizes the short-term effects of protest mobilization. Even scholars who focus on long-term effects often conclude that ongoing mobilization is necessary if movements are to have an enduring impact: as two scholars of the women's movement put the point, "the survival and continued strength of movement politics are essential to ensuring continued movement success."[5] But the case of the tax revolt illustrates that a social movement's full effect on formal politics may unfold years and even decades after mobilization subsides.

The tax revolt, after all, is long gone. The major tax debates of the twenty-first century do not arise from any social movement. No one burned estate tax bills on the steps of the Capitol in 2001, as Roger Sutton and his compatriots had burned their property tax assessments on the steps of the county courthouse in 1977. No mob took to the streets when income tax forms went out in early 2003, as homeowners had done when local property tax bills went out in New Bedford in 1978. In historical terms, the income tax was not even especially unpopular at the start of the twenty-first century.[6]

Still, scholars are right to see the lingering effects of the property tax revolt in the tax policy debates of the twenty-first century. The tax revolt put a new issue on the federal agenda. And the issue stuck there because it was also enshrined in policy at the state level. In particular, the wave of state tax and expenditure limitations (or "TELs") that followed Proposition 13 ensured that tax cuts would stay in the public eye. These TELs were supposed to remove taxes from political competition. But in fact they did not. What they did was to make the overall level of taxation into a permanently salient political issue. These limits did not prevent politicians from raising taxes but merely required them to return to the voters for approval when they did so—thereby requiring the voters to rule regularly on tax increases, and making "Taxes: pro or con?" into the perennial question at election time.

In short, tax limitations in the states transformed how partisan elites selected and defined the issues on which they competed for election. Before Proposition 13 fever swept the country, Republicans and Democrats in office sometimes disagreed about particular tax policies, but they rarely made tax policy the basis of their appeal to voters, and they almost never articulated public positions on taxes *in general*.[7] After Proposition 13, they began to compete on the basis of their general positions on taxes. Tax cuts became a campaign issue. And many Republican leaders began to define themselves and their party in opposition to taxes.

HOW PROPOSITION 13 PUT TAX CUTS ON THE NATIONAL AGENDA

The transformation of party competition began with the transformation of Ronald Reagan. The success of Proposition 13 changed Reagan's views. Before 1978, he had never favored property tax limits. As the governor of California, he had opposed Philip Watson's initiatives to limit property taxes in 1968 and 1972. Reagan believed sincerely in reducing the size of government, but, like many other sincere conservatives, he thought that property tax limitation was the wrong way to go about it. A property tax limit would just cause the state to shift the tax burden onto personal income or corporate profits.[8]

Reagan had always liked tax cuts, but he did not always place great priority on them, because he favored balanced budgets. Cut taxes first, and you risked a deficit. Cut spending first, and lower taxes would follow. The natural choice was therefore to limit spending rather than taxes.[9] That, at least, was the logic that Reagan had followed as governor. In 1972, he appointed a task force on tax reduction that included the conservative economists Milton Friedman, William Niskanen, and William Craig Stubblebine, who drafted a constitutional amendment that would have limited state expenditures to 7 percent of total state income. The proposal illustrates the ideological gap that separated Reagan from the property tax revolt in the early 1970s: it included a state income tax cut but no property tax relief, and Democrats killed it in part by arguing that it would actually require *increases* in the local property tax to make up for the state tax cuts. As Howard Jarvis later recalled, "[Y]ou had to be a genius to figure out whether a yes vote or a no vote was a vote to reduce taxes." Voters rejected the amendment in 1973.[10]

Proposition 13 changed everything. Any presidential hopeful had to pay attention when voters in California—the state with the most electoral votes—approved a tax limit by almost a two-to-one margin. And if the next president was paying attention, then Congress would pay attention, too. "The mood of Washington can be summed up in two words," Senator Muskie, the chair of the Senate Finance Committee, said in the summer of 1978: "Proposition 13."[11] The political scientist John Kingdon, who was in Washington interviewing federal officials and lobbyists about health and transportation policy when Proposition 13 passed, noticed that the same two words suddenly began showing up in his interview transcripts. "They [the interviewees] would refer in an offhand way to a 'Proposition 13 mentality' or a 'Proposition 13 atmosphere,'" he wrote, "meaning a severe public opinion constraint on government spending, higher taxation, and new, expensive programs."[12] Proposition 13 particularly emboldened congressional conservatives, including a pair of Republican legislators, Representative Jack Kemp and Senator William Roth, who had drafted a bill to cut income tax rates by 30 percent across the board. Proposition 13 gave the Kemp-Roth proposal an enormous boost: after the California election, one member of Kemp's staff said, "the last Republican resistance to Kemp-Roth faded away."[13]

Reagan immediately seized on tax cuts as a major campaign theme. He announced to his supporters in the Republican Party that Proposition 13 would light a "prairie fire" of opposition to taxes. He also endorsed the Kemp-Roth proposal and made it the centerpiece of his campaign.[14]

The key to Reagan's embrace of tax cuts was a bold new idea: he could reconcile his new tax-cutting enthusiasm with his balanced-budget beliefs by reasoning that cutting tax rates would stimulate the economy, grow the tax base, and thereby actually *increase* federal tax revenues. This idea, sometimes called a "supply-side" economic policy, was circulating at the time. Reagan got the idea from Kemp, who got it from a *Wall Street Journal* columnist named Jude Wanniski, who got it in turn from an economist named Arthur Laffer, who supposedly explained it to Wanniski and Dick Cheney by doodling a revenue curve on a cocktail napkin when they were out drinking together one afternoon. Supply-side policy was unorthodox even in the Republican Party: Reagan's moderate opponent in the Republican primaries, George H. W. Bush, famously mocked it as "voodoo."[15]

What did all this have to do with the property tax revolt? Advocates of big tax cuts saw Proposition 13 as a crucial test of the view that cutting taxes could actually increase economic growth enough to boost government revenues. Thus, the *Wall Street Journal* editorial board described the California property tax initiative as "an empirical test of the recent fierce debate at the national level over the Kemp-Roth bill to cut federal income tax rates." Wanniski later recalled that he had seen it as the first major test of the supply-side model.[16] Laffer himself described Proposition 13 as "an application of the Laffer Curve" and published a paper cautiously predicting increased tax revenues for California. Reagan was less cautious, predicting that Proposition 13 would result in "a surge of dollars in the state Treasury, brought on by increased spending that results from property tax cuts."[17] The predicted surge never came. But neither did the collapse of California that opponents of Proposition 13 had prophesied. In the immediate aftermath of the initiative, the headline story was how *little* impact it had on state and local finances. "Little Impact Seen in Coast Tax Slash," said the *New York Times*: "Dire Predictions on Proposition 13 Have Not Materialized"; "California Finding Proposition 13 Less Potent than Predicted." The state spent down its enormous budget surplus filling holes in the local budgets. This outcome was enough to show supply-siders that their basic political intuition was correct: you could cut taxes deeply without worrying about deficits.[18]

The aftermath of Proposition 13 made an enthusiastic convert of Reagan. Some commentators argue that Reagan's conversion to the supply-side doctrine was inspired instead by the strong primary election showing of a New Jersey senatorial candidate named Jeffrey Bell, who made supply-side policy the centerpiece of his 1978 campaign. But Bell lost to the liberal Democrat Bill Bradley in November, and the lesson that other Republicans drew from New Jersey after 1978 was that supply-side tax cutting was a dead issue.[19] Reagan drew the opposite lesson because he remained focused on California, not New Jersey.

Reagan, in turn, helped to transform his party's position on taxation. When he accepted the Republican nomination in July 1980, he promised a 10 percent tax cut every year for the next three years. The party platform made much of this pledge, commending "Governor Reagan and Congressional Republicans" for their bold proposal—and devoting much more space than any previous Republican platform to tax policy.[20]

Many partisans on both sides of the aisle thought that Proposition 13 also contributed to Reagan's victory in November. Reagan himself sometimes told the story this way. In a 1985 speech to his conservative activist base, Reagan described Proposition 13—along with the "Sagebrush Rebellion," a campaign led by public officials in western states for the devolution of control over federal lands—as the beginning of the conservative revolution that put him in office: "In the seventies the antitax movement begins. Actually, it was much more than an antitax movement, just as the Boston Tea Party was much more than an antitax initiative. [Laughter] In the late seventies Proposition 13 and the Sagebrush Rebellion; in 1980, for the first time in 28 years, a Republican Senate is elected; so, may I say, is a conservative President."[21] That is how conservative activists would remember the property tax revolt: as a first step on the road to the presidency. It need not have been true to have been an effective myth.[22]

What matters is that politicians *thought* Reagan owed his victory to the tax revolt, and they took Reagan's victory as a mandate to cut taxes. In July 1981, legislators approved the Economic Recovery Tax Act (ERTA), the largest single income tax cut in American history. The perception that Reagan spoke for a grassroots tax rebellion helped persuade legislators to vote for the bill. Reagan encouraged this perception by stirring up public sentiment every time his tax cut came up for a vote in the House. The week before a key House vote in June, for example, Reagan flew to a few key sites around the country to drum up support from local taxpayers' groups—including a pointed visit to Los Angeles, the home town of Howard Jarvis, whom the *New York Times* described on the occasion as "the leader of the effort in California to cut property taxes, known as Proposition 13, which seemed to symbolize for many the spirit of taxpayer revolt in the country that helped elect Mr. Reagan to office last year." On the eve of the final vote,

Reagan went on television to appeal directly to the public and to ask that they contact their representatives to support the tax cut—resulting in what Democratic House Speaker Tip O'Neill called "a telephone blitz like this nation has never seen." In an ingenious comparative study, the sociologist Monica Prasad confirms that the perception of public support was critical to the passage of the tax cut. She contrasts the success of the tax cut to the failure of the gold standard, another policy that was proposed by the same conservative opinion leaders, favored by key Reagan advisors, backed by influential interest groups, and arguably possible with much *less* political effort. She concludes that tax cuts succeeded where the gold standard failed because politicians perceived tax cuts to have a popular mandate—and that this perception was due at least in part to Proposition 13.[23]

WHY THE NEW POLITICS OF TAX CUTTING STUCK

Issues come and go. There are many parts of the Republican Party's 1980 platform that now sound quaint: for example, the party promised to protect voters' privacy from the "vast amounts" of personal information collected by federal agencies; endorsed a balanced budget as one of "the keys to maintaining real growth"; and opposed national performance standards in schools.[24] None of this sounds much like the Republican platform of 2004.

Why, then, did the single-minded emphasis on tax cuts stick? One reason that it stuck has already been hinted at: the tax cut was actually achieved, and people who lived through it saw it as a historic accomplishment. It was the largest tax cut in American history. It *felt* like a historic victory. And it was a formative experience for many people who would go on to become influential power brokers in the Republican Party. Examples are not hard to find. In the spring of 1978, while California voters were considering Proposition 13, a historian named Newt Gingrich was running for his first seat in Congress. So was a former White House staffer from Wyoming named Dick Cheney. A younger man named Grover Norquist was just graduating from Harvard; his first job out of college was capitalizing on Proposition 13 fever by campaigning for a tax limitation amendment to the U.S. Constitution.[25] For these men, and others like them, the tax revolt was a formative moment, and the tax cuts of Reagan's first term felt like its culmination.

This cohort of conservative leaders fought to redefine the Republican Party as the party of tax cuts—or, in the words of one conservative intellectual, "to make sure that the GOP gained a brand name as the tax cutting party."[26] Gingrich, for example, waged a long struggle with moderates in the party who remained convinced that tax increases were sometimes necessary to balance the budget. Gingrich derided their argument for tax increases as an "automatic, old-time Republican answer." He thereby implied that the *new* Republican answer was to cut taxes even when there was a deficit. After President Reagan signed tax increases in 1982 and 1983, Gingrich was instrumental in rewriting the Republican Party platform in 1984 to repudiate further tax increases. In 1990, he broke ranks with President George H. W. Bush and led House Republicans in voting down the president's budget—because it included a tax increase.[27] Four years later, Gingrich helped to draft the *Contract with America*, a Republican manifesto that proposed the largest tax cuts since ERTA. The tax cuts were, he said, the "crown jewel" of the *Contract*. Although Congress watered them down and President Bill Clinton vetoed them, Gingrich saw the favorable vote in the House as a major victory.[28]

Cheney also helped to keep the supply-side idea alive. He was an early convert to the cause. He remained active in conservative Republican politics even as his subsequent career led him out of Congress, first into the post of Defense Secretary under President George H. W. Bush and then into the private sector. When Cheney was elected to the vice-presidency in 2000, he promptly began to push for the Economic Growth and Tax Relief Reconciliation Act (EGTRRA), a bill that once again proposed the largest income tax cut since Reagan's first term. Cheney, like others in the administration, drew an explicit parallel between the two tax cuts. The political lesson he drew from the Reagan era was the same as the lesson that Reagan had drawn from Proposition 13: tax cuts came first; spending would take care of itself later. Or, in Cheney's words, "Reagan proved deficits don't matter."[29]

Norquist did more than anyone else to keep tax cuts at the forefront of the federal agenda. In 1986, the Reagan administration hired him to lobby for a tax reform that cut top income tax rates. After the 1986 tax law passed, Norquist went on to build Americans for Tax Reform into a permanent, single-issue, anti-tax lobbying group. To win his support, politicians have to sign a "Taxpayer Protection Pledge" that commits them to opposing "any and all" income tax increases. Many observers credit Norquist's pledge with increasing the numbers of anti-tax politicians and keeping them in line during the 1990s.[30] Norquist campaigned for George W. Bush in 2000. When President Bush announced a major income tax cut as his first domestic priority on taking office in 2001, Norquist ran the lobbying campaign. It was the first of the administration's annual tax cuts, Norquist later told journalists, implicitly invoking the unrealized promise of the Reagan revolution.[31]

These examples illustrate that the transformation of American politics went beyond the transformation of Ronald Reagan to encompass other political entrepreneurs who eventually rose to power in the Republican Party. The lesson that these politicians learned from the tax revolt era was that tax cuts made good politics. They and others like them have redefined the Republican Party as the tax-cutting party.

THE ROLE OF STATE TAX AND EXPENDITURE LIMITATIONS

Political entrepreneurs are constantly experimenting with new issues and new ways of distinguishing themselves in the political marketplace. Most of the issues they try do not stick. This issue stuck because it worked. And it worked because the political salience of tax cuts was encoded in state law. The wave of state TELs that followed Proposition 13 made the overall level of taxation into a political question. By limiting the growth of state taxes and state spending, these laws made sure that politicians and voters were chronically confronted with the question of how much taxing and spending was too much. The question of tax cuts is now unavoidably at the center of how the parties compete for votes.

Of course, we might ask whether state TELs really made a big difference. Before Proposition 13, few politicians tried to position themselves as anti-tax crusaders. After Proposition 13 fever swept the country, many politicians did. But maybe the same would have happened *without* the wave of tax limits. After all, there were many forces pushing the Republican Party to the right in the last decades of the twentieth century. It is reasonable to think that some of these other forces might have pushed tax cuts onto the political agenda even if the tax revolt had not.

One of the forces pushing in this direction was the increase in economic inequality. The gap between rich and poor Americans has been growing since the early 1970s. Income inequality is important for our political life because income is associated with political views: rich people on average favor conservative economic policies, and poor people on average favor liberal ones. The polarization of Americans into rich and poor might therefore have the effect of pushing voters to the extremes of the political spectrum. Moreover, most of the income polarization in the last three decades has occurred at the top of the distribution—that is, inequality is increasing because the rich are growing richer faster than before.

Politicians appear to be especially responsive to the preferences of their high-income constituents. So increasing income inequality alone might explain why income tax cuts for the richest Americans have arrived on the policy agenda.[32]

Another force pulling the Republican Party rightward was the racial restructuring of American politics. President Lyndon B. Johnson won the loyalty of many newly enfranchised black voters for the Democratic Party by signing the Civil Rights Act in 1964—but he thereby also drove many white voters out of the party. This split created a new opportunity for the Republican Party to make inroads among whites, particularly in the South, by recasting itself as the party of racial conservatism. Party leaders in the 1970s made the most of this opportunity. They rejected federal enforcement of equal rights for blacks, but they did so in language that was studiously race-neutral. References to "taxes" may have become part of this code, a synonym for a federal government that interfered in the racial order by providing welfare to black poor people, desegregating public schools, and enforcing affirmative action in hiring and education. So perhaps it was the racially motivated hostility of white voters to black recipients of government aid that put tax cuts onto the federal agenda. Maybe racial realignment would have been sufficient to put tax cuts at the center of American politics even without the tax revolt.[33]

How much, then, can we really attribute to the effect of state TELs? In principle, there is a simple way to answer this question: we can measure the partisan conflict over taxes before and after TELs in states that enacted them, note any change, and compare that change to what happened in a control group of similar states that never passed a tax limit. Scholars often use this "difference-in-differences" method to test the effects of public policy when an experiment is impossible. In the following section, I will apply this method to two different groups. The first group is Republicans in Congress—the leadership of the party. The second group is grassroots Republican activists—the base of the party. Although I will discuss Democrats as well, my focus is on Republicans because the embrace of tax cuts was asymmetrical. For obvious reasons, there is no advantage in being seen as the party of tax increases.

State TELs and the Party in Congress
The leaders of the Republican Party are its elected officials. Unfortunately, we do not have a consistent series of public opinion surveys of congresspeople. Fortunately, we have something that may be even better: their voting records. It is a simple matter to compare the voting behavior of congresspeople who were

elected from states with tax limitations to the average scores of congresspeople who were elected from states without them. Michael Berkman conducted a comparison like this in 1993. He found that congresspeople elected during the tax revolt were more likely to sponsor or vote for tax cut bills than were their senior colleagues. He also found that their voting records made them especially likely to be rated as ideological conservatives by both liberal and conservative interest groups. Although Berkman did not have a direct measure of exposure to the tax revolt, he relied on regional comparisons to show that the conservative turn was sharpest for senators and representatives from states in the Pacific and Great Lakes regions—precisely where states had most vigorously pursued supply-side tax cuts. Berkman concluded that it was the experience of tax revolts in their home states that taught these legislators to seek political advantage by cutting taxes.[34]

I generalized his approach to examine the voting behavior of congresspeople over the period from 1965 to 2001. Not every Congress votes on the same bills; to make comparisons over time possible, I therefore relied on voting scores created by the political scientists Keith Poole and Howard Rosenthal. Poole and Rosenthal distilled all recorded roll call votes into a score for the position of every individual serving in Congress on a single axis that distinguishes those who favor government intervention in the economy (the left) from those who prefer minimal intervention (the right). The result is a number somewhat analogous to the congressional ratings produced by conservative and liberal interest groups that Berkman used, but it is more precise and more directly comparable over time than those ratings. A higher score on Poole and Rosenthal's "DW-NOMINATE" index indicates greater support for tax cuts and other policies to reduce government.[35]

I compared congresspeople from states with and without state budget limits. The analysis is more complicated than simply comparing scores across states. Congresspeople do not generally change their minds much once elected, so rather than asking whether TELs changed the behavior of people *already* in Congress—which is unlikely—we should ask whether they changed the behavior of people subsequently elected to Congress.[36] We should also adjust for preexisting differences among states, because states that pass TELs are presumably states where the voters are especially hostile to taxes, and such states might be more likely to elect conservatives to Congress regardless of whether or not the state had a tax limit. We should also adjust for year-to-year fluctuations that affected everyone equally. After all, it is a commonplace that the national electorate has liberal and conservative mood swings—for example, voters often react against the party of the sitting president. Some states might have replaced their moderate senators with tax-cutting conservatives simply because a particular senate seat happened to be up for election in a year when the voters were tilting to the right. Finally, because the Poole and Rosenthal voting scores do not mean the same thing in the House and the Senate, we should adjust for differences by comparing representatives to representatives and senators to senators.

Did the people elected to Congress from states with state TELs vote differently from the people who are elected from states without such limitations? When all these adjustments are made, the answer is qualified: yes, though not much. The technical details are in Appendix 3, but they are easily summarized. State budget limits shifted the voting behavior of Congress slightly to the right. A state that enacted a tax or expenditure limit could expect its newly elected representatives in Congress to be about 0.05 points further to the right along Poole and Rosenthal's left-right axis (which runs from −1.3 to 1.3). The rightward shift in the House reflects partisan turnover: voters in these states tended to replace moderate Democrats with conservative Republicans. If we restrict our attention only to Democrats, or only to Republicans, the effect is indistinguishable from zero.

What about the Senate? Here the results are less certain, but they suggest that politicians elected after a TEL were generally more conservative. Democratic senators who came from states with TELs voted no differently from Democratic senators who came from states without them. But Senate Republicans did vote differently depending on whether or not they came from states with TELs. A state passing a tax or expenditure limitation could expect to shift the average voting score of its next Republican senator to the right by about 0.11 points. The difference is not very precisely measured, because there are many fewer senators than representatives: it is statistically significant at the 10 percent level, meaning that we would expect to have a one-in-ten chance of measuring a result this large if the true effect were zero. It is also not a seismic shift. But it is almost as far as the median Senate Republican shifted from the 93rd Congress to the 108th Congress—a period scholars describe as one of polarization, when the Republican Party's center of gravity moved far to the right of where it had been.[37]

Of course, it would probably be asking too much to trace a connection between a particular state tax limitation law and an individual Congress member's vote on the 2001 tax cuts or any other recent bill. Still, there is enough evidence here to suggest that on average, state TELs contributed to the Republican Party's

redefinition as the party of tax cuts. Indeed, the estimates presented here probably underestimate the effect of the tax revolt. The cross-state comparisons presented here assume that politicians learn lessons about politics from watching
their *own* state—but as the previous chapters have shown, politicians in states as
distant as New York and Massachusetts took note when Proposition 13 passed in
California. The impact of the tax revolt on federal politics may be greater than
the state-by-state comparative analysis shows.

State TELs and the Party at the Grassroots

The Republican Party is more than just its elected officials. It is also the base. The
Republican base consists of the loyal, activist core of the Republican Party. The
base includes the die-hard electorate that votes most consistently in Republican
primary elections, the foot soldiers who walk precincts before Election Day, and
the convention delegates who decide party policy. For the purposes of the statistical analysis presented here, we can identify the base as survey respondents who
said they identified with the Republican Party and who reported engaging in two
or more out of a list of five campaign-related activities during the last election.[38]
These people are more affluent, more ideologically consistent, and more conservative than the average American. They are also more likely to express hostility to
taxation. Consider their survey responses. Every two years since 1962, the National Election Survey has asked a representative sample of American adults, "Do
you think that people in the government waste a lot of money that we pay in
taxes, waste some of it, or don't waste very much of it?" The answers are recorded
on a three-point scale, from "not very much" to "a lot." For decades, political scientists have used the answers to this question as part of a standard battery of
questions to diagnose distrust of government.[39] In 2000, 74 percent of Republican activists answered that the government "wastes a lot" of tax money, compared
to 60 percent of all Americans.[40]

The Republican base has played a key role in supporting tax cuts in the
twenty-first century. Republican activists vetted congressional candidates for
their commitment to tax cuts in 2000. They lobbied Congress to put estate tax
repeal and income tax cuts on the agenda. And their enthusiasm on the campaign trail also helped to cement the commitment of President George W. Bush
to tax cuts. Republican aides from the 2000 presidential campaign told the tax
scholars Michael Graetz and Ian Shapiro that "proposing an end to the death
tax [that is, the estate tax] would garner Bush the greatest applause from his audiences during his campaign stump speeches."[41]

A simple before-and-after comparison suggests that state TELs helped to redefine how the Republican base saw the issue of taxes. Consider the survey responses by Republican activists in states that passed tax and expenditure limits. In 1972, before their states had acted to cap government budgets, 60 percent of Republican activists in these states said that the government wastes a lot of tax money. In 2000, after their states had passed tax and expenditure limits, 80 percent of Republican activists in these states said the same thing. Meanwhile, Republican activists in states that never acted to limit taxes actually became *less* inclined to perceive government as wasteful—from 76 percent answering "a lot" in 1972 to 65 percent in 2000.

For a precise measurement, of course, we should adjust these figures to account for preexisting differences among the states. We should also adjust them to compensate for trends in the national mood that might have affected everyone, regardless of party or what state they lived in. The Watergate scandal, for example, undermined most people's faith in government officials, and trust in government generally rebounded in the Reagan years. We should also adjust our figures to account for the fact that the average Republican activist is a different person today than in the 1960s and 1970s: more affluent, more likely to be a man, slightly more likely to be Latino, and, perhaps most important, much more conservative in general. Finally, we should also check for state-specific trends, in order to reassure ourselves that the tax limits preceded the shift in survey responses, and not vice versa. The statistical methods used to make these adjustments are described in Appendix 3.

When all these adjustments are made, the best estimate is that tax limitation increased the anti-tax sentiment of the Republican base by about 10 percentage points—that is, it made the average Republican activist that much more likely to answer that the government wastes a lot of money. This shift is almost as big as the gap between Republican activists and the average American in 2000. Democratic activists, by contrast, became if anything slightly *less* opposed to taxation by this measure, although the shift was small enough that it might have been produced by chance. The findings suggest that the parties polarized on their general attitudes to taxation—and in particular, that the Republican Party has staked out a more anti-tax position—in states that have TELs.

We might still ask which came first, tax limitations or the polarization of the parties on this issue. I have argued that state campaigns for tax limitation put taxes on the partisan agenda. But it is also reasonable to imagine that the chain of causation runs in the other direction: maybe such campaigns were more likely where Republican activists had already begun to redefine their party's position on taxes. So did the tax revolt really contribute to redefining the Republican Party? One way to answer this question is to observe which came first. Figure 6.1 plots the percentage of Republican Party activists who said that government wasted too much tax money, for eight years before and after their states passed tax limits. We can think of this graph as a time-lapse picture of the anti-tax sentiment associated with living in a TEL state: the line represents the difference between Republican activists in TEL states and Republican activists in a control group of states that never passed TELs. Figure 6.1 shows that party activists were not especially hostile to taxes at the time that their states acted to limit the budget: even a year before their states passed TELs, they were somewhat *less* likely than activists in other states to say that government wastes a lot of tax money. Figure 6.1 shows a temporary dip in anti-tax opinion the year that governments passed TELs. But in the long run, Figure 6.1 suggests that Republican activists became *more* hostile to taxation after their states passed TELs. It may be that the right turn in the Republican Party contributed to the passage of TELs, but it is hard to escape the conclusion that the tax revolt also changed the Republican Party.

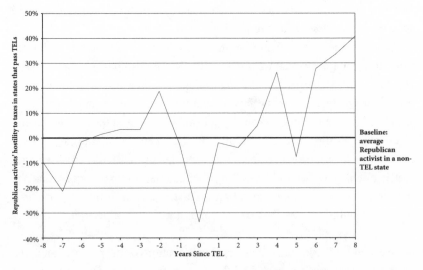

Figure 6.1. Republican activists became more anti-tax after their states passed TELs
SOURCE: Author's analysis of National Election Survey data, 1965–2001.

These comparisons tell us that activists in the Republican Party began to stake out an anti-tax position after their states passed TELs. Hostility to taxes became identified as a partisan issue. Activists who opposed taxes on ideological grounds increasingly found their way into the Republican Party because opposition to taxes became a defining issue for the Republican Party. And state TELs are part of the reason why.

State TELs and the Mass Public

Many commentators have argued that the tax revolt did more than just make tax cuts salient to politicians and party activists. They have argued that the tax revolt imprinted a new anti-tax and anti-government ethic onto the mass public as well. To be sure, as previous chapters showed, the tax revolt began as a response to a specific grievance against the property tax. But the property tax revolt inspired limitations on general taxing and spending powers of state and local government. All of these TELs might have contributed to further undermining the public's trust in government. The downward spiral is easy to imagine: by limiting taxes, you limit the effectiveness of state and local government; and then you complain that an ineffective government is unworthy of your tax dollars and limit taxes some more. Some commentators have seen a vicious circle like this in post–Proposition 13 California.[42] But are they right? Did the tax revolt change public attitudes?

The fiscal effects of tax limitation took some time to manifest. In the long run, however, at least some state and local tax limitations did what they promised. They limited the growth of property taxes and government revenues in general.[43] Governments responded by cutting spending on direct service provision. The most systematic evidence comes from schools, where measures of quality are more easily available than in many other areas of local government provision. Careful studies have shown that property tax limits like Proposition 13 reduced spending per pupil, lowered teacher qualifications, increased class sizes, and—the acid test for skeptical economists—reduced students' test scores.[44] The evidence of deteriorating services in other areas is anecdotal but plausible: more potholes, less maintenance of public facilities from schools to parks, shorter hours and longer lines at local government offices. Journalists noticed these effects, or thought they did, even if economic historians have not yet tried to measure them.[45]

Perhaps these consequences of tax limitation undermined trust in the public sector: the less revenue there is, the more of it people believe is wasted. The hypothesis is plausible. Many scholars have argued that the legitimacy of taxation depends on the perceived benefits of public spending. Scholars of public opinion have also shown that the state and local context can shape the public's trust in government and that people do not always distinguish clearly between local, state, and federal government.[46] Thus, the worsening performance of state and local governments might easily have contributed to a general distrust of *all* government. Tax limitation laws need not have created this general distrust of government from whole cloth; they could have reinforced the threads of distrust that were already there. Perhaps tax limitation simply confirmed and strengthened the public's prior beliefs that government could not be trusted with taxpayers' money.

The best available evidence, however, suggests that TELs did not have any measurable effect on the attitudes of the broader public beyond the Republican base. David Lowery arrived at this negative conclusion in a 1982 study that examined public opinion in California and a handful of comparison states in the two years just before and just after Proposition 13. At the time his study was completed, few states had tax limitations, and the full fiscal effects of those tax limitations had not yet begun to be felt. For this book, I therefore replicated his study with data covering a period of thirty-seven years (from 1964 to 2000) and a grand total of 21,593 people. As with the analysis of Republican activists described above, I focused on the effects of state TELs on general attitudes toward taxation. Appendix 3 reports the details of the analysis to satisfy specialists, but the results can be summarized simply: there was no effect. When asked whether "people in the government waste a lot of money that we pay in taxes," similar people gave similar answers, regardless of whether or not their states imposed limits on state or local taxation and expenditures. TELs did not increase the average person's perception of government waste. Neither did they reduce the average person's perceptions of waste, which is what you might expect if they actually made government more efficient.

The tax revolt changed American politics by changing how political elites talked about taxes and how politicians and party activists framed the choices for voters. Taxes became an issue that predictably captures public attention at election time. The central question about taxes became whether their overall level was too high or too low, not whether they were fairly distributed or well timed or wisely spent. The tax revolt put tax cuts permanently on the partisan agenda. But there is no evidence that the tax revolt changed the fundamental beliefs of the American public. It did not make most American voters more hostile to taxes or less favorable to big government.

THE ROAD NOT TAKEN

What would American politics look like today without the legacy of Proposition 13 and the state budget limits that it inspired? We will never know for sure. But a comparison can give us some idea. Britain once again provides an opportune case for comparison. The British Conservative Party in 1978 was similar to the American Republican Party in many ways. Both President Reagan and Prime Minister Thatcher embraced similar free-market agendas. They brought about similar "neoliberal" transformations in their own conservative parties and in the public policies of their respective societies. The comparison is particularly useful for our purposes because Thatcher, like Reagan, came to power closely identified with a property tax rebellion. In 1979, the Conservative Party election manifesto retreated from the earlier promise to abolish the rates, but it continued to decry burdensome local taxes and promised to restrain local spending. Like the Republican Party platform of 1980, it also promised deep income tax cuts across the board.[47]

Thatcher, like Reagan, asked for and got a series of deep income tax cuts despite a questionable public mandate. Public opinion data suggest that the public in Britain, like the public in America, was ambivalent about tax cuts—when presented with a choice between raising taxes or cutting social spending in 1975, for example, 42 percent of Americans and 38 percent of Britons said they would choose tax cuts.[48] Thatcher, like Reagan, pressed ahead nevertheless.

But Thatcher never had the conversion experience that Reagan underwent in the wake of Proposition 13. She never embraced the idea that tax cuts alone could balance the national budget. She focused on limiting spending rather than cutting taxes, just as Reagan had done before Proposition 13. In 1981, her budget included big cuts to the income tax but raised VAT to compensate.[49] Reagan raised taxes too, in 1982 and 1983. But it is the memory of his 1981 tax cut that lives on in the anti-tax wing of the Republican Party, and nothing like this pure tax cut ever occurred in Britain.

Both Reagan and Thatcher also identified themselves closely with the cause of local tax cuts, but when it came to local taxation, Thatcher continued to cling to the theory that Reagan had espoused before Proposition 13 changed his mind. As governor of California, Reagan had argued that radical property tax cuts were impossible without substituting some other tax. It was precisely this logic that drove Thatcher to replace the domestic rates with the new poll tax. But Proposition 13 changed Reagan's mind. In the run-up to the 1980 elections, Reagan embraced Proposition 13 as the cause that would propel him into the

White House; in the run-up to the 1987 elections, Thatcher announced that the abolition of the rates and their replacement with a poll tax was the "flagship of the Thatcher fleet."[50] The difference was that Reagan was identifying himself with a policy that already existed at the state level. It had been refined by a decade of competition with other policies in California and selected after a decade of experimentation with different models of property tax relief in different states. Most important, it had been tested by the voters and tested by experience; by the time of Reagan's election in 1980, Proposition 13 had not had the disastrous consequences that its opponents predicted. Thatcher, by contrast, was identifying herself with a policy that was untested and, it would turn out, catastrophically unpopular. Proposition 13 helped to win Reagan the presidency; the poll tax lost Thatcher the premiership. Her party colleagues ousted her from the top position in 1991 after the poll tax rebellion revealed her policy to be a failure.

The result is that Reagan's tax cuts live on in today's Republican Party as an inspiring example, while Thatcher's tax policy lives on in the Conservative Party as a cautionary tale. The Conservative Party has abandoned much of Thatcher's legacy. Any talk of deep income tax cuts or social spending cuts in the party today is muted. The party's 2005 election manifesto pledged to match or exceed Labour's spending on health, education, and pensions and to return less than 1 percent of the budget in tax cuts—mainly in the form of local property tax relief targeted to elderly pensioners.[51]

WHY AMERICA IS OBSESSED WITH TAX CUTS

American politicians and American voters in the twenty-first century seem to be fixated on tax cuts. This single-minded focus on cutting taxes has sometimes inspired incredulity and even ridicule overseas. It has also inspired some genuine efforts to understand why American politics display this peculiar trait. Two of the most astute commentators, the British journalists John Micklethwait and Adrian Wooldridge, have traced America's obsession with tax cuts to the first European settlers in the New World. "Distrust of government came over to America on the first English ships," they write. The tax cuts of the twenty-first century, they argue, are just the latest expression of an ingrained cultural predisposition to distrust government.[52]

This chapter has argued for a contrary view. Americans may have a long tradition of anti-statism, but the chronic partisan conflict over big tax cuts is a new and distinctive feature of American politics. The insistence on tax cuts is not a timeless American tradition but is the fruit of the property tax revolt—planted by tax limitation policies, watered by the Reagan Revolution, and flowering in the heart of the Republican Party. As the next chapter shows, there was nothing peculiarly American about the movement itself. But where a comparable wave of tax limit policies was missing, there was no comparably lasting transformative effect on politics.

7 AMERICAN EXCEPTIONALISM RECONSIDERED

HOWARD JARVIS DESCRIBED THE PROPERTY TAX REVOLT as an expression of a distinctively American political tradition. The movement was, he later wrote, a "Second American Revolution," the work of patriots who set out "to prove again that the American system of freedom and liberty is the greatest in the world." Many commentators, even commentators who share few other opinions with Jarvis, agree with his view that there was something uniquely American about the origins of the tax revolt. Americans have a long tradition of hostility to the state. We teach our children that our nation's founding fathers were tax protesters. Public opinion data show that we are less inclined to support activist government than citizens of any other comparably developed democracy. It is easy to assume that Americans rebelled against taxes because it is our national tradition to rebel against government.[1]

Was Jarvis right? This book has presented comparative evidence that administrative modernization caused the property tax revolt, but we might still ask: does administrative modernization cause tax rebellion in general, or only in America? The question is obviously an important one to consider if you are curious about the causes of tax revolts in other countries. But it is also an important question to consider even if you are interested only in the American tax revolt. If Americans are especially quick to protest when their tax privileges are threatened, then the roots of the American tax revolt must lie much deeper than the property tax reforms of the 1960s. And if that is true, then the story that is told in the previous chapters of this book is incomplete.

The comparative analysis of the United States and Britain presented in previous chapters has shown that the modernization of tax assessment caused protest by doing away with traditional tax privileges. In this chapter, I extend the comparison in two different directions in order to assess how general this argument really is. First, I briefly review what scholars have learned about protest against similar taxes that were levied in a very different social context—namely, the land taxes that paid for the agrarian empires of early modern Europe and China. Next, I provide a more detailed look at different taxes levied in a relatively similar context—namely, the income taxes that supported the affluent industrial democracies of the late twentieth century. Each comparison holds some potential causal factors constant and permits others to vary. Together, these comparisons help to clarify the limits of the causal argument advanced in this book.

The comparisons suggest one possible limitation on the scope of the argument. The comparative evidence suggests that modernization of tax assessment commonly provokes protest in peacetime but not during defensive or total wars, when civilians are more willing to sacrifice some of their customary tax privileges in exchange for protection from violence. This finding supports the argument of Chapter 2 that World War II was a missed opportunity to modernize the American property tax. It also suggests that the postwar *Pax Americana* probably helped to lay the foundation for the property tax rebellion.

The main story of this chapter, however, is that the American property tax rebellion fits a surprisingly general historical pattern. The modernization of tax assessment has often provoked revolt where it infringed on traditional tax privileges. Modernizing tax assessment may not be the only way to provoke a tax rebellion, but it is certainly a reliable way to do so. And it is so regardless of whether the taxpayers are suburban homeowners in the United States, rural peasants in China, or central-city shopkeepers in Denmark.

OTHER TIMES, OTHER COUNTRIES, OTHER TAXES

Most previous research on tax revolts concerns violent rebellions by peasants and rural landlords in early modern Europe and Asia. These might seem like unlikely times and places to look for parallels to the late-twentieth-century United States. A brief review of what we know about early modern tax revolts is useful, however, because it helps to clarify which parts of the story so far are peculiar to the American property tax rebellion of the 1970s and which parts of the story might apply to taxes in other times and places.

The general outline of the story is surprisingly familiar. Scholars of early modern tax systems have found that modernization frequently provoked rebellion by doing away with customary privileges. The paradigmatic case is old regime France, the kingdom that lasted from the fifteenth century to the eve of the French Revolution. In this period, French kings and their ministers built a fiscal regime based on privilege. The law codified formal tax privileges for the clergy and the nobility, for various categories of public servants, and for residents of particular regions and particular towns. Informal tax privileges were also rife: well into the eighteenth century, the royal house left the assessment and collection of land taxes to local notables who played favorites and often went easy on their neighbors. The system appears unfair and arbitrary by today's standards, and it appeared that way to many people who lived under it, too. It certainly enriched the powerful. But it also provided some privileged people with a kind of social protection against risks of poverty and old age. The historian Michael Kwass relates the story of the early eighteenth-century widow Elizabeth Vignon, for example, whose village assembly apparently sheltered her for years from paying tax on the full value of her land. This was not exactly fair. But in an era before welfare states and widows' pensions, it was understandable.[2]

In the middle of the seventeenth century, the kings of France began gradually to modernize tax administration—centralizing control over tax assessment in the hands of royal officials called *intendants*, standardizing procedures for measuring the tax base, and eventually even professionalizing the *intendants* to a limited degree.[3] Compared to the professional tax assessors of today, the *intendants* were still hopeless amateurs, and the system was still deeply mired in tradition. But compared to what had come before, the system was shockingly modern. By the early eighteenth century, privileged people, including Elizabeth Vignon, found their wealth assessed at something like its value for the first time. Some, like Vignon, appealed to the courts; others petitioned collectively for redress of their grievances; and still others took up arms.

The collision between modernizing tax administration and customary tax privileges was a crucial ingredient in French tax rebellions. France was unusual for the liberality with which it dispensed tax privileges and for the rigor of its subsequent drive to modernize tax assessment. Comparative studies have shown that the clash between these two principles helps to explain why tax rebellion was so frequent in old regime France, compared to other agrarian empires of the same era; why some regions within France were more rebellious than others; and why the tide of tax rebellion ebbed and flowed over time *within* any particular region of France.[4]

France was unusual, but the history of early modern tax rebellions in other countries shows that the French were not unique in their propensity to protest the loss of privilege. The defense of traditional tax privileges in the face of assessment reform also motivated many of the major agrarian rebellions in the British Isles, for example, from the Pilgrimage of Grace (England, 1536) to the Tithe War (Ireland, 1830). It even played a part in the English Civil War. The English Crown in the sixteenth century relied on property taxes, but by the turn of the century, property assessments were decades out of date. Beginning in 1635, King Charles I authorized new and deeply unpopular annual assessments (called the "ship money," because the taxes were to pay for the navy). King Charles also assessed and taxed many privileged landowners who previously had been altogether exempt from paying for naval upkeep. The result was a wave of unrest that contributed to the outbreak of civil war.[5]

Nor was this pattern confined to Europe. At the other end of the Eurasian landmass, for example, Chinese peasants also rebelled frequently to defend their traditional tax privileges. Qing dynasty tax collectors customarily went easy on peasants at times when the harvest was bad. In some provinces, officials also granted an informal tax privilege to small landholders who paid their taxes indirectly through intermediaries in the gentry, a practice called "proxy remittance." The empire's growing need for tax revenue in the nineteenth century led imperial officials increasingly to centralize control over tax assessment—with mixed success—and to disregard these traditional tax privileges. Where new assessments conflicted with old privileges, peasants rebelled.[6]

All of these examples show that modernization of tax assessment contributed to tax rebellions, but it was not the only cause. In a broad survey of the available research, William Brustein and Margaret Levi find that the imposition of new tax burdens was a necessary ingredient in all of the major regional "anti-state rebellions" in France, England, and Spain from 1500 to 1700, for example, but they also find that there were other ingredients. In order to explain which regions rebelled and which did not, they point to the cohesion of rebels and the vulnerability of monarchs—which in turn depended on such variables as the character of agrarian class structures, the timing of major wars, and the presence of religious conflicts. Most studies of early modern tax revolts by sociologists and social historians highlight these other factors. Comparative studies place particular stress on the prevalence of commerce, which made rural rebellions less likely by increasing the resources available to pay taxes. Recent comparative studies also stress the absence of defensive war. Rural producers might rebel if they were asked to pay for external wars of conquest, but they were much less likely to rebel against taxes that would pay for military defense of their own lands.[7]

Does this body of research have any bearing on the other rich democracies of the twentieth century? Even if the modernization of tax assessment was a reliable cause of protest in the early modern era, there are some reasons to expect that it might not have had the same effect in the twentieth century. Previous chapters have argued that modernization of tax assessment caused tax revolts in the United States and Britain in the twentieth century, but these two countries were unusual precisely because they continued to rely heavily on real property taxes that many tax experts regarded as "medieval."[8] By 1975, in fact, the United States and Britain were the *only* two rich, democratic countries that still collected more than 10 percent of their tax revenues from real estate. The other rich, democratic countries relied more heavily on other, more modern taxes on income and consumption.[9]

The world of the late twentieth century was also different from the world of early modern Europe in many ways that probably reduced the chances of tax revolts. The spread of democracy is one important difference. Taxpayers took up arms to defend their tax privileges when they had few other ways to make their demands felt. Since World War II, however, taxpayers in most of Europe and the rest of the developed world have been able to get their way by voting. They might therefore be less inclined to take other, riskier forms of collective action. When modernization threatened tax privileges in the despotic states of the early modern era, taxpayers rebelled; but when modernization threatened tax privileges in the democratic states of the postwar era, taxpayers might simply vote for change instead of mobilizing a tax revolt.

Economic development is another difference that might lead us to expect fewer tax revolts in the late twentieth century. By 1970, people in the developed countries were unimaginably wealthy by the standards of early modern Europe and Asia. They could surely afford to pay much heavier taxes than their ancestors could. Perhaps the abolition of tax privileges does not cause much protest when people can afford to pay.[10]

On the other hand, there are also reasons to think that the connection between modernization and tax revolt might have been even tighter in the late twentieth century than it was before. For one thing, the welfare states in the developed democracies of the postwar era made unprecedented commitments to protect their citizens from income shocks, whether those shocks were due to sickness, unemployment, or simply bad luck. Citizens of wealthy countries today expect their governments to protect them in ways that even the most privileged noble of eighteenth-century France would have found unimaginable. This expectation might lead taxpayers to defend traditional forms of social protection—including formal and informal tax privileges—all the more vigorously.

For another thing, the growth of taxation during and after World War II made tax privileges immensely more valuable than they had ever been. A tax exemption is a nice thing to have when taxes would otherwise claim 10 percent of your income. But it is an even nicer thing to have when taxes would otherwise claim 30 percent or 50 percent or even 70 percent of your income, as they could in some countries in the late twentieth century. We might therefore expect that traditional tax privileges would become ever more entrenched as tax rates grew ever higher. According to this line of reasoning, tax revolts might, in fact, have become *more* likely in the late twentieth century.

Did the modernization of tax assessment provoke tax revolts in any developed countries of the late twentieth century other than the United States and Britain? Or did the modernization of tax assessment provoke protest only when it applied to traditional land taxes? The next section examines the modernization of the income tax—one of the most characteristic taxes of the twentieth century. It shows that this tax, too, sometimes enshrined customary privileges and that modernizing reforms that threatened these privileges could indeed provoke protest. And modernization could provoke tax protest in countries that had very different cultural legacies from the United States and the United Kingdom.

TWENTIETH-CENTURY INCOME TAX REVOLTS

The first income taxes were introduced as temporary war expedients in industrializing countries in the nineteenth century. They relied on crude techniques to measure income. Assessors either relied on the taxpayer's own sworn declaration or else based their estimate on external signs of opulent living, such as carriages, pocketwatches, and the like. These techniques have been called "presumptive assessment," because they were based on presumption rather than on the direct observation of income.[11] Presumptive assessment required a great deal of local knowledge to be effective at all: the assessor had to know and trust the taxpayer's declaration or else had to have substantial knowledge of the taxpayer's lifestyle. Assessors were therefore local officials, and as such, they were subject to little effective supervision or standardization from the central government. Income tax assessors, like American property tax assessors, had substantial discretion that they could use to award informal tax privileges.[12]

The expansion of market economies in the twentieth century made it possible to assess income more accurately. Income taxation had a key advantage over property taxation in this respect: market income, unlike property, usually leaves a written record that is difficult to hide. Moveable property is easy to conceal from the tax assessor; real estate, although it is harder to hide, is no easier to evaluate, because a property may increase in value without changing in any observable way. By contrast, most sources of income in a market economy produce an observable paper trail—in the form of payrolls, account books, dividend checks, sales receipts, and so forth—that agents of the government can follow if they are motivated and empowered to do so.

Tax officials in the twentieth century adopted two techniques—audit and withholding—that enabled them to follow the paper trail and thereby measure taxable income accurately. Auditing taxpayers' declarations involved inspecting taxpayers' account books and other written records. Withholding effectively conscripted financial institutions and employers as deputy tax agents, by requiring them to subtract income taxes from any wages, salaries, dividends, and interest payments that they made and to remit the tax to the government—a process also called "taxation at source." In effect, taxation at source enabled governments to tax income at the very instant it was received.[13]

Modern income tax assessment, like modern property assessment, was centralized, standardized, and professional. Effective auditing and effective withholding both required centralized supervision of tax inspectors, a body of standard procedures for appraising incomes and calculating the taxes due, and professional assessing staff with the requisite technical accounting skills to advise and audit taxpayers. States that had central income tax bureaucracies were capable of assessing the incomes of most of the working population.

By the end of World War II, most developed countries had modern income tax bureaucracies that relied on a combination of audit and withholding to assess income. The war was the most expensive conflict in the history of the world. As the war escalated, the countries fighting it had to pay salaries for more and more soldiers and had to send more and more expensive equipment to be destroyed on the battlefield. By 1943, the combatant states could afford the war only if they could collect taxes from the majority of the working population. Most of the countries that did not already have modern income tax bureaucracies introduced them.

A handful of countries continued to rely heavily on presumptive assessment, however, and these countries faced substantial protest when they modernized income tax assessment in the postwar era. Three states continued to rely heavily on presumptive assessment for a substantial portion of small

businesses, and they introduced new auditing procedures only several years after the end of the war—France in 1953, Belgium in 1961, and Italy in a series of
piecemeal reforms (in 1971, 1980, and 1992).[14] Two more states replaced the presumptive assessment of wage income by introducing withholding—Norway in
1952 and Denmark in 1967. All of these countries except Norway experienced
tax revolts when they introduced their modernizing tax reforms in the postwar
era; Norway experienced an income tax revolt much later, in 1973.

By contrast, there is no record of any major revolt against the income tax in
the countries that had introduced withholding and auditing requirements during the war—including Australia, Austria, Canada, Finland, Germany, the
Netherlands, Sweden, the United Kingdom, and the United States. Nor is there
any record of a major income tax revolt in Switzerland, a country that, like
France, still has not introduced withholding of income tax from wages and
salaries at the source.[15]

In the remainder of this chapter, I examine the role of modernization more
closely with case studies of postwar income tax rebellions in France and Denmark. These tax revolts are of particular interest because they were the greatest
sustained protest movements against the income tax in the postwar era. They
are also the cases that have produced the most extensive secondary literatures.
And they are of particular interest because they are so different from the United
States. France and Denmark both have long traditions of strong central government, in contrast to the United States, and scholars often see French and
Danish fiscal policies as worlds apart from the American pattern of low taxes
and meager welfare spending. France is a conservative welfare state, which taxes
relatively heavily and spends heavily on benefits earmarked for various middle-
class occupational groups. Denmark is a social democratic welfare state, which
taxes even more heavily and spends heavily on universal benefits for all citizens.[16] As we shall see, however, these countries both experienced protest
movements against their income taxes, and these protest movements resembled
the American property tax revolt in many particulars. Even in these countries,
modernizing reforms to tax assessment provoked rebellion by threatening traditional tax privileges.

THE FRENCH INCOME TAX REVOLT: A TAX
AUDIT TRIGGERS A REBELLION

France entered the postwar era without a modern income tax in place. Although French parliamentarians had introduced the income tax shortly before

World War I, the tax had not undergone the expansion and modernization that it had in many other countries during World War II.

For small-business owners—including shopkeepers and artisan producers—the income tax was based on the principle of presumptive tax or *forfait*. If you qualified for this system, you would not submit a retrospective tax return every quarter to document your profits and calculate your tax liability. Instead, every two years you would stipulate to a prospective estimate of your profits, based on external signs rather than actual records, and that estimate would be the basis for your tax liability for the next two years. In theory, tax officials could decide to audit you sooner, but in practice they rarely did. During a period of inflation, the *forfait* was equivalent to a substantial cash benefit for the taxpayer, who would stipulate to a certain tax liability and then watch it shrink in real terms as money depreciated. Moreover, the estimate was often scandalously low in the first place. "What the small self-employed storeowner declares to the Treasury depends pretty much on his own honesty," wrote one American reporter describing this system. "Fraud has become a method of staying in business, a kind of Government subsidy (without the Government's permission)." It was, that is, a kind of informal social protection against the risk of business failure.[17]

Then the administrative rules changed. Shortly after the liberation of France from German occupation, French officials began to modernize income tax administration. In 1948, they centralized control over tax assessment, bringing together three previously separate administrative departments. This administrative reorganization brought the sales tax auditors and the income tax assessors under the same chain of command—with the result that a sales tax audit could now affect the state's presumptive assessment of taxable income. In 1951, officials took a further step to professionalize tax assessment with the introduction of a national tax academy. And in 1956, they promulgated a single, uniform set of regulations to govern tax assessment and collection.[18]

Artisans and small shopkeepers faced a new fiscal regime. Income taxes were no longer shrinking in real terms, because the government had finally begun to get postwar inflation under control. And the presumptive tax assessment was newly subject to audit. In short, small-business people no longer enjoyed the same customary, informal tax privileges.[19]

As in the United States, it was a tax reassessment that triggered rebellion. On July 22, 1953, the General Tax Directorate (*la Direction Générale des Impôts*) notified thirty shopkeepers and artisans in the small town of Saint-Céré that their sales would be audited the following day. For the last two years, the *forfait* had held down their income taxes while actual sales figures increased under pressure of inflation. Now the pending sales tax audit threatened to increase their income tax assessments.

One of those who was to be audited—a burly blacksmith named Frégeac who was also a member of the city council—organized an emergency meeting of artisans and shopkeepers at city hall. He invited a bookseller named Pierre Poujade, who was also a city council member and chair of the local festivals committee, to help run the meeting. The nine members of the city council and the assembled artisans and shopkeepers of Saint-Céré pledged themselves unanimously to collective resistance.[20]

The events of the following day were anything but politics as usual. Two tax inspectors arrived on schedule on the morning of July 23 to audit a shoe store near the center of town. They found their way blocked by a crowd of merchants and artisans who announced that they were barring all access to the store's account books. There was a brief but tense standoff while the shopkeeper stood by, nervously toying with a pair of boots. The inspectors left, only to return with more colleagues to audit another business that afternoon. Once again, the crowd—led by a menacing Frégeac—turned them away. The inspectors left Saint-Céré without completing a single audit.[21]

It was the start of a movement. Through the summer and fall, the story of the battle of Saint-Céré spread by word of mouth through the surrounding countryside. Traveling salespeople and independent truck drivers spread the word. Poujade crisscrossed the region in his delivery van, tirelessly organizing protest meetings and inspiring imitators wherever he went. In villages and towns throughout southwestern France, retailers and artisan producers rallied to the defense of their colleagues when tax inspectors showed up. The inspectors who returned to Saint-Céré in September encountered an unprecedented mass mobilization that drew retailers and artisans from the whole surrounding region. By fall, the rising tide of protest was known throughout the country as the *Mouvement de Saint-Céré*.[22]

The *Mouvement*, much like the American property tax revolt, was at first a purely reactive mobilization whose participants lacked any broad agreement on matters of ideology or public policy. There are no public opinion polls from the early days of the movement, but the indirect evidence that is available— including studies of the movement's early leadership in the area around Saint-Céré, historical voting patterns, and subsequent opinion surveys—suggests that participants came from all across the political spectrum. Frégeac, for example, had been elected to the city council as a Communist, while Poujade had been elected as a member of the anti-Communist *Rassemblement du Peuple Français*. The far left, and the Communist Party in particular, provided a great deal of early support in larger towns, but the movement also relied on the support of small employers who had traditionally supported the centrist Radical Party.[23] The protesters did not need to agree on broader policy aims as long as they sought only to block tax inspections.

The sole cause uniting the tax rebels was their resistance to the reassessment of revenues. At a regional meeting of tax protesters in October 1953, they adopted an eight-point program, of which the first seven points exclusively concerned taxes, and tax assessment in particular. The program demanded the total cessation of tax audits and an immediate amnesty for tax evaders. It demanded that shopkeepers and artisans receive equal tax treatment with large corporations, cooperatives, and salaried employees—all groups that enjoyed various advantages with respect to the assessment of income. The centerpiece of the program was a demand for "*imposition unique à la base*." This vague phrase implied an end to the double taxation of small business revenues; that is, either sales taxes or income taxes had to go. The protesters otherwise disclaimed all interest in the details of tax policy. They even asserted defiantly (in point five of their program) that it was not their job to devise an acceptable tax reform: that was up to the parliament. The purpose of their union was simply to defend the interests of one narrow tax category: the artisans and small merchants. Six weeks later, the protesters adopted a charter and a dues-paying membership structure, and named themselves the *Union de Défense des Commerçants et Artisans* (UDCA).[24]

French shopkeepers and artisans—like American homeowners—rose up in protest wherever there was a new reassessment. In January 1954, the General Tax Directorate issued instructions to its agents to bring small-business income tax assessments up to date by reassessing all estimated profits (*bénéfices forfaitaires*) throughout the country. As tax inspectors fanned out through the *départements*, the agitation followed, gradually spreading from the rural southwest to encompass most of France. By July 1955, the UDCA newspaper reported that there had been 1,155 collective protests against tax inspection in the two years since the battle of Saint-Céré.[25]

Comparison of regions within France also supports the view that the defense of traditional tax privileges motivated the protests. The only areas where there was no protest to speak of were the most developed industrial regions in the north. These were the regions where relatively few people had qualified for the *forfait* in the first place. Higher levels of economic concentration meant that there were fewer independent businesspeople per capita and that their businesses had higher revenues on average. The issue that moved people to protest elsewhere in France—the abrogation of the informal subsidy that inhered in the *forfait* system—thus had little traction in these regions. There were no protests because comparatively few people had anything to protest.[26]

The authorities' answer to mass tax evasion was further modernization of tax assessment, which only fed the flames of protest. In August 1954, the parliament passed the so-called Dorey Amendment to rationalize tax assessment by bringing income taxes and sales taxes under a single enforcement regime. The Dorey Amendment was a straightforward attempt to modernize tax administration; its purpose was to revise and update for the first time an eighteenth-century law that established criminal penalties for obstructing tax assessors at work. Poujade and other protesters decried it as a Gestapo-like law, and repeal of the amendment assumed pride of place in the movement's demands. In January 1955, the UDCA drew some 100,000 protesters to a rally in Paris to protest the amendment and to vote their support for a tax strike. In March, Poujade and 100 other UDCA protesters disrupted the National Assembly to demand fiscal amnesty and repeal of the amendment. Two weeks later, shopkeepers around the country closed their doors for a one-day strike. The government under Edgar Faure conceded, repealing the Dorey Amendment and instituting less severe penalties.[27]

The tax rebels saw themselves as heirs to a long national tradition of tax resistance. They looked back on the French Revolution as a noble rebellion against unfair and intrusive taxation. They described peasant farmers, merchants, and artisans as defenders of traditional liberty against a bureaucratic state that sought to measure and regulate every aspect of life. Some commentators have even claimed to find continuities between *Poujadisme* and the peasant tax revolts of fourteenth-century France. To Poujade, at least, protest against fiscal inquisition was part of what made France so French.[28]

But for all its appeal to French tradition, the French income tax revolt looks very similar to the American property tax revolt. It was sparked by reassessment and fanned into a fire by the modernization of tax assessment. Protesters took collective action to defend their informal tax privileges from the modernization of the income tax.

THE DANISH INCOME TAX REVOLT: TAX ASSESSMENT SPARKS THE REBELLION

The Danish income tax revolt also bore striking similarities to the American property tax revolt. As with the American property tax revolt, the modernization of tax assessment was the precipitating factor. Like France, Denmark was occupied early in World War II and, unable to defend its borders, opted not to modernize its income tax. The old income tax system was a lot like the American property tax: income was assessed by local officials, with little standardization, and measured with a substantial lag—typically eighteen months—that provided taxpayers with an informal tax break that was especially valuable in times of inflation.[29]

The Danish parliament, or *Folketing*, finally passed legislation to modernize the tax in 1967. The reforms centralized supervision over assessment and created a new computer system to standardize auditing of taxpayer returns. They made the tax into a tax on current income that was withheld at the source. They imposed new record-keeping requirements on employers. They also required self-employed people to submit quarterly provisional tax payments. And they did away with several other popular tax breaks that had protected taxpayers against income shocks. The most important of these was a deduction for all direct taxes paid in the previous year. This deduction was a legacy of the Copenhagen income tax of 1850. Experts were happy to see it abolished because it was unfair to people with rising incomes: because the size of your tax break corresponded to the income taxes you paid *last* year, a big pay raise might make you liable for more taxes than a neighbor or co-worker who had already spent years at your new salary level. But looked at another way, this deduction provided a substantial privilege to people whose incomes were *not* rising. Abolishing the tax break did away with a traditional cushion for people with stagnant or falling incomes.[30]

The implementation of the new Tax at Source Law was a comedy of errors. A change of government and a variety of technical problems delayed implementation until 1970 (with 1969 as a "tax-free" transition year). The newly appointed head of the Tax-at-Source Directorate (*Kildeskattedirektorat*) threatened to quit over a pay dispute in November 1968. Then scandal erupted over the improper assignment of the construction contract for the building that was to house the new directorate.[31] Then the directorate erroneously sent out thousands of threatening collection letters to employers who were, in fact, complying with the law. This incident prompted an apology from Finance

Minister Poul Møller, who announced a series of measures to prevent a repeat of the incident—whereupon it promptly happened again. As the end of the tax year 1970 approached, the staff of the directorate discovered an enormous volume of errors in the data submitted by local tax authorities. It was a good illustration of why assessment modernization was needed, but it was also an enormous complication to discover at the last minute. The directorate undertook to correct the local assessments, but the computer programmer who was assigned to double-check the corrections quit—once again over a pay dispute—and the corrections were only partly completed.[32]

As in the United States, the first assessment under the new system was the signal to start a tax revolt. The very first individual income tax returns under the new system were due on January 31, 1971. In honor of the deadline, the television program *Focus* presented an interview with an unassuming tax lawyer and part-time university lecturer named Mogens Glistrup the evening before. The producers had picked Glistrup out of the phone book. He was competent, but uninspiring, and the first take of the interview was by all accounts dull. But after it was over, Glistrup made several shocking statements over coffee in the network cafeteria, and a reporter dared him to repeat them on the air. Glistrup took the dare and started a movement.[33]

The broadcast interview was electrifying. In the space of two minutes, Glistrup told viewers that loopholes in the tax law allowed everyone to determine his or her own tax rate by the expedient of founding fictitious corporations; that, in effect, this practice was equivalent to printing one's own money; that this was not only legal and moral, but that it was conversely "immoral" to pay taxes; that "a *krone* paid in taxes is a *krone* paid toward the ruin of the country"; and that "tax dodgers today are comparable to the railroad saboteurs under the [Nazi] occupation: they do a dangerous job, but they do it for the good of the country."[34] It was the most provocative two minutes in the history of Danish television. "The broadcast made a fantastic impression on me and many other Danes," recalled Glistrup's later colleague in the *Folketing*, Pia Kjærsgaard. "Just as with the Kennedy assassination, many can remember precisely where they were, and where they were sitting, when they saw it."[35]

The broadcast was the start of Glistrup's legal troubles. Finance Minister Møller announced his intention to file a complaint with the radio board and demanded to see Glistrup's tax return. It turned out that Glistrup practiced what he preached. He admitted in radio debate two weeks later that he had got his official tax rate down to zero, despite his million-*kroner* income. The bar association (*Advokatrådet*) opened an investigation into Glistrup's law practice, and the justice ministry began a parallel investigation into his personal finances. By summer 1971, Glistrup faced the first in a long series of fines and criminal prosecutions for legal malpractice and tax evasion.[36]

The broadcast was also the start of a grassroots movement to draft Glistrup as an anti-tax protest candidate for the *Folketing*. After the show, the telephones at the studio and the major newspapers rang off the hook with calls favorable to Glistrup.[37] He became famous, with semi-regular appearances in public meetings and broadcast media and a column in a major tabloid newspaper.[38] People started organizing to draft him into politics. Throughout 1971 and 1972, at least four minor political parties of the far right approached Glistrup and invited him to stand for election under their banner.[39] He claimed that the far left Socialist People's Party had also approached him. In June 1972, a Conservative Party caucus in the suburban community of Søllerød chose him as its candidate for the *Folketing*. The decision came from the grassroots, and the party leadership—which included Finance Minister Møller—did not welcome it. A district chairman left the caucus meeting in protest, and when the news of the decision reached the national party leadership, the Conservatives' speaker in the *Folketing* announced that he would quit if Glistrup were elected to join his party's delegation. The party's general secretary invalidated the caucus decision and sent it back to a larger, regional body that overturned it. A second attempt by dissident Søllerød Conservatives to elect Glistrup was blocked by the party leadership in the first days of August.[40]

Like the California property tax crisis, the Danish income tax crisis led voters to undertake a massive petition drive to abolish the tax. It began with Glistrup's announcement on August 22, 1972, that he was founding a new protest party. He made the announcement in Copenhagen's Tivoli amusement park at a press conference to promote a book two journalists had written about his life and views. Before the assembled reporters, Glistrup named his new brainchild the Progress Party (*Fremskridtspartiet*) and laid out an unorthodox program whose centerpiece was the abolition of the income tax. It also included a new constitution that would provide for monthly elections, a shrunken *Folketing* of only forty members, repeal of the franchise for voters over sixty years old, and a variety of radical public expenditure cuts including a proposal to reduce the defense budget to the cost of an answering machine that would say "We surrender" in Russian. The press understandably treated the whole thing as a publicity stunt.[41]

Many taxpayers saw it instead as a real opportunity to express their discontent, and the petition drive began immediately. Eager volunteers approached Glistrup after the conference. Glistrup told them that he would need to present the Ministry of the Interior with approximately 17,000 petition signatures in order to secure his party a line on the ballot. By the first party meeting on September 7, the party already had twenty-two volunteer activists and 1,200 signatures.[42] By January 1973, they had met the quota with a total of 17,113 signatures, although there was never an official tally. Glistrup presented the petitions to the Ministry of the Interior in a locked chest. He argued that the bureaucrats of Denmark's Statistical Bureau (*Danmarks Statistik*) could not be trusted to count the signatures of a party that proposed to cut their budget to zero. He therefore demanded that a party representative be permitted to oversee the counting. When the ministry refused to grant this request, Glistrup walked away with the key to the chest. It was a nice bit of theater that helped to keep the petition drive going. The party activists resumed their work and collected 18,000 more signatures between January and July, at which point the ministry verified the signatures and recognized the party.[43]

The Progress Party also organized mass protest meetings—much like the protest meetings against the property tax in Detroit or Chicago or Los Angeles, although organized with a bit more showmanship. People who attended Progress Party protest meetings in 1973 likened the experience variously to a vaudeville show, a religious revival meeting, or—in one particularly unsympathetic account—the Nuremberg Rally. A live pop band typically opened the meeting, followed by Glistrup, who delivered lengthy diatribes against the income tax, the paper-pushers who ran the government, and people who sponged off of the welfare system.[44] He traveled around Denmark at a hectic pace in the spring and fall of 1973, presiding over two to four mass meetings every week. Attendance ranged from a few hundred to 3,000 people, who purchased tickets to attend.[45]

The Progress Party subsequently embraced many other issues, but it was at first a single-issue protest movement focused on abolishing the income tax. The party publicized its campaign with print advertisements that asked, "Do you like INCOME TAXATION AT SOURCE [*KILDESKATTEN*]?" Punning on the idea of taxation "at the source," party placards informed readers that "The Progress Party holds that this tax is the greatest *source* of pollution in Denmark [*Danmarks største forureningskilde*]."[46] The abolition of the income tax was the first demand on every party program and the only concrete policy in the party's three main platform points (the other two were "cutting red tape" [begrænsning af papirvældet] and "simplifying legislation" [sanering af lovgivningen]).[47] All other policy matters were open to debate within the party, and activists promptly debated and dropped Glistrup's other outrageous policy proposals, including the answering machine and the disenfranchisement of the elderly.[48] But subscribing to the abolition of the income tax was a nonnegotiable condition of participation. In the absence of other formal membership criteria, it was the one thing that defined the party.[49]

What made the Danish income tax so odious to taxpayers? It might have seemed to an American in 1973 that they had little to complain about. True, Danish income tax rates were very high for most people, but nominal rates were already on their way down at the time of the tax revolt. Legislators had reduced income tax rates dramatically since their peak in 1968.[50] The Danish government had also indexed tax brackets for inflation beginning in 1970, so bracket creep—the problem of inflation pushing people into higher tax brackets—was not the problem in Denmark that it was in, say, the United States.[51] The Danish income tax did pay for some unpopular means-tested welfare programs, a point that Glistrup made with relish, but the same programs were *much* more unpopular in the United States, and yet there was no comparable revolt against the American income tax.[52] Moreover, the Danish income tax, unlike the American income tax, paid for other social programs—from old-age pensions to health insurance—that were available to all Danish taxpayers and that enjoyed widespread public support.

What made the income tax so hateful was the loss of popular tax privileges. The available data—including surveys of voters and a systematic study of the activists whom the party recruited as candidates in 1973—suggest that support ran particularly high among the groups that had benefited from the old deduction for taxes paid. Small employers were overrepresented among Progress Party voters, and they made up the single largest group of party activists. They resented the burdensome new recordkeeping and reporting requirements imposed by the Tax at Source Law. They were also the only occupational group experiencing slow or negative income growth at the time the Tax at Source Law was implemented.[53] Survey data from the December 1973 election suggest that individuals with falling incomes were especially likely to support the Progress Party.[54] These were precisely people who would have benefited from the old tax privilege.

The Social Democratic government might have survived the tax revolt, but it sealed its fate with a second bout of reform in 1973 that did away with another popular tax privilege and thereby spurred another round of protest. In November, the Social Democrats struck a compromise with the Socialist People's Party to eliminate a homeowners' tax deduction that had been put in place in 1966 to protect people from rising housing prices. The plan to abolish the deduction outraged many working-class homeowners, who rallied around Erhard Jakobsen, a member of the *Folketing* and a prominent figure in the moderate wing of the Social Democrats. Jakobsen had already begun organizing a centrist Social Democratic caucus in response to the growing left-wing presence in the party. The deal to abolish homeowners' tax privileges was his Rubicon. He withdrew from the party on November 6, and the next day he announced the formation of a separate party, the Center Democrats (*Centrumdemokraterne*). The party would contest the next election as a single-issue protest party focused on the preservation of tax preferences for homeowners.[55]

Jakobsen's withdrawal from the Social Democratic Party set in motion a chain reaction that ultimately exploded Danish party politics. The day after he quit the party, he skipped a crucial vote, claiming his car had run out of gas, and thereby deprived the Social Democratic government of its majority. Prime Minister Anker Jørgensen dutifully called an election for December 4, 1973. This would later be known as the "Earthquake Election" or—to Social Democrats— the "Catastrophe Election." Denmark's famously stable four-party system fell to pieces, as voters abandoned all of the major parties in droves. The Progress Party won 16 percent of the vote, becoming the second largest party in the *Folketing*. The Center Democrats placed sixth, with 8 percent. The election even revived the fortunes of the League of Justice, a small tax protest party that could trace its roots to the single-tax movement inspired by the turn-of-the-century writings of the economist Henry George. The tax revolt had arrived in the Danish parliament. American tax protesters could read about the Danish tax protest election the next day on the front page of the *Wall Street Journal*, which reported that "Danish voters dealt a blow to that nation's welfare state tradition."[56]

The Danish income tax revolt, like the French income tax rebellion and the American property tax revolt—and like many other tax revolts of another era—arose because modernizing reforms threatened traditional tax privileges.

AMERICAN EXCEPTIONALISM REVISITED

Mogens Glistrup was delighted when the news of Proposition 13 reached him in Denmark. "Seen through Danish eyes, it is one of the many fortunate omens that the Progress Movement is on the way to becoming a worldwide movement," he wrote in the party newspaper, *Sidste Nyt*. "But meanwhile we can be proud of being far ahead of the Jarvis/Gann people. They are at a much more primitive stage than our thorough, balanced, comprehensive program, which finds expression for example in our annual budget proposals." Glistrup's confidence was unwarranted. By 2001, the Progress Party was dead and its budget proposals were forgotten.[57] Proposition 13, meanwhile, lives on—and continues to underwrite public and partisan support for tax cuts.

That is not to say that the Danish and French tax revolts lacked impact. These two social movements had far-reaching consequences for Danish and French politics. Although the income tax protest faded away quickly, both Poujade and Glistrup managed to keep their parties alive by capitalizing on other political issues. Under the leadership of Poujade, the UDCA turned from a protest organization against the income tax into a political party that embraced a virulent French nationalism. It laid some of the groundwork for the French extreme right of today. Glistrup likewise tried to refashion the Progress Party into a nationalist and anti-immigrant party. Although the Progress Party eventually splintered over conflicts of personality and strategy, one of its descendants became the Danish People's Party—as of 2007, the third largest party in the *Folketing* and a pivotal supporting vote for the Conservative-Liberal coalition government. Nevertheless, the fact that both of these tax protest parties turned toward other issues to sustain themselves illustrates the distance separating them from their American counterpart. Neither the Danish nor the French tax protest parties could sustain much organizational momentum on hostility to taxation alone. Neither tax revolt produced the kind of permanent tax rebellion that characterizes American politics today.

What can this comparison teach us about the American tax revolt? One conclusion from this comparison must be that tax rebellion is not simply an American preoccupation. American political culture may be distinctively anti-statist. But even in some of the largest welfare states in Europe, where voters are much more favorable toward government intervention in the market, voters may rebel against taxes when provoked. It follows that the cause of the American tax revolt was not a distinctively anti-tax culture. The cause of the tax revolt was the institutional condition that the American states of the 1960s and 1970s shared with the French state of 1953 and the Danish state of 1971, namely, the modernization of tax assessment.

The comparison also reminds us what it was about the American property tax reforms that provoked rebellion. Not every tax increase provokes a backlash.

Every rich democratic country increased taxes substantially in the postwar era, but only a few of these countries experienced tax revolts. The tax privileges that voters fought to defend were those that protected people from the market—whether by subsidizing homeownership (as in the United States and Denmark), by cushioning people against the loss of income (as in Denmark), or by sheltering small business from competition (as in France).

There is one final conclusion to be drawn from this comparative exercise. The fact of tax protest in the 1970s is not enough to explain the right turn in the politics of taxation in the United States. Both France and Denmark had tax revolts, yet neither French nor Danish politicians have permanently reoriented their country's politics toward tax cuts in the way that American political leaders have. The origin of the American property tax revolt, like the origins of the French and Danish movements, was a defensive rebellion against income insecurity. As Chapter 5 showed, it was only later—when the right turn in the movement became firmly anchored in public policy at the state level—that the United States turned toward its current and distinctive path.

EPILOGUE
Lessons of the Tax Revolt

THE TAX REVOLT is over. George Wiley, that unlikely progressive spokesperson for the tax rebels, died in 1973. Some of the tax protest organizations that he helped to found live on, but they have moved on to other issues. Howard Jarvis died in 1986. His memory is kept alive in the Howard Jarvis Taxpayers' Association, but this organization is no longer a grassroots insurgency against the California establishment. It has become a part of that establishment, with a full-time lobbying staff in Sacramento dedicated to defending Proposition 13.[1]

But the last consequences of the tax revolt have not yet been felt. The most enthusiastic proponents of tax cuts in Washington are veterans of the tax revolt era who remember it fondly and who dream of leading what Michael Graetz and Ian Shapiro have called a "permanent tax rebellion."[2] The sunset provisions written into the tax cuts Congress passed in recent years ensure that this issue will stay on the agenda for the foreseeable future. The growing federal deficit also ensures that conflicts over the appropriate level of taxation will not go away anytime soon. And the tax limitation laws left to us as a legacy of Proposition 13 promise to keep the issue alive at the state and local levels.

This book has focused on the origins of our chronic conflict over tax policy. But what can this history teach us about the future? Are we doomed to cut taxes, as Grover Norquist notoriously proposed, until our government is so small that "you could drown it in a bathtub"? Should we expect a tax revolt when the federal income tax cuts expire? What about when the clock runs out on the legislation that temporarily abolished the federal estate tax? Are we doomed to choose between tax cuts and tax protest? One lesson of this book is surely that answering questions like these is hazardous: the story of the tax revolt is replete with unintended and unanticipated consequences. American tax politics are changeable, and history has not been kind to social scientists who have ventured predictions about future tax policies based on the assumption that our future will be like our past.[3] But reviewing the story of the book may suggest some conclusions about the future. I will conclude the book, then, with a brief overview of what we might learn from the origins of the property tax revolt and what we might learn from its consequences.

WHAT WE CAN LEARN FROM THE ORIGINS OF THE TAX REVOLT

The book has shown that the tax revolt arose as a defensive movement. Homeowners rose up in protest because reforms to the local property tax threatened traditional tax privileges that had provided them with income security—just as taxpayers have rebelled to defend their traditional tax privileges in times and places ranging from early-eighteenth-century China to late-twentieth-century Scandinavia and Britain.

The book has also argued for a new theory of *why* people fought to defend these privileges. Not every tax increase causes a protest movement. Most tax increases had, and have, no such effect. Homeowners fought to defend their tax privileges in this instance for the same reason that senior citizens fight to defend Social Security and for the same reason that the full panoply of social subsidies that we call the welfare state have proved to be so politically resilient. People took collective action to defend their tax privileges because those privileges protected them from income shocks.[4]

The tax privilege of selective fractional assessment was like social programs in other ways, too. For most of the twentieth century it was protected from political interference because politicians wanted to avoid blame for tax increases. Those who were lucky enough to benefit from illegally low assessments were an especially attentive constituency. Those who paid the price were at first more numerous, but they lacked information about the tax break, and they lacked strong incentives to act collectively. As the decades passed, moreover, the number of attentive beneficiaries increased. So did their material stake in their tax privileges. The informal tax breaks doled out by local assessors grew until they were impossible to dislodge without provoking protest.[5]

If these arguments are correct, then we need not expect a tax revolt in 2010, when the vast majority of recent income tax cuts are scheduled to expire. The situation confronting most Americans today is substantially different from that confronting homeowners in the 1970s. The great tax revolts of the late twentieth century defended tax privileges that were long-established customs of providing people with shelter from the vagaries of the market—by subsidizing retirement savings, as fractional assessment did for American homeowners; or by protecting small and failing businesses against competition, as the *forfait* did for French shopkeepers and artisans; or by favoring people with stagnant or declining incomes, as the Danish direct tax deduction did. The 2001 income tax cuts are not like this. They are not yet entrenched promises. Most of them were not targeted to protect people from market failure; in fact, the overwhelming majority of the benefits went to the richest Americans. Though most taxpayers received some benefit, it is probably safe to assume that relatively few taxpayers have planned their lives and their retirement savings in the expectation that these tax cuts will be made permanent. No doubt we can expect wealthy donors to back a coordinated lobbying campaign in favor of keeping the tax cuts. But a mass social movement against the restoration of higher marginal income tax rates is probably not in the offing.

Provided that Congress acts quickly. As long as economic growth continues to raise American incomes, it will continue to propel more Americans into higher tax brackets. The longer that the restoration of top income tax rates is delayed, the greater the constituency for maintaining the tax cuts, and the greater the stake those constituents have in maintaining the tax cuts. The longer that the Bush tax cuts persist, the greater the chances of grassroots resistance when they are repealed.

WHAT WE CAN LEARN FROM THE OUTCOMES OF THE TAX REVOLT

That does not mean that everything is rosy for Democrats who would repeal the tax cuts. The argument of this book also suggests that even if Congress allows many tax cuts to expire in 2010, the demand for cutting taxes will stay front and center in American politics. The permanent politics of tax cutting is anchored in state and local policy. Property tax limitation laws, and limitations on the growth of state budgets, keep our attention focused on the overall level of taxation. We ask whether taxes are too high—but we neglect to ask whether they come at the right time, whether they are distributed too fairly, or how they are best spent. As long as the issue is framed in this way, some politicians will seek advantage in identifying themselves with a politics of indiscriminate tax-cutting. Our future conflicts over taxation hinge on the future of state and local tax limitation laws.

What, then, are the prospects for these tax limitation laws? The book argues that many of these laws can be understood as tax privileges analogous to social programs. Property tax limitations like Proposition 13 may even be understood as a kind of social insurance against the rising cost of housing—a program like Social Security. What this means in practice will depend on your point of view. People who prefer low taxes and small government can take courage from the example of Social Security. Tax limits, like social insurance programs, are hard to overturn. Commentators on California politics sometimes even borrow a well-known metaphor for Social Security when they describe Proposition 13. They say it is "the third rail of California politics"—the electric rail on the subway, which will kill any politician who is dumb enough to touch it. Abolishing Proposition 13 is off the table because no politician wants to be the one who starts the next tax revolt.

People who worry that tax limitations impair our ability to govern ourselves effectively can also take inspiration from the Social Security analogy. Political support for Social Security is resilient, but it is weaker than it used to be. Opponents have not succeeded yet in abolishing or privatizing the program, but they have developed a set of promising strategies—a playbook, if you will—that can be mined for lessons about how to approach tax limitation laws.

One of these lessons is that fundamental reform of property tax limitations will not happen overnight. The opponents of Social Security are playing a long game. Howard Jarvis, for example, made up his mind in 1935 that the Social Security Act was a bad idea. Forty-four years later, he argued in his autobiography that government old-age insurance should be abolished and replaced with private savings accounts. Although some of the more radical conservatives close to Ronald Reagan's administration shared his view, they recognized the need to "prepare the political ground" before proposing to privatize Social Security outright. It was only in 2005 that even a partial plan to privatize Social Security finally made it onto the public agenda.[6] The plan was defeated, but it is safe to predict that it will return.

Reforming tax limitation laws might not take the better part of a century. But it is a long-term project that will require long-term planning. Reformers tried for decades to get rid of the informal tax privilege of fractional assessment. They failed many times before they succeeded. The formal tax privileges that result from tax limitation will be no different. Anyone who shares the long-term goal of fundamentally reforming tax limitation laws—or of replacing them with another, fairer set of tax privileges—needs to think about preparing the ground over a period of years and probably decades.

The second lesson is that reforming tax limits will require would-be re-formers to create a sense of crisis. Politicians know that people will mobilize to defend social programs from threats. The only way to persuade voters that it is necessary to repeal a program is therefore to persuade them that the program is already threatened and that dismantling some aspects of the program may help to protect the benefits that it provides. Here, too, opponents of tax limits might learn something from opponents of Social Security. In recent decades, the crit-ics of Social Security have labored to foster a public perception that the pro-gram faces impending fiscal collapse. Creating a sense of crisis takes work because—even if the claims of crisis are true—the crisis is not immediately perceptible to voters. Although current projections show the Social Security program to be out of actuarial balance in the long term, for example, they also show that the program could continue without tax increases or benefit cuts un-til 2040.[7] This is not a crisis that anyone perceives immediately. It is felt perhaps least of all by the program's staunchest defenders—its current beneficiaries, most of whom do not expect to be living in 2040. Opponents of the program have therefore adopted a rhetorical strategy of insistent repetition: Social Secu-rity is "going broke," "Social security cannot afford to pay all of the benefits it has promised," "Social security is headed towards bankruptcy."[8]

In the case of tax limitation, it should be easier to persuade the public that a crisis is imminent. Many state and local governments that operate under tax limitations are much closer to fiscal breakdown than the Social Security trust fund is. California, the home of Proposition 13, has so far postponed the reck-oning through a combination of borrowing and accounting gimmickry, but the long-term outlook is bad. At the time of this writing—after a year in which tax revenues were unexpectedly high—the nonpartisan Legislative Analyst's Office predicts an annual operating shortfall of over $4 billion beginning next fiscal year.[9] In the long term, the structural deficit may not be soluble without re-forms that would give state officials more flexibility in deciding whom, how, and when to tax. Colorado's recent experience is instructive: confronted with an unprecedented and immediate budget crisis in 2005, state legislators and voters concluded that the only way to save popular programs—including pop-ular tax privileges such as the state's senior citizen property tax circuit breaker—was to suspend the state's stringent tax limitation for five years.[10]

A third lesson we might draw from efforts to dismantle Social Security is that anyone who wants to reform tax limitations will have to offer taxpayers an alter-native way to protect their incomes, and their retirement incomes in particular.

The conservative strategists who set out to cut Social Security in the 1980s learned that simply proposing cuts was a recipe for sure defeat. People could not be pushed off of social insurance. They had to be weaned away gradually, by offering them an alternative. The opponents of Social Security therefore set about deliberately constructing a "parallel system" of private retirement savings options that would provide people with an alternative to Social Security and thereby erode the vested interests defending the program.[11] Although this strategy has not yet paid off, it looks promising.

The same strategy could be used to reform our system of state and local tax limitation. Property tax limitations like Proposition 13, for example, provide residential and income security for long-term homeowners. Reformers who would do away with these limits will need to offer senior citizens and other homeowners another way to protect themselves from being displaced. The alternative might take the form of another tax privilege: a property tax deferral program, for example, or a deep circuit breaker along the lines that the California legislature nearly passed in 1977. The alternative could take the form of direct spending on housing or income support. It might have to be a combination of many different state and federal policies. The crucial point is simply that property tax limitation is here to stay until there is a substitute way to provide its beneficiaries with long-term security of income and housing.

These lessons, of course, are only possibilities. The history of the tax revolt does not leave us with unconditional predictions. But it does leave us with hope. If the history of the tax revolt teaches anything, it is that Americans are not doomed to repeat the past. Nor are we fated by our traditions to cut taxes until we have drowned our government in a bathtub. The great American tax revolt and the American welfare state emerged from the same social impulse: the demand for social protection from the uncertainties and risks of market society. Everything depends, as George Wiley would have said, on how that impulse is shaped and directed.

Reference Matter

APPENDIX 1
HOW GREAT WAS THE TAX PRIVILEGE
OF FRACTIONAL ASSESSMENT?

THIS BOOK ARGUES that taxpayers rebelled because tax reforms threatened the traditional tax privileges that had provided them with a kind of informal social protection. But were these tax privileges really very important? How did their magnitude compare, for example, to direct government spending on housing and social insurance? To answer this question, I estimated the total value of fractional assessment to residential property owners at three points in time between the end of the Great Depression and the eve of the tax revolt. I would have preferred to have annual estimates, or even one a decade, but comprehensive data on assessed valuations were scarce before the 1960s. I settled for three years at roughly even intervals: 1940, 1956, and 1971.

I calculated the value of fractional assessment on a revenue loss basis—that is, as the total tax revenue lost to local governments because of this tax privilege. Recall from Chapter 1 that a tax privilege is, by definition, a deviation from the normal rules of taxation—in this case, a deviation from the rules of property taxation. The normal rule I take as the starting point for this calculation is the ideal of *ad valorem* property taxation at 100 percent of market value. Some people criticize the view that fractional assessment constituted a subsidy on the grounds that 100 percent is an arbitrary baseline. Local governments can and do compensate for low assessments by raising the tax rate; a 5 percent tax on 100 percent of value is the same as a 10 percent tax on 50 percent of value.[1] The justification for nevertheless taking the ideal of 100 percent valuation as the baseline for calculating the value of fractional assessment is threefold. First, this ideal was the rule that was enshrined in most state constitutions during this period. It was the norm from which most assessors knew they were deviating, and it was the norm to which taxpayers who benefited from fractional assessment knew that they were not being held. Second, it was an ideal that was approximated in the taxation of at least some property. People who benefited from fractional assessment enjoyed a tax privilege not only in comparison to the theoretical ideal of 100 percent valuation but also in comparison to unlucky taxpayers who were in fact taxed at the legal norm. Third, this ideal was, in fact, politically effective. The real or perceived threat of taxation at 100 percent of market value motivated many of the tax rebels, as Chapter 3 showed.

In theory, local governments should have calculated homeowners' total tax liability t as the average tax rate r times the total market value v of taxable homes:

$$t=r^*v \qquad \text{(Equation 1)}$$

In practice, local assessors underestimated the market value of taxable homes, so that tax was levied on total assessed value a that was some fraction of the total market value. We may call that fraction a/v the assessment ratio. The formula in practice was therefore:

$$t=r^*(a/v)^*v=r^*a \qquad \text{(Equation 2)}$$

The difference between these two equations—the ideal tax liability and the actual tax liability—represents the gross value of the tax privilege associated with the practice of fractional assessment. We may define the value of fractional assessment, f, as the difference between equation 1 and equation 2, or the additional property tax that homeowners would have paid if the assessment ratio had been 100 percent. By subtracting equation 2 from equation 1 and rearranging terms, we get:

$$f=r^*(v-a) \qquad \text{(Equation 3)}$$

This is a simple equation, and it is easy to calculate the total value of f with available estimates of the average tax rate, the total value of property, and the total assessed value of property. The available data did not permit me to limit this calculation to owner-occupied homes, so I conducted the calculation for all non-farm residential real property; more than half of the lost taxes can be attributed safely to the fractional assessment of owner-occupied homes. Because the results might seem surprising, Table A1.1 reports the steps of the calculation in detail for anyone who wishes to follow along. The estimated value of fractional assessment was approximately $1.6 billion in 1940, making it easily greater than the total benefits provided by any social spending program and an order of magnitude greater than any government housing subsidy. By 1971, the taxes lost to fractional assessment had grown to $39 billion, but this implicit subsidy had been eclipsed by federal social spending on a few major programs that grew even faster—most notably Social Security ($43.1 billion). Still, on the verge of the tax revolt, the value of fractional assessment was greater than any direct or indirect government housing subsidy, including the home mortgage interest deduction ($3.5 billion) and direct federal spending on housing assistance ($868 million).[2]

These estimates are analogous to the most common estimates of income tax expenditures that provide the basis for recent scholarship on the hidden welfare state.[3] Critics of the tax expenditure concept, however, have argued that simple revenue loss accounting overstates the actual benefit that people receive from any particular tax privilege. If this particular tax expenditure were not available, the argument goes, people might qualify for different tax breaks or adjust their behavior in other ways that would permit them to secure the same benefit. The net value of fractional assessment was probably considerably less than f, for example, because of the federal income tax deduction for state and local taxes. If homeowners had suddenly found their local property tax bills increased by f, many of them would have simply deducted their share of f from the income recorded on their federal income tax returns. Some fraction of the increased local tax would therefore have been refunded to them by the federal government.

There are two answers to this objection. One is that it does not distinguish a tax privilege like fractional assessment from any other social program. As Christopher Howard points out, direct spending programs may be interdependent in much the same way: for example, "cuts in disability insurance may prompt more claims for Supplemental Security Income [SSI]."[4]

The second answer is that even an overly conservative estimate would show fractional assessment to be one of the most important subsidies in the postwar era. It is instructive to calculate a lower-bound estimate of the net value of fractional assessment, on the assumption that federal income tax deductions would take up much of the slack if fractional assessment were suddenly eliminated. I calculated the net tax privilege due to fractional assessment under two extreme assumptions: that 100 percent of homeowners would itemize deductions on their federal income tax returns and that the deduction for the increased property taxes would be valued at the highest marginal income tax rate. These assumptions deliberately overstate the federal income tax deduction for local

Table A1.1. Calculating the Benefit Provided to Taxpayers by the Fractional Assessment of Residential Nonfarm Property, in Current $ Millions

Variable	Description	1940	1956	1971
t_{total}	Property tax revenue of local governments[1]	4,204	12,385	36,726
a_{net}	Assessed value of locally taxable property (excludes exempt property)[2]	108,823	272,200	694,600
$r = t_{total} \div a_{net}$	Average tax rate	3.9%	4.5%	5.3%
$v_{structures}$	Value of private nonfarm residential structures (excluding land)[3]	83,200	330,000	809,500
m	Multiplier for total value of land and structures[4]	1.22	1.31	1.43
$v_{residential} = v_{structures} * m$	Value of private nonfarm residential property (including land and structures)	101,504	432,300	1,157,585
a_{gross}	Gross assessed value of locally assessed real property (includes exempt property)[5]	112,088	280,300	717,800
s	Share of gross assessed value in nonfarm residential real property[6]	54.1%	54.1%	58.4%
$a_{residential} = s * a_{gross}$	Assessed value of locally assessed nonfarm residential real property	60,639	151,642	419,195
$v_{residential} - a_{residential}$	Unassessed value of locally assessed nonfarm residential real property	40,865	280,658	738,390
$f = r * (v_{res} - a_{res})$	Estimated value of fractional assessment, or total property taxes lost to fractional assessment of homes	1,579	12,770	39,041
d	Amount of this extra tax that would be rebated by federal government under deduction for state and local taxes, assuming 100% claim deduction at top marginal income tax rate	1,280	11,621	27,817
$f\text{-}d$	Lower bound: estimated benefit of fractional assessment, net of federal deduction	298	1,149	11,224

See endnotes for sources.

property taxes. They therefore understate the net value of fractional assessment.[5] Even the lower bound estimate of $6.2 billion in 1971 suggests that the value of fractional assessment was greater than all direct and indirect federal housing subsidies combined.

Several cautions are in order about the estimates provided here.

First, this is an exercise in accounting, not causal modeling. I have not explicitly considered what would actually happen to other parameters of the equations (r and v) if a had been suddenly set equal to 1. Economic theory suggests that if fractional assessment had been abolished outright, property values (v) would have fallen as housing came to be seen as a less advantageous investment. Many governments might have responded by lowering tax rates (r). And, of course, the argument of this book implies that tax revolts would have interrupted long before these other adjustments took place. But all of these caveats merely underscore the main point of the accounting exercise: fractional assessment was a highly valued subsidy.

Second, the data are approximate. I have relied on the best data available from the Bureau of the Census and the Bureau of Economic Analysis, but even under the best conditions, true market value (v) is not directly observable. Analysts have generally tried to reconstruct total real property values from aggregate data supplied by the construction industry, under various assumptions about depreciation and the useful lives of different types of property. The results may be sensitive to even small changes in these assumptions. For this appendix I conservatively relied on old estimates of the net capital stock that assumed straightline depreciation. The most recent revisions to the National Income and Product Accounts employ more realistic assumptions that imply substantially greater estimates of the value of housing stock; if these estimates are correct, then it would appear that fractional assessment was more costly even than I have represented it here—indeed, that it was the most generous social program of the postwar era, outstripping even Social Security.[6] Data on assessed values are probably more reliable, but the 1940 data in particular should be taken with a grain of salt. Note also that the figures here probably understate the rate of growth in the importance of fractional assessment to homeowners insofar as they include all nonfarm residential property, not just owner-occupied homes, which benefited disproportionately from fractional assessment.

Third, these estimates of the total value of the tax privilege of fractional assessment do not distinguish between formal and informal tax privileges. Many states formalized fractional assessment over the time period considered here by amending their constitutions expressly to permit the taxation of owner-occupied homes at a smaller fraction of their true value than other property. This table treats such classification laws as tax privileges when evaluated against the baseline of uniform assessment at 100 percent of market value.

It would be edifying to repeat this exercise with contemporary data. Unfortunately, it is not possible. The Census Bureau has not collected or published data on assessed property values since the 1980s because of cuts in the budget that may themselves have resulted indirectly from the tax revolt.

APPENDIX 2
WAS PROPOSITION 13 REALLY A TURNING POINT?

THIS APPENDIX REPORTS a statistical analysis designed to test the argument advanced in Chapter 5 that Proposition 13 was a turning point in the tax revolt. The argument entails two claims. First, it implies that Proposition 13 was avoidable, in the specific sense that voter demand for property tax limitation could have been met with another, more liberal form of property tax relief, such as a circuit breaker or classification law. Second, it implies that Proposition 13, once it passed, changed the dynamics of the property tax revolt such that the odds of property tax limitation in other states were increased.

I tested these claims with an event history analysis that measured how the rate of passage of property tax limitation laws depended on the prior passage of other state laws—while controlling for other variables that might affect the passage of tax limits, such as the property tax rate, the homeownership rate, the availability of the ballot initiative, and so forth.[1] The dependent variable in this analysis was the passage of a state law or constitutional amendment to limit the annual increase in assessed property values or in the aggregate local property tax levy. I used a logit specification with the state-year as the unit of analysis, so the rate can be understood as the annual probability of passing a property tax limit in a given state. Table A2.1 reports the regression results, along with robust standard errors that adjust for the clustering of observations at the state level. For ease of interpretation, I also translated the logit coefficients into the predicted change in the annual probability of passing a tax limit for an average state in 1978, assuming a one-unit change in the associated independent variable. An "average" state was one with continuous variables set at their mean values and dichotomous variables set at their modal values. (For

Table A2.1. How Did Structural Characteristics of States Affect the Annual Probability of Passing Tax and Expenditure Limitations (TELs), 1964–1989?

Results from Discrete-Time Event History Analyses

Variable	Property tax limit		State budget limit		Descriptive statistics	
	Logit (SE)	Change in annual probability	Logit (SE)	Change in annual probability	1978 Mean	1978 SD
Home ownership rate[1]	−0.02		0.09			
(% all single-family homes)	(0.07)	−0.08%	(0.09)	+4%	66.14	5.48
African Americans[2]	0.04		0.02			
(% population)	(0.04)	+4%	(0.05)	+2%	8.99	9.12
Urban residents[3]	0.04		0.05			
(% population)	(0.02)*	+5%	(0.03)	+6%	66.69	14.34
Total state personal income[4]	−0.73		−0.09			
(constant 1983 $1,000s per capita)	(0.30)**	−7%	(0.22)	−1%	11.82	1.92
Union members[5]	0.12		0.06			
(% labor force)	(0.06)**	+12%	(0.05)	+4%	21.61	7.92
Education spending[6]	0.06		−0.07			
(% state personal income)	(0.37)	+0.04%	(0.41)	−0.5%	6.67	0.98
Hostility to property tax[7]	0.008		—	—		
(% calling it "the worst tax")	(0.05)	+0.05%			33.62	8.19
Property tax burden[8]	0.12		—	—		
(% state personal income)	(0.48)	+2%			3.63	1.67
Total tax burden	—	—	0.15			
(% state personal income)			(0.12)	+2%	10.49	1.85
State has ballot initiative?[9]	0.81		0.75			
(1=yes)	(0.82)	+5%	(0.64)	+4%	0.5	0.51
Republican legislature?	−1.44		−1.92			
(1—majority, both houses)	(1.28)	−7%	(1.36)	−6%	0.1	0.30
Prior classification law?[10]	−1.83		—	—		
(1=yes)	(0.92)**	−7%			0.16	0.37
Prior circuit breaker?[11]	−0.57		—	—		
(1=yes)	(0.68)	−6%			0.6	0.49
Midwest (1=yes)	1.18		−0.52			
	(1.21)	+20%	(1.22)	−5%	0.24	0.43
South (1=yes)	−0.27		0.76			
	(1.65)	−2%	(1.38)	+4%	0.32	0.47
West (1=yes)	0.50		1.58			
	(1.41)	+9%	(1.29)	+8%	0.26	0.44
After Proposition 13?	3.91		3.21			
(1=yes)	(0.75)***	+9%	(1.31)**	+7%	1	0
Constant term	−2.99		−17.97			
	(5.88)	9%	(7.41)**	8%		
N (state-years)	542		1,078			
Wald Chi-squared (d.f.)	73.7		74.1			
	(16)***		(13)***			
McFadden's pseudo-R²	0.23		0.24			

* $p<.10$
** $p<.05$
*** $p<.001$
See endnotes for sources.

continuous variables, I standardized the unit in this calculation to equal one standard deviation.)

In order to test the first claim—that another policy could have substituted for tax limitation—I included a dichotomous variable indicating whether a state had previously passed a circuit breaker and another dichotomous variable indicating whether a state had previously passed a classification law. The coefficient of a prior classification law was strong, negative, and significant at the $p<.05$ level in a two-tailed test. This finding supports the view that another policy could have substituted for tax limitation. The coefficient of a prior circuit-breaker law was neither especially strong nor statistically significant, although it was also negative.

In order to test the second claim—that Proposition 13 changed the dynamics of the tax revolt—I included a dichotomous variable equal to one for the years 1978 and later, in order to capture the effect of Proposition 13. The coefficient of this variable was positive, substantively great, and statistically significant. Because this variable could conceivably proxy for any unmeasured variable that increased over time, I tested alternative versions of the model with different years as the turning point. The model that specified 1978 as the turning point was by far the best fit to the data (see Table A2.2).

These are two of the strongest associations in the data. An average state had a 9 percent probability of passing a property tax limit in 1978. The model estimates that if the same state had already passed a classification law, then its annual probability of passing a property tax limit would have been only 2 percent. Prior to the passage of Proposition 13, the same state would have had a probability very close to zero.

Two other findings deserve brief discussion. First, all else being equal, lower-income states within a given region were more likely to pass property tax limitations. This finding is consistent with the book's argument that the property tax revolt was a movement for economic security rather than a revolt of the affluent.

Second, union density was positively associated with the passage of property tax limits. Most labor unions did not favor tax limitation, so the coefficient for union density probably represents an indirect effect. Labor unions were strong proponents of increased local public spending in the 1960s and 1970s. States where spending had risen rapidly were under considerable pressure to increase the elasticity of the local property tax by modernizing assessment.

Chapter 5 also presented qualitative and historical evidence that Proposition 13 inspired state legislators to enact limitations on *state* budgets. These

Table A2.2. Was 1978 Really the Turning Point? Alternative Specifications of the Turning Point in the Event History Models Reported in Table A2.1

Year specified as turning point	Property tax limitation		State budget limit	
	Logit coefficient of turning point variable	t-statistic	Logit coefficient of turning point variable	t-statistic
1974	0.95	0.81	...	...
1975	2.09	2.35	...	...
1976	2.77	3.56	...	...
1977	2.67	4.43	3.72	2.56
1978	3.91	5.23	3.21	2.46
1979	2.40	2.86	0.84	1.12
1980	2.01	2.33	0.06	0.09
1981	0.69	0.92	−1.39	−1.58
1982	−0.21	−0.28	−1.56	−1.80
1983	−0.39	−0.44	−1.50	−1.63
1984	−0.67	−0.65	−1.20	−1.28
1985	−0.26	−0.23	−0.85	−0.89
1986	−0.93	−0.68	−2.11	−1.70
1987	−0.42	−0.30	...	...

See endnotes for sources.

state tax and expenditure limitations (TELs) were not a direct response to the property tax revolt. They did not generally limit the growth of property taxes, except as an ancillary matter; their main purpose was to limit the growth of total state revenues or total state expenditures.

Did Proposition 13 increase the rate at which states passed such TELs? The second model reported in Table A2.1 shows that the answer is yes. It reports the results from a discrete-time event history analysis of potentially binding limitations on the growth of state budgets. The key finding from this model is that the rate of passage was dramatically increased after 1978. There were no other reliable predictors in the model, and the post-1978 increase in the rate of passage of state TELs cannot be explained away by any of the structural trends measured in this model—from the rising affluence of the electorate to changing party control of state government. A test of alternative turning points, reported in Table A2.2, suggests that a plausible case could also be made for 1977. But only one state passed a state-level TEL in 1977 (Colorado), while five states did so in 1978 (Arizona, Hawaii, Michigan, Tennessee, and Texas). The results also make clear that no other year is a plausible candidate, and the qualitative case studies in Chapter 5 leave little doubt that Proposition 13 accelerated the passage of state TELs.

APPENDIX 3
HOW DID TAX LIMITATION POLICIES AFFECT
THE POLITICS OF TAXATION?

THIS APPENDIX PRESENTS the results from statistical models that examine how state-level tax and expenditure limitation laws affect public trust in government and the political parties' positions on tax cuts. I focus on the Republican Party. I include any potentially binding limitation on the growth of state or local government revenues or expenditures. These are "difference-in-differences" models that measure the difference that tax limitations make by comparing before and after measures of the difference between states with and without such limitations.

The first set of analyses reported in this appendix concerns the voting behavior of Congress, as measured by the first (economic) dimension of Poole and Rosenthal's DW-NOMINATE score. Higher scores indicate greater hostility toward government intervention in the economy. Table A3.1 reports the results from separate linear regressions estimating the effect of tax and expenditure limitations on the DW-NOMINATE score of congresspersons elected from a given state. I assigned each congressperson a single DW-NOMINATE score representing the score for his or her first term in Congress. All models included fixed effects for state and year, in addition to a dummy variable for tax and expenditure limitations. All models were significantly different from the null model at $p<.01$. The table reports robust standard errors adjusted for clustering at the state level. The table covers the period 1965–2001.

I next report the results from two regression analyses using time-series panel data on respondents to the American National Election Study. The models reported in Table A3.2 tested whether residence in a state with a tax limitation law affects a respondent's probability of stating that the government wastes

Table A3.1. Did State TELs Shift Congress to the Right on Tax Questions? Linear Regressions of Ideology over Samples of First-Term Congress Members, 1965–2001

Regression sample		Coefficient of tax limit dummy variableon state)	Robust standard error (clustered	N
(1)	All House members	.05	.03*	1,653
(2)	House Democrats only	.008	.03	910
(3)	House Republicans only	.008	.02	741
(4)	All Senators	.10	.07[†]	339
(5)	Senate Democrats only	−.008	.06	183
(6)	Senate Republicans only	.11	.08[†]	154

Author's calculations. See text and endnotes for sources. Positive coefficients indicate greater conservatism on a left-right scale of economic ideology that runs from −1.3 to 1.3.

All regressions include fixed effects for state and year.

[†] $p<.10$, one-tailed.

[*] $p<.05$, one-tailed.

"a lot" of taxpayer money. I included all years from 1964 to 2000. I included a variety of controls for respondent characteristics, dummy variables for years, and fixed effects for each state. (Because a measure of respondent's self-identification as conservative was not available for the whole period, I relied instead on a "feeling thermometer" measure that asked respondents to rate their warmth of feeling toward conservatives on a scale from 0 to 100, with 50 indicating neutrality.) I estimated both logit and linear probability models. I report coefficients from a linear probability model because they are more easily interpretable, but the qualitative pattern of results in the logit model was identical.

I tested for endogeneity by reestimating the model reported in the last column of Table A3.2 with an additional dummy variable indicating that a tax limitation law would be passed in the current or following year. If the apparent effect of tax limitation on public perceptions of waste simply reflected prior beliefs of respondents in these states, then the coefficient of this variable should have been positive. It was negative, suggesting that tax limitation was indeed exogenous.

I also tested whether the apparent effect of tax limitation on the opinions of Republican activists was an artifact of serially autocorrelated errors, using two different procedures both recommended by Marianne Bertrand, Esther Duflo, and Sendhil Mullainathan. First, I estimated the model with robust standard errors clustered at the state level. This procedure adjusts the standard errors for autocorrelation, without arbitrarily imposing a functional form (such as a one-year lag) on the autocorrelation structure. These are the results reported in

Table A3.2. Do TELs Undermine Trust in Government? Linear Models of the Probability That a Respondent Would Say Government Wastes "a Lot" of Money, 1964–2000

	All respondents		Republican base		Democratic base	
	Coeff.	S.E.	Coeff.	S.E.	Coeff.	S.E.
Tax Limit? (1=yes)	−.0006	.01	.09	.04*	−.05	.04
Black? (1=yes)	−.06	.02**	−.03	.17	−.05	.07
Latino? (1=yes)	−.09	.02**	−.24	.10*	−.008	.04
Female? (1=yes)	−.04	.007**	.009	.02	−.08	.03*
Income (quintile 1 to 5)	.009	.003**	.01	.009	−.02	.01†
Conservative thermometer (How "warmly" R feels toward conservatives, on a scale from 0 to 97)	.002	.0002**	.003	.0008**	−.00002	.0007
(Year dummies and state fixed effects omitted from table.)						
N	21,953		1,720		2,092	

Author's calculations. See text and endnotes for sources. Reported standard errors are robust standard errors that adjust for clustering of observations at the state level.

† $p<.10$.

* $p<.05$.

** $p<.01$.

Table A3.1. Second, I also reestimated the model according to the two-step procedure recommended by Bertrand and her co-authors. In step one, I purged the data of time-series information by regressing the dependent variable on year dummies, state fixed effects, and the individual-level covariates. In step two, I regressed the residuals from this equation on the presence of a tax limitation in the treatment group only.[1] The coefficient of tax limitation in this linear probability model remained positive, comparable in magnitude to the result reported in Table A3.1, and statistically significant at $p<.05$ in a one-tailed test ($p<.07$ in a two-tailed test).

ARCHIVAL SOURCES AND THEIR ABBREVIATIONS

Robert Barrett Papers, California State Library, Sacramento.

Campaign Literature Files, California State Library, Sacramento.

Margaret Cleeff Carlson Papers (MCCP), Schlesinger Library, Radcliffe College, Cambridge, Massachusetts.

Fremskridtspartiets Arbejdsarkiv, 1972–1989 (FRPA). Privatarkiv series number 11008. Rigsarkivet (Denmark).

Paul Gann Archive, California State Library, Sacramento.

Richard H. Headlee Papers, 1976–1992, Bentley Historical Library, University of Michigan, Ann Arbor.

William G. Milliken Papers, 1969–1982, Executive Office, Communications Division, RG 88-269, State Archives of Michigan, Lansing.

Movement for Economic Justice (MEJ) Records, 1972–1980. Mss 766. Wisconsin State Historical Society (WSHS), Madison.

New York State Assembly Speaker's Office Subject Files, 1977–1986. Series L0017-86 and series L0017-87. New York State Archives (NYSA), Albany.

New York State Temporary State Commission on the Real Property Tax. Meeting, hearing and research files, 1978–1987. Series 15604-89. New York State Archives (NYSA), Albany.

Skattedepartementet. Kommissionen og Udvalg. Skattelovskommissionen af 1937 (SL1937). Series 0039/199/50. Rigsarkivet (Denmark).

George A. Wiley Papers, 1949–1975. Mss 324, Wisconsin State Historical Society (WSHS), Madison.

NOTES

Acknowledgments

1. Joseph A. Schumpeter, "The Crisis of the Tax State," in *Joseph A. Schumpeter: The Economics and Sociology of Capitalism*, ed. Richard Swedberg (Princeton: Princeton University Press, 1991), 101.

Chapter 1

1. Edmund L. Andrews, "Bush Remark Touches Off New Debate on Income Tax," *New York Times*, August 11, 2004; see also "The Republicans' First Presidential Candidates Debate," *New York Times*, May 3, 2007, http://www.nytimes.com/2007/05/03/us/politics/04transcript.html.

2. Andrea Louise Campbell, "What Americans Think of Taxes" (paper presented at "The Thunder of History: Taxation in Comparative and Historical Perspective," conference held at Northwestern University, Chicago, Illinois, May 3–5, 2007); Susan B. Hansen, *The Politics of Taxation: Revenue without Representation* (New York: Praeger, 1983).

3. Jacob S. Hacker and Paul Pierson, *Off Center: The Republican Revolution and the Erosion of American Democracy* (New Haven: Yale University Press, 2005), 30. Other scholars who have studied the anti-tax wing of the Republican Party also trace its rise to the 1970s. See Sheldon Pollack, *Refinancing America: The Republican Antitax Agenda* (Albany: State University of New York Press, 2003), 57; Michael Graetz and Ian Shapiro, *Death by a Thousand Cuts: The Fight over Taxing Inherited Wealth* (Princeton: Princeton University Press, 2005), 4.

4. There is no firm consensus on the definition of social movements, but this one borrows heavily from various writings of Charles Tilly and Sidney Tarrow. See Doug McAdam, Sidney Tarrow, and Charles Tilly, *Dynamics of Contention* (New York:

Cambridge University Press, 2001), 5–7; Sidney Tarrow, *Power in Movement: Social Movements and Contentious Politics* (New York: Cambridge University Press, 1998), 10; Charles Tilly, "From Interactions to Outcomes in Social Movements," in *How Social Movements Matter*, ed. Marco Giugni et al. (Minneapolis: University of Minnesota Press, 1999).

5. Of course, as Tilly has pointed out, movements develop their own conventional forms of behavior, such as the picket line, the protest march, and so on. For this reason, he now defines the social movement positively in terms of the conventions it embraces rather than negatively in terms of those it rejects: a movement consists of a campaign involving repeated displays of "worthiness, unity, numbers and commitment" and invoking a specific behavioral repertoire consisting of the "creation of special-purpose associations and coalitions, public meetings, solemn processions, vigils, rallies, demonstrations, petition drives, statements to and in public media, and pamphleteering." Charles Tilly, *Social Movements, 1768–2004* (Boulder: Paradigm Publishers, 2004), 3–4. Tilly retains a conceptual distinction between social movements on the one hand and electoral campaigns and other formal political processes on the other, but he and his collaborators now prefer to describe movements as "transgressive" rather than "unconventional": see McAdam, Tarrow, and Tilly, *Dynamics of Contention*, 7. The tax revolt, it will become clear, fits this positive definition, too.

6. This composite portrait almost certainly overstates the degree to which the movement was affluent and white because it is based on surveys of people who voted for tax limitations—the most conservative of the many policy remedies entertained by activists, and the most favorable to affluent, white homeowners. See Paul Courant, Edward Gramlich, and Daniel Rubinfeld, "Why Voters Support Tax Limitation Amendments: The Michigan Case," *National Tax Journal* 33, no. 1 (1980); Helen F. Ladd and Julie Boatwright Wilson, "Who Supports Tax Limitations: Evidence from Massachusetts' Proposition 2½," *Journal of Policy Analysis and Management* 2, no. 2 (1983); David O. Sears and Jack Citrin, *Tax Revolt: Something for Nothing in California* (Cambridge, Mass.: Harvard University Press, 1985). On Rubino, see Clarence Y. H. Lo, *Small Property Versus Big Government: Social Origins of the Property Tax Revolt* (Berkeley and Los Angeles: University of California Press, 1990), 71. On Wiley, see Nick Kotz and Mary Lynn Kotz, *A Passion for Equality: George Wiley and the Movement* (New York: W. W. Norton & Co., 1977). On Tisch, see Nila Aamoth, "Jousting Tax Windmills: Ordinary Citizens Are Carrying Banners for Lower Taxes," *Grand Rapids Photo Reporter*, June 20, 1978.

7. On Anderson and Sampson, see, respectively, Nathan Cobb, "Some People Put Drama in Their Lives by Going to Horror Movies. I Work in Massachusetts Politics," *Boston Sunday Globe*, January 14, 1990; Bert De Leeuw to Morgan Yamanaka, April

22, 1974, Movement for Economic Justice (MEJ) Records, 1972–1980 (MS 766), box 8, folder 11, Wisconsin State Historical Society (WSHS).

8. Robin L. Einhorn, *American Taxation, American Slavery* (Chicago: University of Chicago Press, 2006), 65–66.

9. See, e.g., Milton Friedman, "The Message from California," *Newsweek*, June 19, 1978.

10. The best evidence comes from surveys of people who voted for property tax limitation referenda: they were not taxed more heavily than people who did not. See Richard Attiyeh and Robert F. Engle, "Testing Some Propositions About Proposition 13," *National Tax Journal* 32 (1979); Ladd and Wilson, "Who Supports Tax Limitations"; Robert M. Stein, Keith E. Hamm, and Patricia K. Freeman, "An Analysis of Support for Tax Limitation Referenda," *Public Choice* 40, no. 2 (1983). According to the U.S. Advisory Commission on Intergovernmental Relations (ACIR), an average family in 1975 spent 4 percent of its income on local property taxes, compared to 6 percent on Social Security payroll taxes and almost 10 percent on federal personal income tax—neither of which saw a comparable protest movement. See ACIR, *Significant Features of Fiscal Federalism*, 1976 ed., vol. 1 (Washington, D.C.: ACIR, 1976), 41.

11. See, e.g., James O'Connor, *The Fiscal Crisis of the State* (New York: St. Martin's Press, 1973), 228; Ronald Smothers, "Welfare Activist Plans New Group: Will Leave Rights Post for Economic Justice Drive," *New York Times*, November 17, 1972.

12. In practice, every tax system treats different people differently, and in some cases it may be hard to identify which set of rules is "normal" and which is the exception to the norm. But tax authorities often draw explicit distinctions between the normal rules and exceptions, because part of the political value of tax privileges comes from taxpayers' grateful recognition that they benefit from special treatment.

13. Michael Kwass, *Privilege and the Politics of Taxation in Eighteenth-Century France: Liberté, Égalité, Fiscalité* (New York: Cambridge University Press, 2000), 24, 30.

14. See United States Office of Management and Budget, "Analytical Perspectives, Budget of the United States Government, Fiscal Year 2007" (U.S. Government Printing Office, 2006), 285–328.

15. David Cay Johnston, *Perfectly Legal: The Covert Campaign to Rig Our Tax System to Benefit the Super-Rich—and Cheat Everybody Else* (New York: Portfolio, 2003), 216.

16. ACIR, *The Role of the States in Strengthening the Property Tax*, vol. 1 (Washington, D.C.: ACIR, 1963), 43. Technically, the political efficacy of this informal tax privilege came from the combination of (1) the selective application of fractional assessment to owner-occupied homes and (2) the habit of copying assessment rolls from year to year without reappraisal, so that low initial assessments changed more slowly than market values. At the cost of imprecision, I will call this complex "fractional assessment."

17. Einhorn, *American Taxation*, 141.

18. Glenn W. Fisher and Robert P. Fairbanks, "The Politics of Property Taxation," *Administrative Science Quarterly* 12, no. 1 (1967); David Lowery, "Performance in Assessment Administration: Property Rights Analysis Applied to the Administration of the Property Tax" (Michigan State University, 1981), 65; Diane B. Paul, *The Politics of the Property Tax* (Lexington, Mass.: Lexington Books, 1975).

19. Francis G. Castles, "The Really Big Trade-Off: Home Ownership and the Welfare State in the New World and the Old," *Acta Politica* 33, no. 1 (1998); Dalton Conley and Brian Gifford, "Home Ownership, Social Insurance, and the Welfare State," *Sociological Forum* 21, no. 1 (2006): 58.

20. Christopher Howard, *The Hidden Welfare State: Tax Expenditures and Social Policy in the United States* (Princeton: Princeton University Press, 1997); Kenneth T. Jackson, *Crabgrass Frontier: The Suburbanization of the United States* (New York: Oxford University Press, 1985).

21. Howard, *Hidden Welfare State*, 3, 26.

22. Jacob S. Hacker, *The Divided Welfare State: The Battle over Public and Private Social Benefits in the United States* (New York: Cambridge University Press, 2002); Christopher Howard, *The Welfare State Nobody Knows: Debunking Myths About U.S. Social Policy* (Princeton: Princeton University Press, 2006).

23. The details of the calculation are in Appendix 1.

24. This definition is generalized from a definition of social insurance proposed by Hacker, *Divided Welfare State*, 32. I also take inspiration from Ann Shola Orloff's argument that students of social policy should broaden their attention from "the welfare state," narrowly defined as a set of formal social insurance programs, to the broader category of "systems of social provision and regulation": Ann Shola Orloff, "Social Provision and Regulation: Theories of States, Social Policies, and Modernity," in *Remaking Modernity: Politics, History, and Sociology*, ed. Julia Adams, Elisabeth S. Clemens, and Ann Shola Orloff (Durham: Duke University Press, 2005), 190–224.

25. The following paragraphs draw heavily on the works of Paul Pierson, including *Dismantling the Welfare State? Reagan, Thatcher, and the Politics of Retrenchment* (New York: Cambridge University Press, 1994); *Politics in Time: History, Institutions, and Social Analysis* (Princeton: Princeton University Press, 2005); and "When Effect Becomes Cause: Policy Feedback and Political Change," *World Politics* 45, no. 4 (1993).

26. This imbalance may be exacerbated by a widespread tendency to overvalue existing benefits relative to prospective rewards: psychologists suggest that most of us would rather have a bird in the hand than an even chance at bagging two in the bush, even though the two choices are exactly the same from the point of view of a cost-benefit

analysis. See Eldar Shafir and Robyn A. LeBoeuf, "Rationality," *Annual Review of Psychology* 53 (2002).

27. Pierson, *Dismantling*, 17–19.

28. Pierson, "When Effect Becomes Cause."

29. Richard D. Pomp, "What Is Happening to the Property Tax?" *Journal of Real Estate Taxation* 7, no. 4 (1980); ACIR, *The Property Tax in a Changing Environment: Selected State Studies* (Washington, D.C.: ACIR, 1974). Sociologists will recognize that this definition of modern administration is heavily indebted to Max Weber's classic definition of bureaucracy. Max Weber, *Economy and Society: An Outline of Interpretive Sociology*, vol. 2 (Berkeley: University of California, 1978), 956–58.

30. Quoted in Richard A. Eribes and John S. Hall, "Revolt of the Affluent: Fiscal Controls in Three States," *Public Administration Review* 41, special issue (1981): 111.

31. Quoted in Lester A. Sobel, *The Great American Tax Revolt* (New York: Facts on File, 1979), 125.

32. The National Taxpayers Union campaigned for a balanced budget amendment to the federal constitution: see Robert Dreyfuss, "Grover Norquist: 'Field Marshal' of the Bush Plan," *The Nation*, May 14, 2001; Robert Kuttner, *The Revolt of the Haves: Tax Rebellions and Hard Times* (New York: Simon and Schuster, 1980), 280–82.

33. James Ring Adams, *Secrets of the Tax Revolt* (San Diego: Harcourt Brace Jovanovich, 1984); Marjorie Kornhauser, "Legitimacy and the Right of Revolution: The Role of Tax Protests and Anti-Tax Rhetoric in America," *Buffalo Law Review* 50, no. 3 (2002); Julian E. Zelizer, "The Uneasy Relationship: Democracy, Taxation, and State-Building since the New Deal," in *The Democratic Experiment: New Directions in American Political History*, ed. Meg Jacobs, William J. Novak, and Julian E. Zelizer (Princeton: Princeton University Press, 2003).

34. Nor were white working-class voters the main driving force in welfare backlash more generally. Ellen Reese has documented that low-wage employers mobilized against welfare before and during the Johnson presidency, apparently motivated less by resentment of taxes than by the desire to suppress the reservation wage of unskilled labor. See Ellen Reese, *Backlash against Welfare Mothers: Past and Present* (Berkeley and Los Angeles: University of California Press, 2005).

35. Jonathan Kozol, *Savage Inequalities: Children in America's Schools* (New York: HarperCollins, 1991), 220.

36. David N. Figlio, "Did the 'Tax Revolt' Reduce School Performance?" *Journal of Public Economics* 65 (1997); Isaac Martin, "Does School Finance Litigation Cause Taxpayer Revolt? Serrano and Proposition 13," *Law and Society Review* 40, no. 3 (2006); Kirk Stark and Jonathan Zasloff, "Tiebout and Tax Revolts: Did Serrano Really Cause Proposition 13?" *UCLA Law Review* 50, no. 3 (2003). For arguments that

school finance equalization was to blame, see William Blankenau and Mark Skid-more, "The Relationship between Education Finance Reform and Tax and Expenditure Limitations," *Journal of Regional Analysis and Policy* 32, no. 1 (2002); William A. Fischel, *The Homevoter Hypothesis: How Home Values Influence Local Government Taxation, School Finance, and Land-Use Policies* (Cambridge, Mass.: Harvard University Press, 2001).

37. The role of social movements in the origins of modern social policy is a staple of the sociological literature. The most influential argument emphasizes the role of labor movements, sometimes in coalition with small farmers: see Gøsta Esping-Andersen, *Politics against Markets: The Social Democratic Road to Power* (Princeton: Princeton University Press, 1985); Esping-Andersen, *The Three Worlds of Welfare Capitalism* (Princeton: Princeton University Press, 1990). Other scholars have emphasized the role of poor people's movements (Frances Fox Piven and Richard A. Cloward, *Regulating the Poor: The Functions of Public Welfare*, New York: Pantheon Books, 1971) and women's movements (Theda Skocpol, *Protecting Soldiers and Mothers: The Political Origins of Social Policy in the United States*, Cambridge, Mass.: Harvard University Press, 1992). Some of the best recent work suggests that social movements may have had the greatest impact on the formation of early social policy where they were pushing on an open door—because state officials or capitalists also favored social policy. See Edwin Amenta, *When Movements Matter: The Townsend Plan and the Rise of Social Security* (Princeton: Princeton University Press, 2005); Peter A. Swenson, *Capitalists Against Markets: The Making of Labor Markets and Welfare States in the United States and Sweden* (New York: Oxford University Press, 2002).

38. Edwin Amenta and Michael P. Young, "Democratic States and Social Movements: Theoretical Arguments and Hypotheses," *Social Problems* 46, no. 2 (1999); Hanspeter Kriesi et al., *New Social Movements in Western Europe: A Comparative Analysis* (Minneapolis: University of Minnesota Press, 1995); Doug McAdam, "Conceptual Origins, Current Problems, Future Directions," in *Comparative Perspectives on Social Movements: Political Opportunities, Mobilizing Structures, and Cultural Framings*, ed. James McCarthy, Doug McAdam, and Mayer N. Zald (New York: Cambridge University Press, 1996). On the concept of political opportunity structures, see also David S. Meyer, "Protest and Political Opportunities," *Annual Review of Sociology* 30 (2004); Tarrow, *Power in Movement*; Peter K. Eisinger, "The Conditions of Protest Behavior in American Cities," *American Political Science Review* 67, no. 1 (1973): 11–28.

39. Paul D. Almeida, "Opportunity Organizations and Threat-Induced Contention: Protest Waves in Authoritarian Settings," *American Journal of Sociology* 109, no. 2 (2003); Rachel L. Einwohner, "Opportunity, Honor, and Action in the Warsaw Ghetto Uprising of 1943," *American Journal of Sociology* 109, no. 3 (2003); Jack A. Goldstone and Charles Tilly, "Threat (and Opportunity): Popular Action and State

Response in the Dynamics of Contentious Action," in *Silence and Voice in the Study of Contentious Politics*, ed. Ronald R. Aminzade et al. (New York: Cambridge University Press, 2001); Charles Tilly, *From Mobilization to Revolution* (Reading, Mass.: Addison-Wesley, 1978), 133–38. A handful of exceptional studies focus on the mobilizing power of threats other than state repression: see, e.g., Andrea Louise Campbell, *How Policies Make Citizens: Senior Activism and the American Welfare State* (Princeton: Princeton University Press, 2005); Nella Van Dyke and Sarah A. Soule, "Structural Social Change and the Mobilizing Effect of Threat: Explaining Levels of Patriot and Militia Organizing in the United States," *Social Problems* 49, no. 4 (2002).

40. Sven Steinmo, *Taxation and Democracy: Swedish, British, and American Approaches to Financing the Modern State* (New Haven: Yale University Press, 1993); Carolyn Webber and Aaron Wildavsky, *A History of Taxation and Expenditure in the Western World* (New York: Simon and Schuster, 1986).

41. Traffic routing is a good example of a routine government function that invariably imposes unequal burdens, and it is no coincidence that many community-based social movement organizations in the contemporary United States got their start by contesting the placement of stop signs. Gary Delgado, "The Last Stop Sign," *Shelterforce Online* 102 (1998). On the diffusion and routinization of the social movement repertoire in democratic countries more generally, see, e.g., Robert J. Sampson et al., "Civil Society Reconsidered: The Durable Nature and Community Structure of Collective Civic Action," *American Journal of Sociology* 111, no. 3 (2005); Tilly, *Social Movements*. The political opportunity for protest in democratic countries is surely the main reason why social movements are most pervasive in democracies. But an adequate theory would also have to explain why even the best-run democratic states routinely produce people who have grievances against their governments that are not adequately expressed by voting. My argument about the existence and importance of routine policy threats parallels an argument about routine political opportunities made by Amy Binder: internal conflict is the ordinary condition of most organizations in modern society, and so the political opportunity for protest is, in fact, a chronic potential of modernity. See Amy J. Binder, *Contentious Curricula: Afrocentrism and Creationism in American Public Schools* (Princeton: Princeton University Press, 2002), 21.

42. Doug McAdam, *Political Process and the Development of Black Insurgency, 1930–1970* (Chicago: University of Chicago Press, 1982); Meyer, "Protest and Political Opportunities."

43. This is a central thesis of Lo, *Small Property*.

44. Herbert P. Kitschelt, "Political Opportunity Structures and Political Protest: Anti-Nuclear Movements in Four Democracies," *British Journal of Political Science* 16, no. 1 (1986): 67. Edwin Amenta and Michael P. Young argue that the availability of veto

points shapes not only movement outcomes but also challengers' goals: "Because divisions of powers make it easier for political actors to block new policy . . . collective actions will focus more on preventing policy than on initiating it." Amenta and Young, "Democratic States and Social Movements," 157. On veto points in general, see Evelyne Huber, Charles Ragin, and John D. Stephens, "Social Democracy, Christian Democracy, Constitutional Structure, and the Welfare State," *American Journal of Sociology* 99, no. 3 (1993); Ellen M. Immergut, "The Rules of the Game: The Logic of Health Policy-Making in France, Switzerland, and Sweden," in *Structuring Politics: Historical Institutionalism in Comparative Analysis*, ed. Sven Steinmo, Kathleen Thelen, and Frank Longstreth (New York: Cambridge University Press, 1992).

45. See Pierson, *Dismantling*, 33–34.

46. See Hacker, *Divided Welfare State*, 279; Monica Prasad, *The Politics of Free Markets: The Rise of Neoliberal Economic Policies in Britain, France, Germany, and the United States* (Chicago: University of Chicago Press, 2006), 274.

47. See Kriesi et al., *New Social Movements*, 28.

48. *New State Ice Co. v. Liebmann*, 285 U.S. 262, 311 (1932).

49. See Andrea Louise Campbell and Kimberly J. Morgan, "Federalism and the Politics of Old-Age Care in Germany and the United States," *Comparative Political Studies*, no. 38 (2005); Herbert Obinger, Francis G. Castles, and Stephan Leibfried, "Introduction: Federalism and the Welfare State," in *Federalism and the Welfare State: New World and European Experiences*, ed. Herbert Obinger, Stephan Leibfried, and Francis G. Castles (New York: Cambridge University Press, 2005). Article I, Section 9 of the U.S. Constitution forbids the federal government to levy a "direct tax" unless apportioned among the states according to population; and Amendment X implicitly reserves to the states the power to establish their own statutory framework for taxation. The German constitution, by contrast, explicitly reserves property tax revenues to local and state governments (Art. 106 VI GG), but the rates are set within parameters established by a federal statute, the *Grundsteuergesetz* of August 7, 1973 (GrStG).

50. Amenta, *When Movements Matter*; Edwin Amenta, Drew Halfmann, and Michael P. Young, "The Strategies and Contexts of Social Protest: Political Mediation and the Impact of the Townsend Movement in California," *Mobilization* 4, no. 1 (1999); Kenneth T. Andrews, "Social Movements and Policy Implementation: The Mississippi Civil Rights Movement and the War on Poverty, 1965 to 1971," *American Sociological Review* 66, no. 1 (2001); Marco Giugni, "How Social Movements Matter: Past Research, Present Problems, Future Developments," in *How Social Movements Matter*, ed. Marco Giugni et al. (Minneapolis: University of Minnesota Press, 1999).

51. Cf. Amenta and Young, "Democratic States and Social Movements."

52. The crucial difference is that historical social scientists are never in a position to assign cases to treatment or control groups, whether randomly or otherwise. For insightful methodological discussions of comparative historical analysis that influenced my approach, see Edwin Amenta, "Making the Most of a Case Study: Theories of the Welfare State and the American Experience," *International Journal of Comparative Sociology* 22, no. 1–2 (1991); Gary King, Robert O. Keohane, and Sidney Verba, *Designing Social Inquiry* (Princeton: Princeton University Press, 1994); James Mahoney, "Strategies of Causal Assessment in Comparative Historical Analysis," in *Comparative Historical Analysis in the Social Sciences*, ed. James Mahoney and Dietrich Rueschemeyer (New York: Cambridge University Press, 2005).

Chapter 2

1. California State Assembly Interim Committee on Revenue and Taxation, *A Program of Tax Reform for California*, vol. 12, *A Major Tax Study* (Sacramento: California State Legislature, 1965), 28–54.

2. Ibid., 27, 373.

3. Ibid., 58–59.

4. Article I, Section 9 of the U.S. Constitution precludes a federal *ad valorem* property tax by permitting the federal government to levy a "direct tax" only if it is apportioned among the states according to population.

5. California State Assembly Interim Committee on Revenue and Taxation, *Taxation of Property in California*, vol. 5, *A Major Tax Study* (Sacramento: California State Legislature, 1964), 95–144.

6. Paul V. Corusy, "Improved Property Tax Administration: Legislative Opportunities and Probabilities," in *The Property Tax and Its Administration*, ed. Arthur D. Lynn Jr. (Madison: University of Wisconsin Press, 1969); Paul, *Politics of the Property Tax*, 1–12.

7. Fisher and Fairbanks, "Politics of Property Taxation"; Lowery, "Performance in Assessment Administration"; Paul, *Politics of the Property Tax*, 25–39.

8. ACIR, *Role of the States in Strengthening the Property Tax*, vol. 1.

9. See Jens Peter Jensen, *Property Taxation in the United States* (Chicago: University of Chicago Press, 1931).

10. On the lagging trend of assessments, see Mabel Newcomer, "The Decline of the General Property Tax," *National Tax Journal* 6, no. 1 (1952). See also Malcolm MacNiven Davisson, *Property Tax Reduction in California: A Study of Tax Relief to Property Owners in California, 1931–1936* (Berkeley: University of California, Bureau of Public Administration, 1937).

11. David T. Beito, *Taxpayers in Revolt: Tax Resistance During the Great Depression* (Chapel Hill: University of North Carolina Press, 1989), 16–32; Los Angeles Times, "Imperial Tax Strike Urged," *Los Angeles Times*, December 4, 1932; "San Bernardino County Tax Strike Threatened Unless Costs Go Down," *Los Angeles Times*, November 23, 1932; "Strike Threat on Tax Boost," *Los Angeles Times*, August 18, 1933.

12. Los Angeles Times, "Tax Plan Expounded by Author," *Los Angeles Times*, June 8, 1933.

13. James E. Hartley, Steven M. Sheffrin, and J. David Vasche, "Reform During Crisis: The Transformation of California's Fiscal System During the Great Depression," *Journal of Economic History* 56, no. 3 (1996); Los Angeles Times, "San Diego's Tax Doubled," *Los Angeles Times*, June 13, 1935; "Supervisors Warned of Tax Strike Plan," *Los Angeles Times*, August 3, 1937; "Tax Strike Fear Voiced," *Los Angeles Times*, July 17, 1935; "Tax Strike in Long Beach," *Los Angeles Times*, March 5, 1934; "Tax Strike Threat Made," *Los Angeles Times*, March 31, 1939; "Tax Strikes Threatened," *Los Angeles Times*, August 21, 1934; Marvel M. Stockwell, "The Riley-Stewart Act," in *Studies in California State Taxation 1910–1935*, ed. Marvel M. Stockwell (Berkeley: University of California Press, 1939).

14. Jensen, *Property Taxation in the United States*; U.S. Treasury Department Committee on Intergovernmental Fiscal Relations, *Federal, State, and Local Government Fiscal Relations* (Washington, D.C.: Government Printing Office, 1943).

15. Marilyn S. Johnson, *The Second Gold Rush: Oakland and the East Bay in World War II* (Berkeley: University of California Press, 1995), 4–8, 34–45; Kevin Starr, *Embattled Dreams: California in War and Peace, 1940–1950* (New York: Oxford University Press, 2002), 68.

16. Howard Jarvis and Robert Pack, *I'm Mad as Hell* (New York: New York Times, 1979), 240; Roger W. Lotchin, *Fortress California, 1910–1961: From Warfare to Welfare* (Urbana and Chicago: University of Illinois Press, 2002), 42, 132.

17. California State Board of Equalization, "Biennial Report, 1941–1942" (California State Board of Equalization, 1942), 25; Jarvis and Pack, *Mad as Hell*, 246. It took years for the government to compensate Jarvis for the loss of his inventory, and he claimed that the latex turned up years later in a federal warehouse, unused and, after years of disuse, unusable.

18. On the market as a social precondition for assessment, see Gabriel Ardant, *Théorie Sociologique de L'impôt* (Paris: S.E.V.P.E.N., 1965), 557.

19. On public opinion, see Hadley Cantril, *Public Opinion, 1935–46* (Princeton: Princeton University Press, 1951), 320–21; Andrea Campbell, "What Americans Think of Taxes"; James T. Sparrow, " 'Buying Our Boys Back': The Mass Foundations of Fiscal Citizenship, 1942–1954," *Journal of Policy History* 20, no. 2 (2008). On the relationship between war and popular consent to taxation, see, e.g., Edgar Kiser and April Linton, "Determinants of the Growth of the State: War and Taxation in Early Modern France

and England," *Social Forces* 80, no. 2 (2001); Michael Mann, "State and Society, 1130–1815: An Analysis of English State Finances," *Political Power and Social Theory* 1 (1980); Alan T. Peacock and Jack Wiseman, *The Growth of Public Expenditure in the United Kingdom*, 2nd ed. (London: Allen and Unwin, 1967); Karen A. Rasler and William R. Thompson, "War Making and State Making: Governmental Expenditures, Tax Revenues, and Global Wars," *American Political Science Review* 79, no. 2 (1985).

20. Donald Marr Nelson, *Arsenal of Democracy: The Story of American War Production* (New York: Harcourt, Brace and Company, 1946); John Witte, *The Politics and Development of the Federal Income Tax* (Madison: University of Wisconsin Press, 1985), 125–26.

21. U.S. Treasury Department Committee on Intergovernmental Fiscal Relations, *Federal, State, and Local Government Fiscal Relations*, 411.

22. Ursula K. Hicks, *Public Finance* (London: James Nisbet and Co., Ltd., 1956 [1947]), 242.

23. C. Lowell Harriss, "The British Revaluation of Real Estate for Local Taxation," *National Tax Journal* 5, no. 3 (1952); Allan McConnell, "The Recurring Crisis of Local Taxation in Post-War Britain," *Contemporary British History* 11, no. 3 (1997): 44.

24. Kjeld Philip, *Intergovernmental Fiscal Relations* (Copenhagen: Institute of Economics and History, 1954), 152–58.

25. *Parliamentary Debates*, Commons, 5th ser., vol. 444 (1948), col. 996.

26. Winston W. Crouch, "Local Government Under the British Labour Government," *The Journal of Politics* 12, no. 2 (1950).

27. *Parliamentary Debates*, Commons, 5th ser., vol. 444 (1948), col. 1020–1044.

28. Robert Murray Haig, "Federal-State Financial Relations: A Conscientious Governor Studies a Senate Document," *Political Science Quarterly* 59, no. 2 (1944): 162.

29. Tom Gregory, *History of Yolo County, California with Biographical Sketches of the Leading Men and Women of the County Who Have Been Identified with Its Growth and Development from the Early Days to the Present* (Los Angeles: Historic Record Company, 1913), 229–32, 510–11.

30. California State Board of Equalization, *Annual Report* (California State Board of Equalization, 1951), 6.

31. Ibid., 5. The quotation is attributed to Pierce by William R. MacDougall and Jacob M. Jaffe, "Prospects for Assessment Reform: An Overview," in *Property Tax Reform: The Role of the Property Tax in the Nation's Revenue System*, ed. ACIR (Washington, D.C.: ACIR, 1973).

32. California State Assembly Interim Committee on Revenue and Taxation, *Taxation of Property*, 127.

33. Ibid., 332.

34. Malcolm M. Davisson, "Fundamental Revision of Municipal Revenue Pattern Is Underway," *Western City* 22, no. 10 (1946): 40.

35. California State Senate Interim Committee on Revenue and Taxation, *State and Local Property Taxes in California: A Comparative Analysis*, vol. 3, *Report* (Sacramento: California State Legislature, 1951), 507; League of California Cities, "California League Conference Calls for Action Program on Property Tax," *Western City* 22, no. 10 (1946): 31.

36. Frederic L. Alexander, "Current and Future Problems Confronting Counties," in *Papers Presented at 1946 Conference, County Assessors of California and State Board of Equalization* (Sacramento: California State Board of Equalization, 1946), 68.

37. Dixwell Pierce, "Remarks," in *Papers Presented at 1946 Conference, County Assessors of California and State Board of Equalization* (Sacramento: California State Board of Equalization, 1946), 9.

38. California State Board of Equalization, *Biennial Report* (Sacramento: California State Board of Equalization, 1946), 10, emphasis added.

39. League of California Cities, "Directors Approve Program of Legislative Objectives for Cities," *Western City* 23, no. 1 (1947): 30.

40. League of California Cities, "Directors Review Pending Legislation Affecting Cities as Session Re-Convenes," *Western City* 23, no. 3 (1947): 36.

41. Lawrence Brooks De Graaf and Jackson K. Putnam, *Oral History Interview with Richard Nevins: Oral History Transcript* (Fullerton: California State University, Fullerton, for the State Government Oral History Program, California State Archives, 1992), v–vi, 3–6, 206; Steven P. Arena, *History, California State Board of Equalization: The First One Hundred Years, 1879–1979*, ed. California State Board of Equalization (Sacramento: California State Board of Equalization, 1980), 135.

42. Richard Nevins, "Address," in *Papers Presented at 1960 Conference, County Assessors of California and State Board of Equalization, Fifty-Eighth Annual Conference* (Sacramento: California State Board of Equalization, 1960), 4.

43. California State Assembly Interim Committee on Revenue and Taxation, *Program of Tax Reform*, 21–22.

44. California State Assembly Interim Committee on Revenue and Taxation, *Taxation of Property*, 141; California State Legislature, *California Assembly Journal*, February 6, 1962, 122; Richard Nevins, "Should There Be a Standard Assessment Ratio?" in *Papers Presented at 1961 Conference, County Assessors of California and State Board of Equalization, Fifty-Ninth Annual Conference* (Sacramento: California State Board of Equalization, 1962), 83.

45. Kuttner, *Revolt of the Haves*, 30–32; Paul, *Politics of the Property Tax*, 94.

46. California State Assembly Interim Committee on Revenue and Taxation, *Taxation of Property*, 140–41.

47. Paul, *Politics of the Property Tax*, 100.

48. California State Assembly Interim Committee on Revenue and Taxation, *Program of Tax Reform*, 21.

49. Ibid., 73, 329.

50. Ibid., 26, 58.

51. Ibid., 25; California State Legislature, *Assembly Final Histories* (Sacramento: California State Legislature, 1965), 698; David R. Doerr, "Capsule History of the California Tax Structure, Part IV, Chapter Two: The Tax and Spend Years, 1959–1967," *Cal-Tax Digest* 1, no. 10 (1997): 13. On the role of rural counties, see De Graaf and Putnam, *Oral History Interview with Richard Nevins*, 240.

52. ACIR, *Significant Features of Fiscal Federalism*, 1979 ed., vol. 1 (Washington, D.C.: ACIR, 1979).

53. Paul, *Politics of the Property Tax*, 64–66, 88.

54. *Bettigole v. Assessors of Springfield*, 343 Mass. 223 [1961]. See Jane H. Malme, "Mandate for Assessment Uniformity: The Massachusetts Experience," *Property Tax Journal* 1, no. 3 (1982): 176; Paul, *Politics of the Property Tax*, 37, 88.

55. *Town of Sudbury v. Commissioner of Corporations and Taxation*, 366 Mass. 558, 560 (1973).

56. Paul, *Politics of the Property Tax*, 88.

57. New York State Commission of Investigation, *Report by the Commission of Investigation of the State of New York of an Investigation Concerning Real Estate Tax Assessments in the City of New York* (New York: New York State Commission of Investigation, 1973), 101–13.

58. Kuttner, *Revolt of the Haves*, 126.

59. New York State Temporary State Commission on State and Local Finances, *Report of the Temporary State Commission on State and Local Finances*, vol. 2, *The Real Property Tax* (Albany: New York State Temporary State Commission on State and Local Finances, 1975), 11, 72.

60. Ibid., 63, 74, 75.

61. Kuttner, *Revolt of the Haves*, 31–33; Paul, *Politics of the Property Tax*, 108–9.

62. Ronald Welch, "A New Generation Takes Over" (paper presented at the Fifteenth Annual Conference of the Western States Association of Tax Administrators, Seattle, Washington, September 6, 1966), 1. See also Kuttner, *Revolt of the Haves*, 33; George Murphy, "Wolden Guilty of Bribery," *San Francisco Examiner*, May 29, 1966.

63. Paul, *Politics of the Property Tax*, 101.

64. Ibid., 110; California State Legislature, *California Assembly Journal*, April 6, 1966, 152.

65. Doerr, "Capsule History," 13; Nicholas Petris and Gabrielle Morris, *Dean of the California Legislature, 1958–1996: An Oral History Transcript* (Berkeley:

Regional Oral History Office, the Bancroft Library, University of California, 1996), 273.

66. See De Graaf and Putnam, *Oral History Interview with Richard Nevins*, 208; Paul, *Politics of the Property Tax*, 102.

67. California State Legislature, *California Assembly Journal*, June 30, 1966, 1567; Paul, *Politics of the Property Tax*, 110–11.

68. *Town of Sudbury*, 567; see also Kuttner, *Revolt of the Haves*, 153; Malme, "Mandate," 177–78.

69. Malme, "Mandate," 179.

70. Kuttner, *Revolt of the Haves*, 310–12; Malme, "Mandate," 179–81.

71. Kuttner, *Revolt of the Haves*, 162.

72. Ibid., 310; Malme, "Mandate," 179–83.

73. *Hellerstein v. Town of Islip*, 33 N.Y. 2d 1, 16 (1975).

74. Kuttner, *Revolt of the Haves*, 154; Joseph F. Zimmerman, "Financing the State," in *The Politics and Government of New York State*, ed. Joseph F. Zimmerman (New York: New York University Press, 1981), 342.

75. E. J. Dionne, Jr., "Carey's Loss on Veto May Be His Gain," *New York Times*, December 5, 1981, 28; Marilyn Rubin and Fran Joseph, "The New York City Property Tax: A Case Study in Structural Change and Administrative Response," *Property Tax Journal* 7, no. 1 (1988): 88–91.

76. Pomp, "What Is Happening to the Property Tax?"

77. California State Assembly Interim Committee on Revenue and Taxation, *Taxation of Property*, 302.

78. U.S. Bureau of the Census, *Historical Statistics of the U.S.*, vol. 2 (Washington, D.C.: U.S. Government Printing Office, 1970), 646 (series N238–345).

Chapter 3

1. "SM County Group Burns Tax Assesment Notices," *Palo Alto Times*, April 20, 1977, n.p.; "Board Favours Tax Relief Bid," *San Mateo Times and Daily News leader*, April 26, 1977, n.p.; Movement for Economic Justice (MEJ) Records (Mss 766), box 18, folder 2, Wisconsin State Historical Society (WSHS), Madison.

2. This is the title of Robert Kuttner's indispensable book on the tax revolt.

3. The similarity is not just superficial: a military draft is, in effect, a tax paid in labor (and blood) rather than in money.

4. Citizens Action League, "The People Speak: Testimony of the Citizens Action League," October 21, 1976, pp. 1–2, MEJ Records, box 18, folder 2, WSHS.

5. Lo, *Small Property*, 123; Philip E. Watson, Steven Edington, and Richard Candida Smith, *Tax Reform and Professionalizing the Los Angeles County Assessor's Office: An Oral History Interview* (Los Angeles: Oral History Program, University of California, Los Angeles, 1988), 29–32.

6. California State Assembly Interim Committee on Revenue and Taxation, *Taxation of Property*, 40–41, 110–12; Kuttner, *Revolt of the Haves*, 37–39; Lo, *Small Property*, 123–24; Watson, Edington, and Smith, *Tax Reform and Professionalizing*, 42–44.

7. Kuttner, *Revolt of the Haves*, 37.

8. Lo, *Small Property*, 71.

9. Ibid., 72–73, 77, 226 n. 10. Watson's office is described in Kuttner, *Revolt of the Haves*, 37.

10. Kuttner, *Revolt of the Haves*, 351; George A. Wiley, "Notes on Trip to Milwaukee, Wisconsin," May 8, 1973, George A. Wiley papers (henceforth "Wiley papers") (Mss 324), box 42, folder 2, WSHS.

11. James P. Gannon, "Taxpayers in Revolt: Citizens Band Together to Fight Levy Boosts at State, Local Levels," *Wall Street Journal*, May 11, 1970; David Murray, "Midwest," *New York Times*, October 12, 1972; William Robbins, "Taxpayer Revolt Gains in Chicago Suburbs," *New York Times*, August 20, 1977; William Tucker, "Spread of Untaxed Land Stirs Resistance," *New York Times*, January 30, 1977. On the Universal Life Church, see David Axelrod, "Tax Protesters Seek Pennies from Heaven," *Chicago Tribune*, August 22, 1977.

12. "A Brief History of the Fannin County Taxpayers Association," MEJ Records, box 20, folder 14, WSHS.

13. Arkansas Community Organization for Reform Now, "ACORN Cites Developments in Its Campaign for Pulaski Tax Equalization," June 21, 1974, MEJ Records, box 21, folder 4; "Muskie Begins Tax Probe." *Property Tax Newsletter*, no. 3, n.d. (1973), MEJ Records, box 20, folder 14; Movement for Economic Justice, *Property Tax Organizing Manual*, 1973, p. 14, MEJ Records, box 33, folder 1, WSHS. "House Probes Reappraisal Programs," *Fair Taxes Now* (newsletter), no. 1, July 2, 1973; "Tax Break for Rural Property Owners," *Fair Taxes Now*, no. 2, July 24, 1973; "Fair Taxes Now, Save Our Cumberland Mountains and Tennessee Citizens for Wilderness Planning Hold Property Tax Meeting in Oak Ridge," *Fair Taxes Now*, no. 5, October 10, 1973; "Citizens for Lower Taxes Discuss Unfair Property Taxes with Davidson County Legislators." *Fair Taxes Now*, no. 5, October 10, 1973, MEJ Records, box 19, folder 1, WSHS.

14. "Tax Association Confronts Board," February 14, 1973, MEJ Records, box 20, folder 14, WSHS. This was scapegoating: food stamps were federally funded and had nothing to do with the local property tax.

15. Si Kahn, *How People Get Power: Organizing Oppressed Communities for Action* (New York: McGraw-Hill, 1970); Si Kahn and Kathy Kahn, "The National Forests in

Appalachia: A Study in Taxes, Profits and People," 1972, MEJ Records, box 20, folder 13, WSHS.

16. Movement for Economic Justice, *Property Tax Organizing Manual*, 1973, 47, MEJ Records, box 33, folder 1, WSHS.

17. "Meet Joe Tinney, City Assessor," July 17 (1975), MEJ Records, box 18, folder 3, WSHS; Raul Ramirez, "Assessor Takes His Lumps Again from Crowd," *San Francisco Examiner*, July 18, 1975.

18. Kuttner, *Revolt of the Haves*, 311. See Michael Ansara to Phillip M. Stern and Neil Gifford Stern, October 17, 1977, MEJ Records, box 9, folder 11, WSHS. On the founding of Fair Share, see *Annual Report of the Movement for Economic Justice*, February 1, 1974, MEJ Records, box 1, folder 3, WSHS; and memos from George Wiley to Mark Splain, May 10, 1973, and Mark Splain to George Wiley, May 25, 1973, MEJ Records, box 9, folder 2, WSHS.

19. Ramirez, "Assessor Takes His Lumps"; Dick Robblee, Central Seattle Community Council Federation to Julia Mark, Movement for Economic Justice, May 16, 1975, MEJ Records, box 22, folder 6, WSHS; "What Chicago Taxpayers Are Doing," *Beyond Just Gripes*, no. 1, November 1972, MEJ Records, box 18, folder 11, WSHS; "Tax Action Day," *Tax Justice News from the TEA Party* (Pennsylvania), no. 1, May 1973, MEJ Records, box 20, folder 14, WSHS; "Citizens Force Coal Company Appraisal Hikes," *Fair Taxes Now*, no. 2, July 24, 1973, MEJ Records, box 19, folder 1, WSHS.

20. Bruce L. Brown to Julia Mark, March 15, 1974, MEJ Records, box 21, folder 10, WSHS; See, e.g., Connecticut Citizen Action Group, *A Citizen's Handbook for Property Taxes: How to Check Your Property Tax Assessment*, n.d., MEJ Records, box 20, folder 14, WSHS; TEA Party (Pennsylvania), *Introduction: About Property Taxes*, n.d., MEJ Records, box 20, folder 14, WSHS; Missouri Tax Justice Project, *A Homeowner's Guide to Property Tax Appeals*, n.d., MEJ Records, box 18, folder 9, WSHS.

21. Tax Reform Research Group, "Property Tax Reappraisals: Special Double Issue." *People and Taxes* 1, no. 8 (1973), 1–30.

22. Jon Kaufman to Mike Miller, July 23, 1975, MEJ Records, box 5, folder 7, WSHS. The lobbyist, Jon Kaufman, was also a former National Welfare Rights Organization staff member. See Jonathan Kaufman, Résumé, n.d., MEJ Records, box 18, folder 4, WSHS.

23. Paul, *Politics of the Property Tax*, 26.

24. The social movement scholars Douglas McAdam, Sidney Tarrow, and Charles Tilly argue that such a "scale shift" from local, episodic protest to broader, sustained protest is a necessary stage in the development of a social movement: McAdam, Tarrow, and Tilly, *Dynamics of Contention*, 332.

25. Robert O. Self, *American Babylon: Race and the Struggle for Postwar Oakland* (Princeton: Princeton University Press, 2003).

26. "Taxpayers' Tour of Downtown S.F.," July 10, 1975, MEJ Records, box 18, folder 3, WSHS. On the origins of CAL, see Mike Miller, "A Brief History of the Organization and Development of the Citizen Action League," May 23, 1975, MEJ Records, box 9, folder 3, WSHS.

27. Paul Gann, "Paul Gann Biography," n.d., Paul Gann Archive, box 1376, folder 1, California State Library, Sacramento; Paul Gann, "Background," n.d. (1980), Paul Gann Archive, box 1376, folder 1, California State Library, Sacramento; Paul Gann and Gabrielle Morris, *Oral History Interview* (Sacramento: California State Archives Oral History Project, 1988), 4.

28. CAL, "Tax Platform: A Statement of Principles," October 14, 1976, MEJ Records, box 18, folder 2, WSHS; "The People Speak: Testimony of the Citizens Action League," October 21, 1976, MEJ Records, box 18, folder 2, WSHS; "CAL Lobby Day," April 27, 1977, MEJ Records, box 18, folder 2, WSHS; "Taxpayers' Capitol Protest," *Oakland Tribune*, April 28, 1977, n.p., MEJ Records, box 18, folder 2, WSHS; CAL, December 9, 1977, "Are Property Taxes 'Taking the Shirt Off Your Back'?!" MEJ Records, box 18, folder 2, WSHS.

29. I coded the presence of initiatives from the state-by-state coverage in M. Dane Waters, *Initiative and Referendum Almanac* (Durham, N.C.: Carolina Academic Press, 2003), supplemented by Massachusetts Secretary of State, "Massachusetts Statewide Ballot Measures 1919–2000," 2001.

30. We know this from the careful detective work of Clarence Lo, who combed the archives of four local newspapers in the Los Angeles area for descriptions of all of the property tax protests that were reported in the period from 1950 to 1978. He found dozens of events—typically protest meetings involving a few hundred people "seated in an auditorium or another public facility for a long period of time"—but the activists he quoted suggested that there were many more that went unreported. For example, one activist claimed that there had been twenty-five protest meetings in Los Angeles County in 1966, whereas Lo found only a combined total of four protest meetings described in newspaper reports for the fiscal years ending in 1966 and 1967. See Lo, *Small Property*, 77, 104, 202. The activist may have been exaggerating, but the consensus of scholars in this field is that newspapers do underreport protests by something like this order of magnitude. See Jennifer Earl et al., "The Use of Newspaper Data in the Study of Collective Action," *Annual Review of Sociology* 30 (2004); Ruud Koopmans and Dieter Rucht, "Protest Event Analysis," in *Methods of Social Movement Research*, ed. Bert Klandermans and Suzanne Staggenborg (Minneapolis: University of Minnesota Press, 2002); Gregory M. Maney and Pamela E. Oliver, "Finding Collective Events: Sources, Searches, Timing," *Sociological Methods and Research* 30, no. 2 (2001).

31. Robert M. Clatanoff, *Patterns of Property Tax Administration in the United States* (Chicago: International Association of Assessing Officers, 1986); ACIR, *The Role of the States in Strengthening the Property Tax*, vol. 1. The data on maps and certification come from surveys conducted in 1979. The data on computers come from surveys conducted in the early 1980s. Thus it is possible that protest preceded modernization and not vice versa. To be sure that the temporal order was consistent with the theory that modernization caused protest, I also tested the hypothesis with data on property tax reforms from 1973, using data from MacDougall and Jaffe, "Prospects." The relationship held.

32. AFL-CIO Public Employee Department, "Analysis of Proposition 13 prepared by PED Research Department," June 29, 1978, Campaign Literature Files, folder: Prop. 13—1978, California State Library, Sacramento.

33. The average for all states in 1970 was 9 percent black, 66 percent urban, 65 percent of households owner-occupied, and property taxes just under 4 percent of personal income; Illinois was 13 percent black, 83 percent urban, and 59 percent owner-occupied, with property taxes just over 4 percent of personal income. The data sources are described in the notes to Appendix 2.

34. David K. Fremon, *Chicago Politics Ward by Ward* (Bloomington and Indianapolis: Indiana University Press, 1988), 246.

35. Illinois Economic and Fiscal Commission, *Property Tax in Illinois: Selected Problems and Proposals* (Springfield: Illinois Economic and Fiscal Commission, 1973), F1–F2.

36. David V. May, "Property Tax for Public Schools," *Illinois Issues* 3, no. 10 (1977); ACIR, *Property Tax in a Changing Environment*, 101–2.

37. Illinois Economic and Fiscal Commission, *Property Tax in Illinois*, 33; ACIR, *Property Tax in a Changing Environment*, 101.

38. Joan E. Lancourt, *Confront or Concede: The Alinsky Citizen-Action Organizations* (Lexington, Mass.: Lexington Books, 1979), 27; Derek Shearer, "CAP: New Breeze in the Windy City," *Ramparts* 11 (1973).

39. Chicago Tribune, "Assessor Aide Sympathetic to Tax Problems but Cynical," *Chicago Tribune*, February 2, 1972; Illinois Economic and Fiscal Commission, *Property Tax in Illinois*, C1–C13. The outside study is described in Dona P. Gerson, "Inflation of Property Values Combined with Increased Tax Levies: Tax Revolt in Cook County," *Illinois Issues* 4, no. 1 (1978).

40. Chicago Tribune, "Call Session to Protest County Tax," *Chicago Tribune*, March 16, 1972.

41. Chicago Tribune, "120 Owners Willing to Go on Tax Strike," *Chicago Tribune*, February 14, 1972.

42. Gerald West, "CAP Asks to End Real Estate Tax," *Chicago Tribune*, February 14, 1972.

43. Chicago Tribune, "CAP Tells Board: Freeze Property Tax," *Chicago Tribune*, May 16, 1972. Chicago Tribune, "Daley Away, Protesters Have Day," *Chicago Tribune*, June 22, 1972.

44. Shearer, "CAP: New Breeze."

45. Harry C. Boyte, *The Backyard Revolution: Understanding the New Citizen Movement* (Philadelphia: Temple University Press, 1980), 80.

46. Pat Kriznis and Alvin Nagelberg, "Golden Years Tarnished," *Chicago Tribune*, February 29, 1972.

47. See, e.g., Chicago Tribune, "Tax Woe Spreads to Homer Township," *Chicago Tribune*, March 16, 1972.

48. Chicago Tribune, "Tax Protesters Rally: Fifteen Removed from House," *Chicago Tribune*, March 1, 1973; Thomas Seslar, "State Legislature OKs Tax Breaks for the Elderly," *Chicago Tribune*, June 21, 1972; St. Louis Tax Reform Group, "What Chicago Taxpayers are Doing," *Beyond Just Gripes* (newsletter), no. 1 (November 1972), n.p., MEJ Records, box 18, folder 11; Citizens Action Program, "House Freeze Property Tax Levy," *Citizens Action Program ACTION*, vol. 3, no. 5 (June 1973), n.p., Wiley papers, box 42, folder 6. On the failure of the freeze bill, see John Elmer, "Legislature Quits—for the Night," *Chicago Tribune*, July 2, 1973.

49. Fremon, *Chicago Politics Ward by Ward*, 247; Gerson, "Inflation of Property Values."

50. Illinois Economic and Fiscal Commission, *Property Tax in Illinois*, 29.

51. Gerson, "Inflation of Property Values"; Ed McManus, "Chicago: Illinois Property Tax Revolution?" *Illinois Issues* 4, no. 8 (1978); Robbins, "Taxpayer Revolt"; Ed McManus, "'Strike Fever' Hits Taxpayers," *Chicago Tribune*, August 7, 1977; Ed McManus, "Tax Protesters Ask Deadline Extension," *Chicago Tribune*, August 16, 1977; Ed McManus, "Tax Rebellion Is Spreading in North Suburbs," *Chicago Tribune*, August 14, 1977.

52. Ed McManus, "Tax Rebels' Cries Ring in Suburbs," *Chicago Tribune*, June 4, 1978.

53. Ed McManus, "Citizens Seize on Obscure Law in Effort to Cut Local Tax," *Chicago Tribune*, September 10, 1978.

54. Ed McManus, "Group Pushes for Illinois Tax Vote," *Chicago Tribune*, June 8, 1978.

55. William Griffin, "Tax Fighters Form Three Factions in Petition War," *Chicago Tribune*, August 6, 1978.

56. Waters, *Initiative and Referendum Almanac*, 190.

57. St. Louis Tax Reform Group, Proposal, November 1, 1972, MEJ Records, box 18, folder 8, WSHS.

58. Mary Ann Fiske to "Dear Friends," April 3, 1973, MEJ Records, box 18, folder 7, WSHS.

59. Ibid.

60. Mary Ann Fiske to John (Franzén), April 5, 1973, MEJ Records, box 18, folder 7, WSHS.

61. St. Louis Tax Reform Group, *The Case for Property Tax Reform*, n.d. (November 1973), MEJ Records, box 18, folder 8, WSHS.

62. Mary Ann Fiske and Kathi Sharkey to Bert (De Leeuw), October 27, 1975, MEJ Records, Box 18, Folder 9, WSHS; "History of Citizen Action," n.d., MEJ Records, box 18, folder 9, WSHS.

63. Marcia Stepanek, "Pat Quinn: A Man Politicians Love to Hate," *Illinois Issues* 6, no. 1 (1980); Kenneth H. Winn, "It All Adds Up: Reform and the Erosion of Representative Government in Missouri, 1900–2000," Missouri State Archives, 2000, available from http://www.sos.mo.gov/archives/pubs/article/article.asp.

64. George A. Wiley to Mark Splain, "Chelsea Pilot Project," May 25, 1973, MEJ Records, box 9, folder 2, WSHS; "Staff Members of the Massachusetts Alliance for a Fair Share," MEJ Records, box 9, folder 2, WSHS; Mark Splain to George Wiley, May 10, 1973, MEJ Records, box 9, folder 2, WSHS.

65. Robert Parlow, "Chelsea's Many Tanks: Property Tax Assessment of the Oil Storage Facilities in Chelsea, Massachusetts," Report No. 15 from the Massachusetts Public Finance Project, January 1974, MEJ Records, box 9, folder 13, WSHS.

66. Michael Ansara to Phillip M. Stern and Neil Gifford Stern, October 17, 1977, MEJ Records, box 9, folder 11, WSHS.

67. Ansara to Stern, October 17, 1977, MEJ Records, box 9, folder 11, WSHS.

68. Lo, *Small Property*, 181–82.

69. Kathy Gorman, Fr. Tom Corrigan, and Teresa Foley to "Members and Friends," n.d. (1978), box 1, no folder, Margaret Cleeff Carlson Papers (MCCP), Schlesinger Library, Radcliffe College, Cambridge, Massachusetts.

70. Jack Conway, "Conway Offices Now Circulating Petitions for Guaranteed Property Tax Relief Referendum," n.d., box 2, no folder, MCCP; David E. Sullivan to Margaret C. Carlson, September 11, 1978, box 2, no folder, MCCP; "Giant Realtor Tax Relief Rally," October 20, 1978, Margaret Cleeff Carlson Papers, box 2, no folder, MCCP.

71. McConnell, "Recurring Crisis," 46.

72. Neill Nugent, "The Ratepayers," in *Respectable Rebels: Middle Class Campaigns in Britain in the 1970s*, ed. Roger King and Neill Nugent (London: Hodder and Stoughton, 1979), 30.

73. Ibid., 34.

74. Ibid., 34–38. Conservative Party, "Putting Britain First: October 1974 Conservative Party General Election Manifesto," 1974.

75. Nugent, "Ratepayers," 38.

76. David Butler, Andrew Adonis, and Tony Travers, *Failure in British Government: The Politics of the Poll Tax* (Oxford and New York: Oxford University Press, 1994), 61.

77. Allan McConnell, *State Policy Formation and the Origins of the Poll Tax* (Aldershot: Brookfield, 1995), 80.

78. Butler, Adonis, and Travers, *Failure*, 62; McConnell, *State Policy Formation*, 56, 90–91, 115.

Table 3.1

Clatanoff, *Patterns*; Waters, *Initiative and Referendum Almanac*. The table includes only those states that permitted the ballot initiative for the entire period at issue. The association between assessment reforms and qualifying petitions in these states is statistically significant at the $p<.01$ level (chi-squared $=14.9$, 4 degrees of freedom).

Chapter 4

1. West, "CAP Asks."

2. Gerson, "Inflation of Property Values"; McManus, "Chicago"; McManus, " 'Strike Fever' "; McManus, "Tax Rebellion Is Spreading"; Robbins, "Taxpayer Revolt."

3. Kotz and Kotz, *Passion for Equality*, 266–71.

4. Rick Perlstein, *Before the Storm: Barry Goldwater and the Unmaking of the American Consensus* (New York: Hill and Wang, 2001), 166.

5. Jarvis and Pack, *Mad as Hell*, 227.

6. According to Jarvis, Secretary of Education Wilson Riles was "of low IQ" (see Peter Schrag, *Paradise Lost: California's Experience, America's Future* [Berkeley: University of California, 1998], 146); Jarvis's opponents in the public sector were "dummies, goons, cannibals, or big mouths" (Time, "Maniac or Messiah?" *Time*, June 19, 1978).

7. See Lisa McGirr, *Suburban Warriors: The Origins of the New American Right* (Princeton: Princeton University Press, 2001), 238.

8. Jarvis and Pack, *Mad as Hell*, 16–17.

9. Kuttner, *Revolt of the Haves*, 37; Los Angeles Times, "Retired Industrialist Heads Drive to End Property Tax," *Los Angeles Times*, February 25, 1968, WS1.

10. Jarvis and Pack, *Mad as Hell*, 283–84.

11. Kotz and Kotz, *Passion for Equality*, 248–49.

12. Smothers, "Welfare Activist Plans New Group."

13. Kotz and Kotz, *Passion for Equality*, 295–301.

14. For evidence of Wiley's initial focus on the income tax, see Misseduc Foundation, "A Proposal for the Establishment of a Tax Justice Project," January 30, 1973, MEJ records, box 22, folder 9, WSHS. On the interest of local groups in property taxes, see John Franzén to "Dear Friends," April 9, 1973, MEJ records, box 22, folder 10, WSHS;

John Franzén to Ted Behr, August 2, 1973, MEJ records, box 18, folder 5, WSHS; John Franzén to Dortha Charles, May 23, 1973, MEJ Records, box 22, folder 3, WSHS; and Larry McNeil to John Franzén, October 11, 1973, MEJ records, box 22, folder 4, WSHS.

15. See Movement for Economic Justice, "Property Tax Project," MEJ Records, box 20, folder 13, WSHS.

16. Movement for Economic Justice, *Property Tax Organizing Manual*, 1973, 60, 64, MEJ Records, box 33, folder 1, WSHS. On the origins of the manual, see John F[ranzén] to Bert [DeLeeuw] et al., memorandum, August 21, 1973, MEJ Records, box 22, folder 9, WSHS.

17. Movement for Economic Justice, "Summary of Tax Reform Meeting—Harvard Faculty Club," March 13, 1973, MEJ Records, box 22, folder 7, WSHS. In addition to Wiley and Thurow, the others in attendance were Anthony (Tony) Baldwin, Peter Edelman, Thomas (Tom) Glynn, Edwin Kuh, Helen Ladd, Richard Musgrave, Alicia Munnell, Anne Peretz, Paul Simon, Stanley Surrey, and James Wetzler. As Thurow was no doubt aware, $15,000 was a magic number to Wiley, who defined the potential "majority constituency" of the MEJ as all Americans at or below this income level. See "A Proposal for the Establishment of the Tax Justice Project of the Movement for Economic Justice," n.d., MEJ Records, box 22, folder 9, WSHS.

18. Jesse Burkhead, *State and Local Taxes for Public Education* (Syracuse: Syracuse University Press, 1963).

19. See People and Taxes, "Property Tax Reappraisals: Special Double Issue," *People and Taxes* 1, no. 8 (1973): 24; "Fair Taxes Now, Save Our Cumberland Mountains and Tennessee Citizens for Wilderness Planning Hold Property Tax Meeting in Oak Ridge," *Fair Taxes Now*, no. 5, October 10, 1973, MEJ Records, box 19, folder 1, WSHS.

20. Tax Task Force, Metro-Act of Rochester, Inc., "Replacement of the Real Property Tax in Monroe County by a County-Wide Income Tax," MEJ Records, box 20, folder 13, WSHS. Metro-Act was originally organized by Saul Alinsky under the name "Friends of FIGHT" to support an organizing project in Rochester's black ghetto. Sanford D. Horwitt, *Let Them Call Me Rebel: Saul Alinsky—His Life and Legacy* (New York: Alfred A. Knopf, 1989), 505.

21. St. Louis Tax Reform Group, n.d. (1973), "The Case for Annual Re-Assessment: A Study of Piecemeal Re-Assessments in Six St. Louis City Neighborhoods," MEJ Records, box 18, folder 7, WSHS; St. Louis Tax Reform Group, "Tax Reform Group Seeks End to Property Tax," November 14, 1973, MEJ Records, box 18, folder 8, WSHS; Americans Nonpartisan for Tax Equity (ANTE), "Property Tax Unfair for the Majority," *Taxaction*, September 1974, MEJ Records, box 18, folder 1, WSHS.

22. On elite allies, crises, and elite competition as conditions for protest movement success, see McAdam, "Conceptual Origins"; Meyer, "Protest and Political Opportunities"; Frances Fox Piven and Richard Cloward, *Poor People's Movements: Why They Succeed, How They Fail* (New York: Vintage Books, 1979).

23. Kuttner, *Revolt of the Haves*, 37.

24. President's Commission on School Finance, *Schools, People, and Money: The Need for Education Reform* (Washington, D.C.: U.S. Government Printing Office, 1972).

25. James W. Naughton, "President Seeks to Ease School Tax on Property," *New York Times*, December 3, 1971.

26. Robert B. Semple, Jr., "President Plans Value-Added Tax to Help Schools," *New York Times*, February 1, 1972. On the importance of property-tax-conscious suburban voters to Nixon's re-election plans, see Stephen E. Ambrose, *Nixon*, vol. 2, *The Triumph of a Politician, 1962–1972* (New York: Simon and Schuster, 1989), 432–33; Matthew Lassiter, "Suburban Strategies: The Volatile Center in Postwar American Politics," in *The Democratic Experiment*, ed. Meg Jacobs, William J. Novak, and Julian E. Zelizer (Princeton: Princeton University Press, 2003).

27. David L. Kirp, "Judicial Policy-Making: Inequitable Public School Financing and the Serrano Case (1971)," in *Policy and Politics in America: Six Case Studies*, ed. Allan P. Sindler (Boston: Little, Brown and Company, 1973); Paul A. Minorini and Stephen D. Sugarman, "School Finance Litigation in the Name of Educational Equity," in *Equity and Adequacy in Education Finance: Issues and Perspectives*, ed. Rosemary Chalk, Helen F. Ladd, and Janet S. Hansen (Washington, D.C.: National Academy Press, 1999).

28. *Serrano v. Priest* (Serrano I), 5 Cal. 3d 584, 96 Cal. Rptr. 601, 487 P. 2d 1241 (1971); see Richard F. Elmore and Milbrey Wallin McLaughlin, *Reform and Retrenchment: The Politics of California School Finance Reform* (Cambridge, Mass.: Ballinger, 1982). A 1976 decision also called *Serrano v. Priest* (Serrano II, 18 Cal. 3d 728, 135 Cal. Rptr. 345, 557 P. 2d 929) is the basis for William Fischel's influential argument that the legal case caused the tax revolt. See William A. Fischel, "Did John Serrano Vote for Proposition 13? A Reply to Stark and Zasloff's 'Tiebout and Tax Revolts: Did Serrano Really Cause Proposition 13?'" *UCLA Law Review* 51 (2004); William A. Fischel, "Did Serrano Cause Proposition 13?" *National Tax Journal* 42, no. 4 (1989); William A. Fischel, "How Serrano Caused Proposition 13," *Journal of Law and Politics* 12 (1996).

29. James W. Naughton, "Two Senators Reject Value-Added Tax," *New York Times*, February 1, 1972; New York Times, "Nader Criticizes Muskie Tax Role," *New York Times*, January 5, 1972. Muskie held hearings about the property tax and—even after losing the Democratic nomination to McGovern—put forward his property tax relief bill as promised. But the bill died in committee, and Muskie gave up on it, perhaps because it

no longer helped his presidential ambitions. The Subcommittee on Intergovernmental Relations of the Committee on Government Operations, United States Senate, Ninety-Second Congress, Second Session, *The Impact and Administration of the Property Tax*, 1972; Kuttner, *Revolt of the Haves*, 137–38; *Congressional Record* 1973: 8093, 14496–14512.

30. ACIR, *Financing Schools and Property Tax Relief: A State Responsibility* (Washington, D.C.: ACIR, 1973), 4, 16.

31. Russell B. Vlaanderen and Erick L. Lindman, "Intergovernmental Relations and the Governance of Education: A Report to the President's Commission on School Finance" (Denver, Colo.: Education Commission of the States, 1971).

32. Eileen Shanahan, "Officials Oppose Nixon Plan to Cut Tax on Property," *New York Times*, December 15, 1972; ACIR, *Financing Schools*; ACIR, *Public Opinion and Taxes* (Washington, D.C.: ACIR, 1972), 4; Warren Weaver, "Governors Score Value-Added Tax," *New York Times*, June 8, 1972.

33. David A. Caputo, "Richard M. Nixon, General Revenue Sharing, and American Federalism," in *Richard M. Nixon: Politician, President, Administrator*, ed. Leon Friedman and William F. Levantrosser (New York: Greenwood Press, 1991); Joan Hoff, *Nixon Reconsidered* (New York: Basic Books, 1994), 69–70.

34. McConnell, *State Policy Formation*, 90–91.

35. Butler, Adonis, and Travers, *Failure*, 22, 25.

36. Ibid., 64.

37. Ibid., 63–64; McConnell, *State Policy Formation*, 95–96, 125.

38. Butler, Adonis, and Travers, *Failure*, 90. Department of the Environment, "Paying for Local Government" (Great Britain: Her Majesty's Stationery Office, 1986), 26.

39. Tony Travers, *The Politics of Local Government Finance* (London: Allen and Unwin, 1986), 88–91, 164–83.

40. Butler, Adonis, and Travers, *Failure*, 71, 97.

41. Ibid., 102–4; McConnell, *State Policy Formation*, 174.

42. A British poll from 1987 showed that 25 percent approved of the plan to substitute a poll tax for local property taxes: Butler, Adonis, and Travers, *Failure*, 259. An American poll from 1972 showed that 32 percent approved of the plan to substitute a VAT for local property taxes: ACIR, *Financing Schools*, 26.

43. See, e.g., Desmond King and Stewart Wood, "The Political Economy of Neoliberalism: Britain and the United States in the 1980s," in *Continuity and Change in Contemporary Capitalism*, ed. Herbert Kitschelt et al. (New York: Cambridge University Press, 1999); Pierson, *Dismantling*.

44. Immergut, "Rules of the Game," 63.

45. Classic reference points for the literature on states as laboratories of democracy in-

clude Daniel J. Elazar, *American Federalism: A View from the States* (New York: Harper and Row, 1984); Jack L. Walker, "The Diffusion of Innovations Among the American States," *American Political Science Review* 63, no. 3: 880–99.

46. Steven D. Gold, "Homeowner Property Taxes, Inflation and Property Tax Relief," *National Tax Journal* 34, no. 2 (1981); Steven D. Gold, *Property Tax Relief* (Lexington, Mass.: Lexington Books, 1979). Other catalogs of possible reforms are provided in Peter Barnes, n.d., "How to Cut Property Taxes," box 41, folder 8, George A. Wiley Papers, 1949–1975 (Mss 324), WSHS; Movement for Economic Justice, *Property Tax Organizing Manual*, 1973, 61–64, MEJ Records, box 33, folder 1, WSHS.

47. Gold, *Property Tax Relief*, 55.

48. De Graaf and Putnam, *Interview with Richard Nevins*, 239; Dean Tipps, "California's Great Property Tax Revolt: The Origins and Impact of Proposition 13," in *State and Local Tax Revolt: New Directions for the '80s*, ed. Dean Tipps and Lee Webb (Washington, D.C.: Conference on Alternative State and Local Policies, 1980).

49. R(hode) I(sland) Coalition for People's Legislation, "Public Hearing on Tax Rebate Bill," April 24, 1973, MEJ Records, box 20, folder 13, WSHS. On Massachusetts: Kuttner, *Revolt of the Haves*, 312.

50. CAL, "Tax Platform: A Statement of Principles," October 14, 1976, MEJ Records, box 18, folder 2, WSHS; "The People Speak: Testimony of the Citizens Action League," October 21, 1976, MEJ Records, box 18, folder 2, WSHS; "CAL Lobby Day," April 27, 1977, MEJ Records, box 18, folder 2, WSHS; "Taxpayers' Capitol Protest," *Oakland Tribune*, April 28, 1977, n.p., MEJ Records, box 18, folder 2, WSHS; CAL, December 9, (1977), "Are Property Taxes 'Taking the Shirt Off Your Back'?!" MEJ Records, box 18, folder 2, WSHS.

51. Mary Ann Fiske to Julia (Mark), November 16, 1973, MEJ Records, box 18, folder 7, WSHS.

52. St. Louis Tax Reform Group, n.d. (1973), "The Case for Property Tax Reform," MEJ Records, box 18, folder 8, WSHS. See Piven and Cloward, *Regulating the Poor*.

53. Jonathan Rowe, "Canadian Elderly Defer Property Taxes," *Taxation* 2, no. 12, December 1975, MEJ Records, box 18, folder 1, WSHS.

54. Movement for Economic Justice, *Property Tax Organizing Manual*, 1973, 61, MEJ Records, box 33, folder 1, WSHS.

55. Sherry Tvedt, "Enough Is Enough: The Origins of Proposition 2½" (MA thesis, Massachusetts Institute of Technology, 1981), 39.

56. ACIR, *Tax and Expenditure Limits on Local Governments: An Information Report* (Bloomington: Center for Urban Policy and the Environment, Indiana University, 1995); Philip G. Joyce and Daniel R. Mullins, "The Changing Fiscal Structure of the State and Local Public Sector: The Impact of Tax and Expenditure Limitations," *Public Administration Review* 51, no. 3 (1991).

57. John M. Allswang, *The Initiative and Referendum in California, 1898–1998* (Stanford, Calif.: Stanford University Press, 2000), 95–96; Jarvis and Pack, *Mad as Hell*, 32–33; Kuttner, *Revolt of the Haves*, 36–42.

58. Jarvis and Pack, *Mad as Hell*, 36–39; Allswang, *Initiative and Referendum*, 103.

59. Jarvis and Pack, *Mad as Hell*, 40; Kuttner, *Revolt of the Haves*, 42–43; Frank Levy, "On Understanding Proposition 13," *The Public Interest* 56 (1979).

60. James M. Buchanan, "The Potential for Taxpayer Revolt in American Democracy," *Social Science Quarterly* 59, no. 4 (1979): 694.

61. Anne Marie Biondo, " 'Cut Taxes!' the Howard Jarvis Cry Rang out in Lansing Thursday," *[Michigan] State News*, July 7, 1978; Cheryl E. Johnson, "Area Official Wants to Halve Property Taxes on Ballot," *Flint Journal*, 1978; Kuttner, *Revolt of the Haves*, 151.

62. John H. Bowman, "Recent Changes in Property Taxation and Their Implications for Balance in State and Local Revenue Systems," in *The Quest for Balance in State-Local Revenue Structures*, ed. Frederick D. Stocker (Washington, D.C.: Lincoln Institute of Land Policy, 1987).

63. On uniformity clauses, see Robin L. Einhorn, "Species of Property: The American Property-Tax Uniformity Clauses Reconsidered," *Journal of Economic History* 61, no. 4 (2001); Wade J. Newhouse, *Constitutional Uniformity and Equality in State Taxation* (Buffalo: William S. Hein and Co., Inc., 1984).

64. Schrag, *Paradise Lost*, 145.

65. Allswang, *Initiative and Referendum*, 106; Kuttner, *Revolt of the Haves*, 69.

66. Movement for Economic Justice, *Property Tax Organizing Manual*, 1973, 61–64, MEJ Records, box 33, folder 1, WSHS.

67. Massachusetts Secretary of State, "Massachusetts Statewide Ballot Measures."

68. Lo, *Small Property*, 181–82.

69. Massachusetts Fair Share, "Dear Members and Friends . . . ," n.d. (1978), box 1, no folder, MCCP.

70. Bowman, "Recent Changes in Property Taxation and Their Implications for Balance in State and Local Revenue Systems"; Kuttner, *Revolt of the Haves*, 315.

71. Department of the Environment, "Paying for Local Government."

72. On the subnational governments as access points for social movements, see, e.g., Amenta and Young, "Democratic States"; Elizabeth S. Clemens, *The People's Lobby: Organizational Innovation and the Rise of Interest Group Politics in the United States, 1890–1925* (Chicago: University of Chicago Press, 1997); Kriesi et al., *New Social Movements*.

73. Huber, Ragin, and Stephens, "Social Democracy"; Immergut, "Rules of the Game"; Stephan Leibfried, Francis G. Castles, and Herbert Obinger, " 'Old' and 'New' Politics

in Federal Welfare States," in *Federalism and the Welfare State: New World and European Experiences*, ed. Herbert Obinger, Stephan Leibfried, and Francis G. Castles (New York: Cambridge University Press, 2005).

74. Kuttner, *Revolt of the Haves*, 275–306.

75. Jarvis and Pack, *Mad as Hell*, 283.

Chapter 5

1. Untitled speech dated March 5 (1973), Wiley papers (Mss 324), box 10, folder 3, WSHS. See also "A Conference on Taxes and Redistribution of Wealth" (flyer), MEJ Records (Mss 766), box 22, folder 8, WSHS.

2. See, e.g., O'Connor, *Fiscal Crisis*, 228.

3. Time, "Maniac or Messiah?"

4. See Fr. Anthony Baumann to Burt [Bert] DeLeeuw, n.d., MEJ Records, box 20, folder 13, WSHS.

5. Kuttner, *Revolt of the Haves*, 39.

6. For the new meaning of "tax revolt," see, e.g., Steven D. Gold, "State Tax Increases of 1983: Prelude to Another Tax Revolt?" *National Tax Journal* 37, no. 1 (1984); Hansen, *Politics of Taxation*, 229–34; David Lowery and Lee Sigelman, "Understanding the Tax Revolt: Eight Explanations," *American Political Science Review* 75, no. 4 (1981); Lee Sigelman, David Lowery, and Roland Smith, "The Tax Revolt: A Comparative State Analysis," *Western Political Quarterly* 36, no. 1 (1983). The literature on the effects of property tax limitation is voluminous: for a few highlights, see Katharine L. Bradbury, Christopher J. Mayer, and Karl E. Case, "Property Tax Limits, Local Fiscal Behavior, and Property Values: Evidence from Massachusetts Under Proposition 2½," *Journal of Public Economics* 80 (2001); David M. Cutler, Douglas W. Elmendorf, and Richard Zeckhauser, "Property Tax Limitations in Retrospect: The Example of Massachusetts," *Proceedings of the National Tax Association* 89 (1997); Richard F. Dye and Therese J. McGuire, "The Effect of Property Tax Limitation Measures on Local Government Fiscal Behavior," *Journal of Public Economics* 66 (1997); Daniel R. Mullins and Philip G. Joyce, "Tax and Expenditure Limitations and State and Local Fiscal Structure: An Empirical Assessment," *Public Budgeting and Finance* 16, no. 1 (1996); Arthur O'Sullivan, Terri A. Sexton, and Steven M. Sheffrin, *Property Taxes and Tax Revolts: The Legacy of Proposition 13* (Cambridge, England: Cambridge University Press, 1995); Anne E. Preston and Casey Ichniowski, "A National Perspective on the Nature and Effects of the Local Property Tax Revolt, 1976–1986," *National Tax Journal* 44, no. 2 (1991); Ronald J. Shadbegian, "Did the Property Tax Revolt Affect Local Public Education? Evidence from Panel Data," *Public Finance Review* 31, no. 1 (2003).

7. David Stockman, *The Triumph of Politics: How the Reagan Revolution Failed* (New York: Harper and Row, 1986); Thomas Edsall and Mary Byrne Edsall, *Chain Reaction: The Impact of Race, Rights, and Taxes on American Politics* (New York: W. W. Norton and Co., 1991), 131; Schrag, *Paradise Lost*, 132; Self, *American Babylon*, 326.

8. ACIR, *Changing Public Attitudes on Governments and Taxes* (Washington, D.C.: ACIR, 1991).

9. Allswang, *Initiative and Referendum*, 96.

10. Jarvis and Pack, *Mad as Hell*, 40; Lo, *Small Property*, 139.

11. De Graaf and Putnam, *Interview with Richard Nevins*, 270; Kuttner, *Revolt of the Haves*, 43.

12. Jarvis and Pack, *Mad as Hell*, 45–46; Kuttner, *Revolt of the Haves*, 62; Schrag, *Paradise Lost*, 150.

13. Gann and Morris, *Oral History Interview*, 18, 35; Jarvis and Pack, *Mad as Hell*, 47; Kuttner, *Revolt of the Haves*, 62; Daniel A. Smith, *Tax Crusaders and the Politics of Direct Democracy* (New York: Routledge, 1998), 70–71.

14. A subsequent initiative statute passed in 1986 established a simple majority voter approval requirement for all local taxes, and yet another initiative in 1996 wrote this requirement into the state constitution. Kim S. Rueben and Pedro Cerdán, *Fiscal Effects of Voter Approval Requirements on Local Governments* (San Francisco: Public Policy Institute of California, 2003), 9.

15. On the sheer scale of this effort in historical perspective, see Allswang, *Initiative and Referendum*, 105. The descriptions of particular campaign tactics in this paragraph come from Jarvis and Pack, *Mad as Hell*, 43, 49–52; Lo, *Small Property*, 170–71; Smith, *Tax Crusaders*, 76.

16. Tim Sampson and Ron Sundergill, "The Citizens' Action League Kicks off Statewide 'Lifeline' Tax Campaign," November 11, 1976, MEJ Records, box 18, folder 2; Office of Senator Nicholas C. Petris, "The Tax Justice Act of 1977," n.d. (January 18, 1977), MEJ Records, box 18, folder 2, WSHS; "Who Supports SB 154?" MEJ Records, box 18, folder 2, WSHS. Although the first draft of the bill limited relief to tax paid on the first $60,000 of market value, this provision was later dropped.

17. Susan Rouder, "What's a Taxpayer to Do?" *California Living*, July 17, 1977; "CAL Delegation Leader Instruction Sheet," MEJ Records, box 18, folder 2, WSHS.

18. "Citizens Action League Claims Victory with Passage of SB 154 out of Senate Finance Committee Today," May 9, 1977, MEJ Records, box 18, folder 2, WSHS.

19. Tipps, "California's Great Property Tax Revolt," 76; Kip Sullivan et al., "Citizens Action League to Confront Senator Marks," October 7, 1977, MEJ Records, box 18, folder 2, WSHS.

20. "Break the Log Jam on Taxes," n.d. (November 1977), MEJ Records, box 18, folder 2, WSHS; "We Want Property Tax Relief Now!" n.d. (November? 1977), MEJ Records, box 18, folder 2, WSHS; Kip Sullivan et al., "Citizens Action League to Confront Senator Marks," October 7, 1977, MEJ Records, box 18, folder 2, WSHS.

21. "Are Property Taxes 'Taking the Shirt Off Your Back'?!", n.d. (December 1977), MEJ Records, box 18, folder 2, WSHS; "Citizens Action League Ends Vigil and Rallies to Renew Efforts for Property Tax Relief," December 7, 1977, MEJ Records, box 18, folder 2, WSHS.

22. Kuttner, *Revolt of the Haves*, 71.

23. Jarvis is quoted in Kuttner, *Revolt of the Haves*, 78; Schrag, *Paradise Lost*, 146; Time, "Maniac or Messiah?" 21.

24. Jarvis and Pack, *Mad as Hell*, 50; Kuttner, *Revolt of the Haves*, 73–74.

25. Sears and Citrin, *Tax Revolt*, 29.

26. De Graaf and Putnam, *Interview with Richard Nevins*, 279–80; Kuttner, *Revolt of the Haves*, 74–75; Schrag, *Paradise Lost*, 149; Sears and Citrin, *Tax Revolt*, 28.

27. Kuttner, *Revolt of the Haves*, 75; Sears and Citrin, *Tax Revolt*, 192.

28. De Graaf and Putnam, *Interview with Richard Nevins*, 279–80; Kuttner, *Revolt of the Haves*, 75–76.

29. Sears and Citrin, *Tax Revolt*, 191.

30. Field Institute, *Survey Code Book, Date File Nos.: Fi7802, Fi7803, Fi7804, Fi7805, Fi7806* (San Francisco: Field Institute, 1978), 64, 112.

31. Ibid., 108.

32. Stark and Zasloff, "Tiebout and Tax Revolts."

33. Bob Deisenroth and Lila Hildreth, "Hymn of the Embattled Taxpayer," Robert Barrett Papers, folder 5, California State Library, Sacramento.

34. Sears and Citrin, *Tax Revolt*, 171–79. Sears and Citrin found that "symbolic racism"—racially motivated opposition to government redistribution—also made a small but measurable contribution to whether people held favorable opinions of Proposition 13 and two other tax limitation measures. But racist attitudes apparently had no effect on behavioral measures of support for the tax revolt, including voting, signing petitions, and talking to others about the issue: Sears and Citrin, *Tax Revolt*, 166–70, 208–12, 303n4.

35. The definitive analysis of the Proposition 13 vote is Sears and Citrin, *Tax Revolt*. But see also Jack Citrin and Frank Levy, "From 13 to 4 and Beyond: The Political Meaning of the Ongoing Tax Revolt in California," in *The Property Tax Revolt: The Case of Proposition 13*, ed. George G. Kaufman and Kenneth T. Rosen (Cambridge, Mass.: Ballinger Publishing Co., 1981); Fischel, *Homevoter Hypothesis*; William F.

Gayk, "The Taxpayers' Revolt," in *Postsuburban California: The Transformation of Orange County Since World War II*, ed. Rob Kling, Spencer Olin, and Mark Poster (Berkeley and Los Angeles: University of California Press, 1991); Martin, "School Finance Litigation"; Max Neiman and Gerry Riposa, "Tax Rebels and Tax Rebellion," *Western Political Quarterly* 39, no. 3 (1986); Stark and Zasloff, "Tiebout and Tax Revolts."

36. Lindley H. Clark Jr., "Monetary Maverick: Milton Friedman, Man of Many Roles, Now Is a Tax Revolutionary," *Wall Street Journal*, July 17, 1978; Jarvis and Pack, *Mad as Hell*, 107–9, 113.

37. See, e.g., Fischel, "How Serrano Caused Proposition 13"; Schrag, *Paradise Lost*, 143–44.

38. The estimated effect of classification laws is statistically significant at the 5 percent level, meaning that if the true effect of classification laws was zero, then the chance that we might calculate a coefficient of this size would be less than one in twenty. The estimated effect of circuit-breaker laws is not significant at conventional levels, meaning that it could easily be due to chance.

39. Richard Boeth et al., "The Big Tax Revolt," *Newsweek*, June 19, 1978; U.S. News and World Report, "Nationwide Cry: 'Cut Our Taxes!'" *U.S. News and World Report*, June 19, 1978; Time, "Sound and Fury over Taxes," *Time*, June 19, 1978.

40. Remembering a name is a harder cognitive task than merely recalling vaguely that one has heard something about a topic, but the comparison still tells us something about how well known Proposition 13 was. Results calculated from the American National Election Survey, 1978.

41. Warren E. Miller and National Election Studies/Center for Political Studies, *American National Election Study, 1978: Codebook*, Third ICPSR Edition (Ann Arbor, Mich.: Inter-University Consortium for Political and Social Research, 2000 [1978]), 261. The wording of the question may have skewed responses toward Proposition 13 by how it presented the two sides of the debate: on the one hand, a demonstrated tax cut ("which *reduced* property taxes"), and on the other hand, an unsubstantiated allegation ("Opponents *said it would*").

42. Office of Senator Nicholas C. Petris, "Major Property Tax Relief Bill Introduced," January 18, 1977, MEJ Records, box 18, folder 2, WSHS.

43. David Lowery and Lee Sigelman found that they were able to explain only 6 percent of the variance in expressed support for "a measure similar to Proposition 13" in the ANES sample with a twenty-five-variable regression model that included race, gender, age, income, education, partisan identity, homeownership, and a large battery of public opinion items. In other words, support for Proposition 13 cut across all of these social cleavages. See Lowery and Sigelman, "Understanding the Tax Revolt."

But homeowners, the elderly, white people, and people whose property taxes were increasing rapidly were overrepresented among those who voted for property tax limitations in every state where the issue was studied. See Courant, Gramlich, and Rubinfeld, "Why Voters Support Tax Limitation Amendments"; Helen F. Ladd and Julie Boatwright Wilson, "Why Voters Support Tax Limitations: Evidence from Massachusetts' Proposition 2 ½," *National Tax Journal* 35, no. 2 (1982); Stein, Hamm, and Freeman, "Analysis of Support."

44. Jon Kaufman to Lois Mazor, Sherwood Forest Foundation, June 12, 1974, MEJ Records, box 5, folder 7, WSHS.

45. Robert S. Erikson, Gerald C. Wright, and John P. McIver, *Statehouse Democracy: Public Opinion and Policy in the American States* (New York: Cambridge University Press, 1993), 16, 103; Walker, "Diffusion of Innovations."

46. Wall Street Journal, "California Votes to Slash Property Taxes, Stealing Headlines from Candidates," *Wall Street Journal*, June 8, 1978.

47. MCCP, Associated Industries of Massachusetts Public Affairs Action Committee Message, June 16, 1978, box 1; MCCP, memo entitled "I recommend the following timetable," n.d., box 1.

48. MCCP, Committee for Guaranteed Property Tax Relief news release, October 20, 1978, box 2.

49. MCCP, handwritten speech ("With just 13 days left . . ."), box 2, AIM envelope.

50. Tvedt, "Enough Is Enough," 46.

51. Massachusetts Legislative Research Council, *Limiting Taxation and Spending by State and Local Governments* (Boston: Massachusetts Legislative Research Council, 1980), 371; Tvedt, "Enough Is Enough," 41–42.

52. Charles Kenney, "Who Gave Us 2 ½?" *Boston Globe*, October 31, 1980, 21.

53. This description of the drafting process is based on Edward F. King, oral history interview, October 22, 2001; and Don Feder, oral history interview with author (by telephone), October 30, 2001.

54. Smith, *Tax Crusaders*, 106–7.

55. Ibid.; Kuttner, *Revolt of the Haves*, 316; Tvedt, *Enough Is Enough*, 33, 45.

56. Adams, *Secrets of the Tax Revolt*, 325; Smith, *Tax Crusaders*, 112.

57. Smith, *Tax Crusaders*, 115; Tvedt, "Enough Is Enough," 66.

58. Kuttner, *Revolt of the Haves*, 279; Bill Shaker to Dick Headlee, March 21, 1977, and Bill Shaker to Dick Headlee, April 20, 1977, Richard H. Headlee Papers, 1976–1992, box 1, folder: General Correspondence—1977, Bentley Historical Library, University of Michigan, Ann Arbor.

59. Lewis K. Uhler to James Barrett, January 17, 1977, Richard H. Headlee Papers, box 1, folder: General Correspondence—1977.

60. Lewis K. Uhler to Richard H. Headlee, February 2, 1977, Richard H. Headlee Papers, 1976–1992, folder: General Correspondence—1977.

61. Kuttner, *Revolt of the Haves*, 293.

62. Detroit News, "Tax Limit Drive Gets a Plug from Jarvis," *Detroit News*, July 26, 1978.

63. John MacDonald, "Tax Reformer Tisch Comes on Bigger Than Life," *Times Herald*, July 26, 1978.

64. Sue Burzynski, "Jarvis Lives up to Billing," *State Journal*, July 7, 1978.

65. Hugh McDiarmid, "MEA Takes Full Credit for Defeat of Spending Limit," *Detroit Free Press*, November 4, 1976, n.p., Richard H. Headlee Papers, 1976–1992, folder: General Correspondence—1976.

66. John A. Rapanos to William G. Milliken, June 12, 1978, box 365, folder 5, Governor William G. Milliken Papers, 1969–1982, Executive Office, Communications Division, RG 88-269, State Archives of Michigan.

67. William G. Milliken to John A. Rapanos, August 11, 1978, box 365, folder 5, William G. Milliken Papers, 1969–1982, Executive Office, Communications Division, RG 88-269, State Archives of Michigan, Lansing; William G. Milliken to Dr. Norman P. Weinheimer, August 24, 1978, box 365, folder 5, William G. Milliken Papers, 1969–1982, Executive Office, Communications Division, RG 88-269.

68. Letter from Philip Pagliarulo, July 23, 1978; box 1, folder: Public Hearing 7/27/78 Nassau/Suffolk, New York State—Temporary State Committee on Real Property Taxation (NYS-TSC), New York State Archives, Albany (NYSA).

69. Testimony of Jim Lack, July 26, 1978; box 1, folder: Public Hearing 7/27/78 Nassau/Suffolk, NYS-TSC, NYSA.

70. Newsletter of the Senior Homeowners Association, Spring Valley, n.d. (November 1978?), box 7, binder: Rockland Hearing, NYS-TSC, NYSA.

71. Statement by Abe Seldin, Chairman of the Nassau County Board of Assessors, box 1, folder: Public Hearing 7/27/78 Nassau/Suffolk, NYS-TSC, NYSA.

72. Statement of the North Shore Council of Home Owners Associations, Inc., box 7, unlabeled binder [New York City Hearing, January 4–5, 1979], NYS-TSC, NYSA.

73. Statement of Erastus Corning, December 7, 1978, box 5, unlabeled binder [Albany Hearing, December 7–8, 1978], NYS-TSC, NYSA.

74. Warren G. Loewy, Superintendent, Hammondsport Central School, "Remarks to the Temporary State Commission on Real Property Taxation," October 19, 1978, box 5, binder: Binghamton Hearing, NYS-TSC, NYSA.

75. On the composition of the commission, see memo from Edwin Margolis to Stanley Fink, March 7, 1979, box 17, folder: Real Property Tax Full Value Assessment, New York State Assembly Speaker's Office Subject Files, 1977–1986 (NYS-ASO), Records Series L0017-86, NYSA.

76. Untitled chapter draft, 1, 17, box 1, folder: Tax and Expenditure Limits, NYS-TSC, NYSA.

77. "Tax and Expenditure Limits in New York State," box 2, folder: Tax and Debt Limits, NYS-TSC, NYSA.

78. New York State Temporary State Commission on the Real Property Tax, *Report of the Temporary State Commission on the Real Property Tax* (Albany: Author, 1979).

79. Memo from Irwin J. Landes to Stanley Fink, April 6, 1979, box 17, folder: Real Property Tax Full Value Assessment, NYS-ASO, NYSA.

80. Memo from Irwin J. Landes to Stanley Fink, March 2, 1979, box 17, folder: Real Property Tax Full Value Assessment, NYS-ASO, NYSA.

81. Rubin and Joseph, "New York City Property Tax," 88–91; New York Times, "Votes in Albany on Overriding Veto of Property Tax Measure," *New York Times*, December 5, 1981.

82. For illustrative data on England, see J. G. Gibson, "Voter Reaction to Tax Change: The Case of the Poll Tax," *Applied Economics* 26, no. 9 (1994): 81–108.

83. A. D. R. Dickson, "The Peculiarities of the Scottish: National Culture and Political Action" (1988): 365.

84. Cf. Butler, Adonis, and Travers, *Failure*, 260; Roper Center for Public Opinion Research (USHARRIS.041273, R1A).

85. R. Barker, "Legitimacy in the United-Kingdom: Scotland and the Poll Tax," *British Journal of Political Science* 22 (1992); Butler, Adonis, and Travers, *Failure*, 129.

86. Barker, "Legitimacy in the United-Kingdom," 527–29.

87. Danny Burns, *The Poll Tax Rebellion* (San Francisco: A. K. Press, 1992), 26, 39, 45, 47.

88. Ibid., 63, 84–86; Butler, Adonis, and Travers, *Failure*, 149.

89. Burns, *Poll Tax Rebellion*, 87–92; Butler, Adonis, and Travers, *Failure*, 149–53.

90. Butler, Adonis, and Travers, *Failure*, 150–51, 64–66.

91. The government also introduced a new tax break for lone householders, who had done comparatively well under the poll tax. Ibid., 176–78.

92. Edgar Kiser and April Linton, "The Hinges of History: State-Making and Revolt in Early Modern France," *American Sociological Review* 67, no. 6 (2002).

93. See the analysis in Appendix 2. For the dates of state TELs, see Shadbegian, "Did the Property Tax Revolt Affect Local Public Education?"

Table 5.1

John H. Bowman, "Real Property Classification: The States March to Different Drummers," *Proceedings of the National Tax Association* 79 (1986); Bowman, "Recent Changes in Property Taxation and Their Implications for Balance in State and Local

Revenue Systems," Commerce Clearing House, *State Tax Handbook* (Chicago: Commerce Clearing House, Various); ACIR, *Significant Features of Fiscal Federalism*, 1992 ed., vol. 1 (Washington, D.C.: ACIR, 1992), 140–42; ACIR, *Significant Features of Fiscal Federalism: Budget Processes and Tax Systems*, 1995 ed., vol. 1 (Washington, D.C.: ACIR, 1995), 130–37; ACIR, *Tax and Expenditure Limits on Local Governments.*

Chapter 6

1. Jarvis and Pack, *Mad as Hell*, 3.

2. Adam Clymer, "Reagan Urges Party to Support Tax Cuts," *New York Times*, June 25, 1978.

3. Edsall and Edsall, *Chain Reaction*, 131; Schrag, *Paradise Lost*, 132; Robert O. Self, *American Babylon: Race and the Struggle for Postwar Oakland*, 326; Michael Kazin, *The Populist Persuasion: An American History* (New York: HarperCollins, 1995), 263.

4. Graetz and Shapiro, *Death by a Thousand Cuts*, 29.

5. Joyce Gelb and Vivian Hart, "Feminist Politics in a Hostile Environment: Obstacles and Opportunities," in *How Social Movements Matter*, ed. Marco Giugni, Doug McAdam, and Charles Tilly (Minneapolis: University of Minnesota Press, 1999), 176.

6. Hacker and Pierson, *Off Center*, 40, 53; Campbell, "What Americans Think of Taxes."

7. See Susan B. Hansen, *Politics of Taxation*, 90, 177.

8. Kuttner, *Revolt of the Haves*, 42; Dick Turpin, "Reagan and Watson Clash over Prop. 14 at Realtors' Meeting," *Los Angeles Times*, October 12, 1972.

9. Prasad, *Politics of Free Markets*, 56–57.

10. Garin Burbank, "Governor Reagan's Only Defeat: The Proposition 1 Campaign in 1973," *California History* 72, no. 4 (1993/94); Jarvis and Pack, *Mad as Hell*, 39; Mickey Levy, "Voting on California's Tax and Expenditure Limitation Initiative," *National Tax Journal* 28, no. 4 (1975).

11. Michael B. Berkman, *The State Roots of National Politics: Congress and the Tax Agenda, 1978–1986* (Pittsburgh: University of Pittsburgh Press, 1993).

12. John W. Kingdon, *Agendas, Alternatives, and Public Policies* (New York: Addison Wesley Longman, 1995), 97.

13. Bruce Bartlett, "Revolution of 1978," *National Review* 30, no. 43 (1978). Democratic resistance to Kemp-Roth also began to weaken noticeably as a result of the tax revolt: Witte, *Politics and Development*, 208–9.

14. Clymer, "Reagan"; Prasad, *Politics of Free Markets*, 57.

15. Prasad, *Politics of Free Markets*, 49; Jude Wanniski, "Sketching the Laffer Curve" (2005); Albert R. Hunt and James M. Perry, "Reagan, Bush Strive to Repair the Image of a 'Dream Ticket,'" *Wall Street Journal*, July 18, 1980.

16. Wall Street Journal, "The California Tax Derby," *Wall Street Journal*, August 29, 1978; Jude Wanniski, *The Way the World Works*, 2nd ed. (New York: Simon and Schuster, 1983), xi.

17. Charles W. Kadlec and Arthur B. Laffer, "The Jarvis-Gann Tax Cut Proposal: An Application of the Laffer Curve," in *The Economics of the Tax Revolt: A Reader*, ed. Arthur B. Laffer and Jan B. Seymour (New York: Harcourt Brace Jovanovich, 1978); Alfred L. Malabre Jr., "Tax-Cut Theorist," *Wall Street Journal*, December 1, 1978; Los Angeles Times, "Reagan Believes Prop. 13 Will Spark Tax Revolt," *Los Angeles Times*, June 24, 1978.

18. On the immediate aftermath of Proposition 13, see Kuttner, *Revolt of the Haves*, 72–73, 81–91; Robert Lindsey, "California Finding Proposition 13 Less Potent Than Predicted," *New York Times*, June 5, 1979; Robert Lindsey, "Dire Predictions on Proposition 13 Have Not Materialized," *New York Times*, March 7, 1979; Schrag, *Paradise Lost*, 151–63; Wallace Turner, "Little Impact Seen in Coast Tax Slash," *New York Times*, February 11, 1979.

19. Wanniski, *The Way the World Works*, xii.

20. Ronald Reagan, "Acceptance Speech," July 17, 1980, http://www.presidency.ucsb.edu/shownomination.php?convid=19, accessed August 24, 2006; Republican Party Platform of 1980, July 15, 1980, http://www.presidency.ucsb.edu/showplatforms.php?platindex=R1980, accessed August 24, 2006. On the increasing space devoted to taxes, see Hansen, *Politics of Taxation*, 90–91.

21. Ronald Reagan, "Remarks at the Annual Dinner of the Conservative Political Action Conference," March 1, 1985, in John Woolley and Gerhard Peters, *The American Presidency Project* [online], Santa Barbara: University of California (hosted), http://www.presidency.ucsb.edu/ws/?pid=38274, accessed August 24, 2006.

22. As the political scientists David Sears and Jack Citrin pointed out shortly after Reagan made this speech, most scholars of voting behavior saw the election as a referendum on Carter rather than an endorsement of Reagan's tax policy: Sears and Citrin, *Tax Revolt*, 269.

23. Prasad, *Politics of Free Markets*, 55; Stockman, *Triumph of Politics*, 230; Steven R. Weisman, "President Is Buoyed by Vote on Budget," *New York Times*, June 26, 1981; Witte, *Politics and Development*, 299.

24. Republican Party, "Republican Party Platform of 1980," July 15, 1980, http://www.presidency.ucsb.edu/showplatforms.php?platindex=R1980, downloaded August 24, 2006.

25. Dreyfuss, "Grover Norquist"; Kuttner, *Revolt of the Haves*, 280–82.

26. Chris Edwards, "Social Policy, Supply Side, and Fundamental Reform: Republican Tax Policy, 1994–2004," in *The Republican Revolution 10 Years Later,*

ed. Chris Edwards and John Samples (Washington, D.C.: Cato Institute, 2005), 46.

27. Dan Balz and Ronald Brownstein, *Storming the Gates: Protest Politics and the Republican Revival* (Boston: Little, Brown and Co., 1996), 40, 128.

28. Newt Gingrich, "The GOP Revolution Holds Powerful Lessons for Changing Washington" in *The Republican Revolution 10 Years Later*, ed. Chris Edwards and John Samples (Washington, D.C.: Cato Institute, 2005); Linda Killian, *The Freshmen: What Happened to the Republican Revolution?* (Boulder: Westview Press, 1998), 73.

29. Ron Suskind, *The Price of Loyalty: George W. Bush, the White House, and the Education of Paul O'Neill* (New York: Simon and Schuster, 2004), 291.

30. Balz and Brownstein, *Storming the Gates*, 180–81; Graetz and Shapiro, *Death by a Thousand Cuts*, 27.

31. Norquist is quoted in Matthew Benjamin, "You Gotta Have a Gimmick: The Senate Approves a Dividend Tax Cut—but It Took Some Real Finagling," *U.S. News and World Report* 134, no. 18 (2003): 39.

32. On rising income inequality, see Martina Morris and Bruce Western, "Inequality in Earnings at the Close of the Twentieth Century," *Annual Review of Sociology* 25 (1999). On the relationship between income inequality and the policy agenda see especially Larry M. Bartels et al., "Inequality and Governance," in *Inequality and American Democracy: What We Know and What We Need to Learn*, ed. Lawrence R. Jacobs and Theda Skocpol (New York: Russell Sage Foundation, 2005); Nolan McCarty, Keith T. Poole, and Howard Rosenthal, *Polarized America: The Dance of Ideology and Unequal Riches* (Cambridge, Mass.: The MIT Press, 2006). On responsiveness, see Martin Gilens, "Public Opinion and Democratic Responsiveness: Who Gets What They Want from Government?" (Russell Sage Foundation Social Inequality Program Working Paper, 2003).

33. Edsall and Edsall, *Chain Reaction*, 214. The transformation is also described in Edward G. Carmines and James A. Stimson, *Issue Evolution: Race and the Transformation of American Politics* (Princeton: Princeton University Press, 1989). For evidence that racially motivated hostility to government redistribution contributed to support for tax limitation, see Sears and Citrin, *Tax Revolt*, 166–70, 208–12.

34. Berkman, *State Roots*, 141.

35. The DW-NOMINATE index is two-dimensional; I focus here on the first dimension, which distinguishes congresspeople based on their propensity to favor government intervention in the economy. See Keith T. Poole, *Spatial Models of Parliamentary Voting* (New York: Cambridge University Press, 2005).

36. Keith T. Poole, "Changing Minds? Not in Congress!" (University of California, San Diego, 2003).

37. The median Republican senator in the 93rd Congress was at .261 on the left-right dimension; the median Republican senator in the 108th Congress was at .379. All of these figures calculated from DW-NOMINATE scores summarizing the first through 108th Congresses and downloaded on August 15, 2006, from ftp://poole-androsenthal.com/junkord/SL01108A1 and ftp://pooleandrosenthal.com/junkord/HL01108A1_PRES.DTA.

38. See Hacker and Pierson, *Off Center*, 27. The five activities are trying to influence others to vote for a party or candidate; attending political meetings; "do[ing] any work for one of the parties or candidates"; wearing a campaign button or sticker; and donating money to a party or candidate.

39. Margaret Levi and Laura Stoker, "Political Trust and Trustworthiness," *Annual Review of Political Science* 3 (2000).

40. These and subsequent statistics calculated from the American National Election Studies Cumulative Data File, 1948–2000.

41. Graetz and Shapiro, *Death by a Thousand Cuts*, 135; Hacker and Pierson, *Off Center*, 54–55.

42. Daniel L. Rubinfeld, "California Fiscal Federalism: A School Finance Perspective," in *Constitutional Reform in California: Making State Government More Effective and Responsive*, ed. Bruce E. Cain and Roger G. Noll (Berkeley: UC Berkeley Institute of Governmental Studies, 1995); Schrag, *Paradise Lost*.

43. Cutler, Elmendorf, and Zeckhauser, "Property Tax Limitations in Retrospect"; Dye and McGuire, "Effect of Property Tax Limitation"; Preston and Ichniowski, "National Perspective"; Ronald J. Shadbegian, "Do Tax and Expenditure Limitations Affect Local Government Budgets? Evidence from Panel Data," *Public Finance Review* 26, no. 2 (1998). Two simulation studies based on general equilibrium models also conclude that property tax limits limit government growth, although they derive different conclusions about whether these laws help or hurt the growth of the private sector: see William F. Fox and Kenneth E. Quindry, "State and Local Government Fiscal Constraints: Public Sector and Private Sector Effects," *Public Finance Quarterly* 12, no. 4 (1984); Edward C. Waters, David W. Holland, and Bruce A. Weber, "Economic Impacts of a Property Tax Limitation," *Land Economics* 73, no. 1 (1997).

44. See Thomas A. Downes, Richard F. Dye, and Therese J. McGuire, "Do Limits Matter? Evidence on the Effects of Tax Limitations on Student Performance," *Journal of Urban Economics* 43 (1998); Thomas A. Downes and David N. Figlio, "Do Tax and Expenditure Limits Provide a Free Lunch? Evidence on the Link Between Limits and Public Sector Service Quality," *National Tax Journal* 52, no. 1 (1999); Figlio, "Did the 'Tax Revolt' Reduce School Performance?"; David N. Figlio, "Short-Term Effects of a 1990s-Era Property Tax Limit: Panel Evidence on Oregon's Measure 5," *National*

Tax Journal 51, no. 1 (1998); David N. Figlio and Kim S. Rueben, "Tax Limits and the Qualifications of New Teachers," *Journal of Public Economics* 80 (2001).

45. Schrag, *Paradise Lost*, 155–57.

46. Mark Baldassare, "Trust in Local Government," *Social Science Quarterly* 66, no. 3 (1985); Marc J. Hetherington and John D. Nugent, "Explaining Public Support for Devolution: The Role of Political Trust," in *What Is It About Government That Americans Dislike?* ed. John R. Hibbing and Elizabeth Theiss-Morse (New York: Cambridge University Press, 2001); Eric M. Uslaner, "Is Washington Really the Problem?" in Hibbing and Theiss-Morse, *What Is It About Government?* ed. John R. Hibbing and Elizabeth Theiss-Morse (New York: Cambridge University Press, 2001).

47. "Conservative manifesto, 1979," http://www.psr.keele.ac.uk/area/uk/man/con79 .htm, retrieved August 24, 2006.

48. Richard M. Coughlin, *Ideology, Public Opinion and Welfare Policy: Attitudes toward Taxes and Spending in Industrialized Societies* (Berkeley: UC Berkeley Institute of International Studies, 1980), 152.

49. Prasad, *Politics of Free Markets*, 104–5.

50. Los Angeles Times, "Reagan Believes."

51. Conservative Party, "Value for Money and Lower Taxes," http://www.conservatives .com/tile.do?def—anifesto.uk.lowertaxes.page, accessed October 21, 2006.

52. John Micklethwait and Adrian Wooldridge, *The Right Nation: How Conservatives Won* (New York: Penguin Press, 2004), 320.

Chapter 7

1. Adams, *Secrets*; Jarvis and Pack, *Mad as Hell*, 8; Kornhauser, "Legitimacy"; Zelizer, "Uneasy Relationship."

2. Kwass, *Privilege*, 50–51.

3. Reforms permitted the finance minister to revoke an *intendant*'s commissions if he performed poorly, and they implemented merit-based pay; Kwass describes this as a limited professionalization. See ibid., 33, 51–57.

4. Gabriel Ardant, *Histoire de l'Impôt, Livre II: Du XVIIIe au XXIe Siècle*, vol. II (Paris: Fayard, 1975), 763–819; Karen Barkey, "Rebellious Alliances: The State and Peasant Unrest in Early Seventeenth-Century France and the Ottoman Empire," *American Sociological Review* 56, no. 6 (1991); Kiser and Linton, "Hinges of History."

5. Jack A. Goldstone, *Revolution and Rebellion in the Early Modern World* (Berkeley: University of California, 1991), 98.

6. R. Bin Wong, *China Transformed: Historical Change and the Limits of European Experience* (Ithaca: Cornell University Press, 1987), 238–47.

7. For highlights of the systematic comparative literature, see Ardant, *Théorie Sociologique*, 751–867; William Brustein, "Class Conflict and Class Collaboration in Regional Rebellions, 1500 to 1700," *Theory and Society* 14, no. 4 (1985); William Brustein and Margaret Levi, "The Geography of Rebellion: Rulers, Rebels, and Regions, 1500 to 1700," *Theory and Society* 16, no. 4 (1987); Kiser and Linton, "Hinges of History."

8. See Dennis Hale, "The Evolution of the Property Tax: A Study of the Relation between Public Finance and Political Theory," *Journal of Politics* 47, no. 2 (1985); Edwin R. A. Seligman, "The General Property Tax," in *Essays in Taxation* (New York: Macmillan, 1931).

9. Organisation for Economic Co-operation and Development (OECD), *Revenue Statistics of OECD Member Countries, 1965–2003* (Paris: OECD, 2003), 78.

10. Gabriel Ardant, *Théorie Sociologique*, 751–62, argues that underdeveloped markets were in fact a primary cause of tax rebellions in early modern Europe.

11. Edwin R. A. Seligman, *The Income Tax: A Study of the History, Theory, and Practice of Income Taxation at Home and Abroad* (New York: Macmillan, 1914), 35.

12. See, e.g., ibid., 80, 237.

13. Sylvain R. F. Plasschaert, *Schedular, Global, and Dualistic Patterns of Income Taxation* (Amsterdam: International Bureau of Fiscal Documentation, 1988).

14. For data on income tax reforms, see Great Britain Board of Inland Revenue, *Income Taxes Outside the Commonwealth* (London: Her Majesty's Stationery Office, 1956–1966); *Income Taxes Outside the United Kingdom* (London: Her Majesty's Stationery Office, 1966–1983).

15. I defined a "tax revolt" as a sustained, collective challenge to authority that was primarily focused on demanding changes in tax policy, and a "major income tax revolt" as a tax revolt involving over 1,000 people directed against the national income tax. Using slightly different criteria, Harold Wilensky found major tax revolts only in Denmark and the United States in the period from 1965 to 1975: Wilensky, *Rich Democracies: Political Economy, Public Policy, and Performance* (Berkeley and Los Angeles: University of California Press, 2002). I located the Norwegian and French movements after a comprehensive search of the secondary literature, including idem; Douglas A. Hibbs Jr. and Henrik Jess Madsen, "Public Reactions to the Growth of Taxation and Government Expenditure," *World Politics* 33, no. 3 (1981); Maria A. Confalonieri and Kenneth Newton, "Taxing and Spending: Tax Revolt or Tax Protest," in *Beliefs in Government*, vol. 3, *The Scope of Government*, ed. Ole Borre and Elinor Scarbrough (Oxford, U.K.: Oxford University Press, 1995); Peter Flora, ed., *Growth to Limits: The Western European Welfare States Since World*

War II (Berlin and New York: Walter de Gruyter, 1986); Arnold J. Heidenheimer, Hugh Heclo, and Carolyn Teich Adams, "Taxation Policy," in *Comparative Public Policy: The Politics of Social Choice in America, Europe and Japan*, ed. Heclo, Adams, and Heidenheimer (New York: St. Martin's Press, 1990); B. Guy Peters, *The Politics of Taxation: A Comparative Perspective* (Cambridge, Mass.: Basil Blackwell, 1991). With the assistance of Paula Garcia-Reynaga, Eric Van Rite, and Nadav Gabay, I located the remaining tax revolts with a comprehensive keyword search of the full text of *Keesing's Record of World Events* and the *New York Times* for articles on all of these countries for the period from 1960 to 2000. This search confirmed the Danish and French cases and produced evidence of the Belgian and Italian income tax protests.

16. See Esping-Andersen, *Three Worlds*; Monica Prasad, "Why Is France So French? Culture, Institutions, and Neoliberalism, 1974–1981," *American Journal of Sociology* 111, no. 2 (2005).

17. Harry Giniger, "Tax Collector's Nightmare," *New York Times*, February 20, 1955, 62. On the *forfait* system in general, see Martin Norr and Pierre Kerlan, *The Tax System in France*, ed. Harvard University International Program on Taxation, *World Tax Series* (Chicago: Commerce Clearing House, 1966), 345–68.

18. Dominique Borne, *Petits Bourgeois en Révolte? Le Mouvement Poujade* (Paris: Flammarion, 1977), 64–67; Gérard Tournié, *La Politique Fiscale sous la 5e République* (Toulouse: Privat, 1985), 25.

19. Borne, *Petits Bourgeois en Révolte?* 48–52, 64–67.

20. Pierre Poujade, *J'ai Choisi le Combat* (St.-Céré: Société Générale des Éditions et des Publications, 1955), 25–29.

21. Ardant, *Histoire de l'Impôt*, vol. 2, 641–42; Poujade, *J'ai Choisi Le Combat*, 29–31.

22. Stanley Hoffman et al., *Le Mouvement Poujade* (Paris: Presses de la Fondation Nationale des Sciences Politiques, 1956), 41, 45.

23. On the early role of Communists, see ibid., 38–40. On the social base of the Poujadists and the Radicals, see Seymour Martin Lipset, "Social Stratification and 'Right-Wing Extremism,'" *British Journal of Sociology* 10, no. 4 (1959): 365–68.

24. Hoffman et al., *Mouvement Poujade*, 46, 53. The eighth point on the UDCA program was a demand for equal treatment in the administration of the French welfare state—"equality of rights and responsibilities in social security, family allowances, and pensions"—which reflected dissatisfaction with the segregation of artisans and merchants in their own risk pool for the purposes of social insurance. See Peter Baldwin, *The Politics of Social Solidarity: Class Bases of the European Welfare State, 1875–1975* (New York: Cambridge University Press, 1990), 248–68.

25. Borne, *Petits Bourgeois en Révolte?* 65; Hoffman et al., *Mouvement Poujade*, 63.

26. See the illuminating analysis prepared by Gabriel Ardant from the reports of anti-tax protest compiled by the *Direction Générale des Impôts*: Ardant, *Théorie Sociologique*, 824–27.

27. Ardant, *Histoire de l'Impôt*, vol. 2, 643–44; Hoffman et al., *Mouvement Poujade*, 19, 62, 77–80. See "Tax Strike Voted by French Group," *New York Times*, January 25, 1955; Lansing Warren, "French Assembly Opens Tax Debate," *New York Times*, March 29, 1955. Estimates of participation in the Paris rally varied from 50,000 to 200,000: see Giniger, "Tax Collector's Nightmare"; Hoffman et al., *Mouvement Poujade*, 54.

28. Ardant, *Histoire de l'Impôt*, vol. 2, 645; Ardant, *Théorie Sociologique*, 823. On Poujade's rhetoric, see Hoffman et al., *Mouvement Poujade*, 210–13. On the history of French resistance to fiscal inquisition, see Kimberly J. Morgan and Monica Prasad, "The Origins of Tax Systems: A French-American Comparison" (paper presented at the Policy History Conference, Charlottesville, Virginia, June 2, 2006); Charles Tilly, *The Contentious French: Four Centuries of Popular Struggle* (Cambridge, Mass.: Harvard University Press, 1986).

29. Skattedepartementet, "Oversigt over den gældende indkomst- og formuebeskatning i Danmark," 1953, Rigsarkivet (Denmark), Skattedepartementet, Kommissionen og Udvalg, Skattelovkommissionen af 1937, Record Series 0039/199/50, box 9. See also Gunnar Thorlund Jepsen, *Skattepolitik* (Copenhagen: Handelshøjskolens Forlag, 1996), 143–45; Kjeld Philip, *Skattepolitik* (Copenhagen: Gyldendal, 1965), ch. 9.

30. For especially clear discussions of the incidence of this complicated tax deduction, see Jepsen, *Skattepolitik*, 143–45; Philip, *Skattepolitik*, 181–84. For a general overview of the reforms, see Great Britain Board of Inland Revenue, "Denmark," in *Income Taxes Outside the United Kingdom 1971* (London: Her Majesty's Publishing Office, 1971). The administrative work created for small employers is documented in Jane Wickman, *Fremskridtspartiet: Hvem Og Hvorfor?* (Copenhagen: Akademisk Forlag, 1977).

31. *Avisårbogen* (1968): 137–39, 147, 184, 187, 197–99.

32. Poul Hammerich, *Det Store Flip, 1968–72*, vol. 6, *Danmarkskrønike* (Copenhagen: Gyldendal, 1984), 23; *Avisårbogen* (1970): 102–5, 119.

33. Flemming Christian Nielsen, *Anarkisten: En Biografi Om Mogens Glistrup* (Copenhagen: Lindhardt og Ringhof, 2000), 19–25; Mogens Glistrup, "Tirret Til Handling," *Fremskridt* 4, no. 13 (1976); Morten Hahn-Pedersen, *Historien om et nul: Mogens Glistrup og fremskridtsbevægelsen 1971–73* (Odense: Odense Universitetsforlag, 1981), 28; Hammerich, *Det Store Flip*, 242–43.

34. For a transcript of the interview, see Bjarne Larsen, *Fremskridtspartiets Organisation: En Analyse Og Kritik Af Fremskridtspartiets Struktur under Anvendelse Af Maurice Duvergers Begrebsapparat* (Århus: Institut for Statskundskab, 1977), 194; for an inside view from the studio, see Hammerich, *Det Store Flip*, 71.

35. Pia Kjærsgaard, *Men Udsigten Er God: Midtvejserindringer* (Copenhagen: Peter Sschenfeldts Nye Forlag, 1998), 59.

36. Hahn-Pedersen, *Historien om et nul*, 26, 30; Hammerich, *Det Store Flip*, 244–48.

37. Nielsen, *Anarkisten*, 28; Hammerich, *Det Store Flip*, 244.

38. Hahn-Pedersen, *Historien om et nul*, 30–31; Hammerich, *Det Store Flip*, 247–48; Larsen, *Fremskridtspartiets Organisation*, 73. The same tabloid, *Extra-Bladet*, picked up on the anti-tax mood with an aggressive advertising campaign that involved spray-painting anti-tax slogans, such as "You're getting ripped off on your taxes [*Du bli'r snydt i skat*]," on public buses (see Hammerich, *Det Store Flip*, 88).

39. Hahn-Pedersen, *Historien om et nul*, 31; Hibbs and Madsen, "Public Reactions," 420; Hanne Rasmussen and Mogens Rüdiger, *Tiden Efter 1945*, vol. 8, *Danmarks Historie* (Copenhagen: Gyldendal, 1990), 203–6, 211.

40. Hahn-Pedersen, *Historien om et nul*, 31–33; Larsen, *Fremskridtspartiets Organisation*, 73–74.

41. Hahn-Pedersen, *Historien om et nul*, 35; Larsen, *Fremskridtspartiets Organisation*, 76, 89. Bjarne Castella and Vilhelm Joost, *Mogens Glistrup: Mand Med Meninger* (Copenhagen: Vinten, 1976). Everybody remembers the answering machine prank, but the Progress Party abandoned this demand very early in the protest campaign.

42. Hahn-Pedersen, *Historien om et nul*, 39; Larsen, *Fremskridtspartiets Organisation*, 77.

43. Some of these signatures may have duplicated signatures that were collected with the first 17,113. Officials finally opened the locked chest in November 1973 in order to verify that the signatures turned in by another new party did not overlap with signatures for the Progress Party. The officials confirmed that the chest was filled with apparently valid voter petitions, but they did not count the signatures because the Progress Party had already collected enough other valid signatures to be officially recognized (Larsen, *Fremskridtspartiets Organisation*, 79). See also Hahn-Pedersen, *Historien om et nul*, 44–45.

44. Hahn-Pedersen, *Historien om et nul*, 46; Gunnar Rasmussen, *Det småborgerlige oprør* (Copenhagen: Demos, 1977), 48.

45. Party Secretary Lise Simonsen recorded the date and location of every meeting, in many cases with attendance figures, in her 1973 appointments calendar (Hahn-Pedersen, *Historien om et nul*, 45–46). With special permission from Simonsen, the historian Morten Hahn-Pedersen examined the calendar in 1980, and he also spot-checked some of its attendance figures against newspaper reports. He concluded on this basis that average attendance lay below the 1,500 reported by Gunnar Rasmussen (*Det småborgerlige oprør*, 47), but he does not report his own estimate of the average.

46. "Holder De af KILDESKATTEN," n.d., box 546, emphasis added, Fremskridtspartiets Arbejdsarkiv, 1972–1989 (FRPA), Privatarkiv nr. 11008, Rigsarkivet (Denmark).

47. "Det vil vi i FREMSKRIDTSPARTIET," April 1973, p. 1, box 545, FRPA; see also "Foreløbigt udkast," October 23, 1972, p. 1, box 546; and "Udkast," October 23, 1972, p. 1, box 533. The exact wording of the three main points varied from document to document. Glistrup once expressed them in English as "Doing away with income taxes," "Cutting down the power of red tape," and "Thinning out the jungle of laws." Mogens Glistrup, "The Danish Progress Party (Fremskridtspartiet)" (paper presented at the Symposium on the Role of Political Parties in the Development of Parliamentary Democracy, Council of Europe, Strasbourg, February 15, 1972), box 545, FRPA. Note that whatever the wording or translation, the abolition of the income tax is the only concrete policy proposal that is implied in this list.

48. Hahn-Pedersen, *Historien om et nul*, 55–56; Larsen, *Fremskridtspartiets Organisation*, 149. See FRPA, C. O. Larsen, "Forsvarspolitik," n.d., box 529; FRPA, Tage Kaarsted, "The Image and Role of the Danish Progress Party" (paper presented at the Symposium on the Role of Political Parties in the Development of Parliamentary Democracy, Council of Europe, Strasbourg, February 15, 1978), 3, box 545. Kai Pedersen, *Fremskridtspartiet: De Første 25 År I Dansk Politik* (Copenhagen: Fremskridtspartiets forlag, 1997), 41.

49. "Udkast," October 23, 1972, p. 1, box 533; "FREMSKRIDTSPARTIET," n.d. [January 31, 1973], pp. 1–2, box 546, FRPA; "Det vil vi i FREMSKRIDTSPARTIET," April 1973, p. 3, box 545, FRPA.

50. Great Britain Board of Inland Revenue, *Income Taxes Outside the United Kingdom*, vol. 2 (London: H. M. Stationery Office, 1973).

51. OECD, *Personal Income Tax Systems Under Changing Economic Conditions* (Paris: OECD, 1986), 67.

52. In the mid-1970s, 58 percent of Americans said that the government spent too much on assistance for the poor, compared to 10 percent of Danes. See Coughlin, *Ideology*, 112.

53. From 1970 to 1971, the Danish Statistical Bureau estimated that the average taxable income of the self-employed fell by 7 percent in the industrial sector, by 1 percent in trade and transport, and by 3 percent in the liberal professions; it increased by just 2 percent for self-employed people in the agricultural sector. By contrast, the average income for skilled and unskilled workers in private industry *increased* by 12 percent. See Danmarks Statistik, *Statistisk Årbog 1974*, vol. 78 (Copenhagen: Danmarks Statistik, 1974), 468–69. For discussions of the occupational composition of Progress Party voters, see Jørgen Goul Andersen and Tor Bjørklund, "Structural Changes and New Cleavages: The Progress Parties in Denmark and Norway," *Acta Sociologica* 33, no. 3 (1990); Ingemar Glans, "Fremskridtspartiet—Småborgerlig Revolt, Högerreaktion Eller Generell Protest?" in *Valg Og Vælgeradfæard: Studier I Dansk Politik*, ed. Jørgen Elklit and Ole Tonsgaard (Copenhagen: Forlaget Politica, 1986); Erik Jørgen Hansen, "The Progress Party in Denmark Is a Class Party—but Which Class?" *Acta Sociologica* 25, no. 2 (1982); Wickman, *Fremskridtspartiet*. The best systematic evidence on the occupations of early

party activists (as opposed to later party voters) comes from an analysis of the grass-roots slate of candidates that the party put forward in December 1973, of whom 37 percent were self-employed. Peter Foverskov, "Den Politiske Rekrutteringsproces Omkring Folketingsvalget 1973," in *Dansk Politik I 1970'erne: Studier Og Arbejdspapirer*, ed. Mogens N. Pedersen (Copenhagen: Samfundsvidenskabeligt Forlag, 1979).

54. My own analysis of the Danish Panel Election Study, 1971–1973 (N=479), suggests that people whose self-reported income in 1972 was less than their self-reported income in 1970 were particularly likely to vote for the Progress Party in December 1973 (18 percent, compared to 13 percent for those whose reported income stayed constant or rose). I estimated a linear probability model to control for gender, age, self-employment, years of education, and self-reported income bracket as of 1972 and found that people who had fallen into a lower income bracket (on the seven-bracket scale used by the survey) were nine percentage points more likely than others to vote for the Progress Party (p<.10, two-tailed). Results were substantially identical with a logistic regression.

55. Lars Bille, "Den Politiske Udvikling November 1966 Til Februar 1975," in *Danmark 1966–1975: En Historisk Økonomisk Oversigt*, ed. H. Juul Madsen, Lars Bille, and Mark Poulsen (Copenhagen: Berg, 1975), 33–36; Lars Bille, *Partier I Forandring: En Analyse Af Dansk Partiorganisationers Udviling 1960–1995* (Odense: Odense Universitetsforlag, 1997), 64; Gøsta Esping-Andersen, "Social Class, Social Democracy and State Policy: Party Policy and Party Decomposition in Denmark and Sweden" (Ph.D. thesis, University of Wisconsin, 1978), 478, 486–87.

56. *Wall Street Journal*, December 5, 1973: 1.

57. Mogens Glistrup, "Sidste Nyt 1 4/12-79," FRPA, box 534. For the coroner's verdict on the party, see Lars Bille, "Politisk Kronik 2. Halvår 2001," *Økonomi og Politik* 75, no. 1 (2002).

Epilogue

1. "Howard Jarvis Taxpayers' Association," http://www.hjta.org, accessed November 6, 2006.

2. Graetz and Shapiro, *Death by a Thousand Cuts*, 282.

3. Norquist is quoted in Laura Blumenfeld, "Sowing the Seeds of GOP Domination," *Washington Post*, January 12, 2004, A1. John Witte famously predicted in 1985 that congressional proposals for loophole-closing income tax reform would never succeed—as they did in 1986. See Witte, *Politics and Development*, 385–86. But subsequent history has vindicated Witte's prediction that the congressional propensity to insert and expand loopholes would reassert itself with a vengeance after 1986.

4. Christopher Howard has questioned this analogy between the politics of tax privileges and the politics of direct social spending, finding that the federal income tax deduction

for home mortgages did not give rise to any interest organizations of beneficiaries comparable to the American Association of Retired Persons (Howard, *Hidden Welfare State*, 114). But homeowners did mobilize to defend selective fractional assessment, which was the greater subsidy.

5. This argument is deeply indebted to the work of Paul Pierson, especially *Dismantling the Welfare State*.

6. Jacob S. Hacker, *The Great Risk Shift: The Assault on American Jobs, Families, Health Care, and Retirement and How You Can Fight Back* (New York: Oxford University Press, 2006), 129; Jarvis and Pack, *Mad as Hell*, 298–300.

7. Federal Old-Age and Survivors Insurance and Federal Disability Insurance Trust Funds Board of Trustees, *The 2006 Annual Report of the Board of Trustees of the Federal Old-Age and Survivors Insurance and Federal Disability Insurance Trust Funds* (Washington, D.C.: U.S. Government Printing Office, 2006).

8. "President Participates in Conversation on Social Security Reform," January 11, 2005, http://www.whitehouse.gov/news/releases/2005/01/20050111-4.html, accessed November 6, 2006; Americans for Tax Reform, *Independence Day Recess Packet on Social Security*, June 30, 2005, http://www.atr.org/content/pdf/2005/jun/063005fact_summary.pdf, accessed November 6, 2006; George W. Bush, "State of the Union Address," February 2, 2005, http://www.whitehouse.gov/news/releases/2005/02/20050202-11.html, accessed November 6, 2006.

9. Elisabeth G. Hill, *Overview of the 2007–08 May Revision* (Sacramento: California State Legislative Analyst's Office, 2007), 3. Social Security is not projected to have an annual shortfall until 2017, and it has a more substantial financial cushion. See Board of Trustees, *The 2007 Annual Report of the Board of Trustees of the Federal Old-Age and Survivors Insurance and Federal Disability Insurance Trust Funds*, 16.

10. Mark P. Couch and Chris Frates, "TABOR's Vise to Be Eased," *Denver Post*, November 2, 2005.

11. Hacker, *Great Risk Shift*, 55–56.

Appendix 1

1. The Tax Reform Research Group took this view: "Most taxpayers think 'fractional assessment' gives them a break. But it's really just a cruel hoax. Taxes don't go down, because the local government just raises the tax rate." Quoted in Paul, *Politics of the Property Tax*, 5.

2. U.S. Bureau of the Census, *Statistical Abstract of the United States, 1973* (Washington, D.C.: U.S. Government Printing Office, 1973), 287.

3. Hacker, *Divided Welfare State*; Howard, *Hidden Welfare State*.

4. Howard, *Hidden Welfare State*, 25.

5. There is a further reason that this adjustment understates the value of fractional assessment: if more people deducted state and local taxes from their adjusted gross income, fewer people would take the standard deduction. So the net increase in federal tax breaks resulting from the loss of informal local tax privileges would be less than it seems.

6. For a discussion of how the new depreciation assumptions affect estimates of the net value of residential structures, see Arnold J. Katz and Shelby W. Herman, "Improved Estimates of Fixed Reproducible Tangible Wealth, 1929–1995," *Survey of Current Business*, May 1997.

Table A1.1

1. Newcomer, "The Decline of the General Property Tax," 40; U.S. Bureau of the Census, *Taxable Property Values and Assessment-Sales Price Ratios*, 1957 ed. (Washington, D.C.: U.S. Government Printing Office, 1957), 21; Bureau of the Census, *Taxable Property Values and Assessment-Sales Price Ratios*, 1972 ed. (Washington, D.C.: U.S. Government Printing Office, 1972), 33.

2. The 1940 figure is from U.S. Bureau of the Census, *Statistical Abstract of the United States, 1942* (Washington, D.C.: U.S. Government Printing Office, 1942), 253; later figures are from Bureau of the Census, *Taxable Property Values and Assessment-Sales Price Ratios*, 1977 ed. (Washington, D.C.: U.S. Government Printing Office, 1977), 5.

3. John C. Musgrave, "New Estimates of Residential Capital in the United States, 1925–1973," *Survey of Current Business* 54, no. 10, Table 2. These figures are the estimated total values of private nonfarm residential stock, net of depreciation.

4. This multiplier equals the total value of land and structures divided by the total value of structures alone. Multipliers for 1950, 1956, 1960, 1970, and 1973 were calculated from data in Musgrave, "New Estimates," Table A. The value for 1971 was imputed to be identical to the values for 1970 and 1973; the value for 1940 was imputed by linear extrapolation.

5. Values for 1956 and 1971 are from Bureau of the Census, *Taxable Property Values*, 1977 ed., 5. The value for 1940 is imputed to be 103 percent of net assessed value, based on the ratio reported in this volume for 1956.

6. The shares for 1956 and 1971 were reported in Bureau of the Census, *Taxable Property Values*, 1957 ed., 25; and Bureau of the Census, *Taxable Property Values*, 1972 ed., 6. The share for 1940 was imputed at the 1956 value.

Appendix 2

1. Janet M. Box-Steffensmeier and Bradford S. Jones, *Event History Modeling: A Guide for Social Scientists* (New York: Cambridge University Press, 2004).

Table A2.1

1. U.S. Bureau of the Census, *Historical Census of Housing Tables: Homeownership* (U.S. Bureau of the Census, 2000 [accessed March 26, 2002]); available from http://www.census.gov/hhes/www/housing/census/historic/owner.html, U.S. Bureau of the Census, *Housing Characteristics 2000: Census 2000 Brief: Census Publication C2kbr/01-13* (Washington, D.C.: U.S. Bureau of the Census, 2000).

2. National Cancer Institute, *SEER Population Files* (National Cancer Institute, 2002 [accessed April 12 2002]); available from http://seer.cancer.gov/USPops/.

3. U.S. Bureau of the Census, *Urban and Rural Population: 1900 to 1990* (U.S. Bureau of the Census, 1995 [accessed March 26, 2002]); available from http://www.census.gov/population/censusdata/urpop0090.txt. I reconstructed data for intercensal years by linear interpolation.

4. U.S. Bureau of Economic Analysis, *Regional Accounts Data* (U.S. Bureau of Economic Analysis, 2002 [accessed March 26, 2002]); available from http://www.bea.doc.gov/bea/regional/spi/.

5. Barry T. Hirsch, David A. Macpherson, and Wayne G. Vroman, "Estimates of Union Density by State," *Monthly Labor Review* 124, no. 7 (2001).

6. Calculated from data in U.S. Bureau of the Census, *Governmental Finances, Series GF* (Washington, D.C.: U.S. Bureau of the Census, various years).

7. This variable was measured almost annually at the level of the census region (Northeast, Midwest, West, and South); I imputed values for missing years by linear interpolation. ACIR, *Changing Public Attitudes on Governments and Taxes*.

8. Calculated from data in U.S. Bureau of the Census, *Governmental Finances*.

9. Council of State Legislatures, *The Book of the States* (Lexington, Ky.: Council of State Legislatures, various years).

10. Bowman, "Real Property Classification"; Bowman, "Recent Changes in Property Taxation"; Commerce Clearing House, *State Tax Handbook*; ACIR, *Significant Features of Fiscal Federalism* (1992), 140–42.

11. ACIR, *Significant Features of Fiscal Federalism* (1995), 130–37.

Appendix 3

1. Marianne Bertrand, Esther Duflo, and Sendhil Mullainathan, "How Much Should We Trust Differences-in-Differences Estimates?" *Quarterly Journal of Economics* 119, no. 1 (2004).

INDEX

A.B. 80 (California), 45–46
A.B. 2270 (California), 41, 45, 46
Ability-to-pay principle, 76
Abolition of property tax, federalism and
failure of, 79–83
Abolition of Domestic Rates Etc. (Scotland)
Act, 121
Activist government, public opinion data on
support for, 146
Actual tax liability, difference between ideal
tax liability and, 176
Ad valorem taxes, 6, 52; advantages for gov-
ernment, 6; property tax as, 6; in U.S.
Constitution, 199n4
Advisory Commission on Intergovernmental
Relations, U.S. (ACIR), 82
Affluent, creation of tax breaks for the, 14
Aid to Families with Dependent Children
(AFDC), benefits provided by, 10
Alinsky, Saul, 59, 65
All-Britain Anti-Poll Tax Federation,
123
America. *See* United States
American National Election Study, 185
Americans for Tax Reform, 133
Americans Nonpartisan for Tax Equity
(ANTE), 79
Anderson, Barbara, 3–4
Anti-Poll Tax Federation, 123
Anti-Poll Tax Unions, 123
Antipoverty groups, endorsement of Tax
Justice Act by, 102–4
Anti-statism, 16, 144

Arizona: limitation of growth of tax revenues
in, 91; petition drives for property tax
relief in, 60
Arkansas, tax protests in, 55
Assessed value, 105
Assessment: of income, 151–52, 153; of
income, role in sparking rebellion
against Danish income tax, 158–63; mod-
ernization of, 12, 146–47; presumptive,
151; of property, 26–27, 43, 44, 46–47; of
property, efforts of public officials to
delay modernization of, 26–27. *See also*
Fractional assessment; Reassessment in
tax protest movement
Assessment ratios, 27, 28, 40, 176
Assessment reform in Massachusetts, 46–47
Assessors, 7; dispensation of informal tax
privileges by, 27–28
Associated Industries of Massachusetts
(AIM), 70, 113
Association of County Councils, 85
Association of District Councils, 85
Association of Metropolitan Authorities, 85
Atlanta, property tax strikes in, 29
Audits, 152
Australia, withholding and auditing require-
ments of, 153
Austria, withholding and auditing require-
ments of, 153

Baker, Howard, 117
Baker, Russell, 14
Bakolis, Michael, 66

239